Dancing in the Dark

Dancing in the Dark

The Privilege of Participating
in the Ministry of Christ

Graham Buxton

paternoster
press

Copyright © 2001 Graham Buxton

First published in 2001 by Paternoster Press

07 06 05 04 03 02 01   7 6 5 4 3 2 1

Paternoster Press is an imprint of Paternoster Publishing,
PO Box 300, Carlisle, Cumbria, CA3 0QS, UK
and Paternoster Publishing USA,
Box 1047, Waynesboro, GA 30830–2047
www.paternoster-publishing.com

British Library Cataloguing in Publication Data
A catalogue record for this book is available from the British Library

1–84227–088–5

Cover Design by Compudava
Typeset by WestKey Ltd, Falmouth, Cornwall
Printed in Great Britain by
Omnia Books Ltd, Glasgow

LORD OF THE DANCE

'Dance, then, wherever you may be,
I am the Lord of the Dance,' said he,
'And I'll lead you all, wherever you may be,
And I'll lead you all in the dance,' said he.

Sydney Carter

JEU D'ESPRIT

Flame-dancing Spirit, come,
Sweep us off our feet and
Dance us through our days.
Surprise us with your rhythms,
Dare us to try new steps, explore
New patterns and new relationships.
Release us from old routines,
To swing in abandoned joy
And fearful adventure.
And in the intervals,
Rest us,
In your still centre.

Ann Lewin
from *Carols and Kingfishers: Reflections on the Journey*
(Peterborough: Foundry Press, 1997), page 61.

THE DANCE (thanks to T.S. Eliot)

That is where the dance is.
In the deep green stillness,
The flickering darkness.
There the Spirit dances
In the hidden heart of things.

Sometimes it is the capering,
Gambolling dance of childhood,
Sometimes the sinuous,
Sensuous circling of lovers.
Sometimes a stately pavane,
With every movement part of a controlled pattern.
Sometimes it is more like wrestling
Than dancing.

But always it is at the centre,
Where the darkness and the light
Touch and embrace.

And always it is in the stillness
Where the movement is felt.

Given to each other,
The movement and the stillness,
The darkness and the light,
Create the dance.

Veronica Faulks

Contents

Foreword

Graham Buxton has made a much needed and significant contribution to the new and growing discipline of practical theology with his book *Dancing in the Dark*. Though he writes from an Australian, Anglican context, his critical interaction with contemporary post-modern culture has global, evangelical and ecumenical relevance. This is a book that knows no national or ecclesial boundaries; it is a book that belongs in every pastor's 'must read' stack.

I once wrote an essay entitled 'Clergy Burnout as a Symptom of Theological Anaemia'. In that essay I suggested that there is a sick theology and a healthy theology which contributes to either a sick or a healthy ministry. I went on to suggest that a healthy theology contains healing for the healer and freedom for the fighter of God's battles. It is a theology of a loving God who knows that to be God is to be responsible, even for our faltering and fallible efforts. A sick theology tends to invest the calling of God in the needs of the world rather than to follow Christ in serving the Father on behalf of the world. A theology which produces dissonance and distress in the minister reflects a ministry that is theologically impoverished. A theology which cripples and destroys the self-esteem and sense of worth of a minister is not made better by 'success' in ministry. A theology in which there is no 'sabbath rest' for the one who does the work of the ministry is a theology of the curse, not a theology of the cross. What is lacking in the lives of many who pastor and lead churches is a clear understanding of the inner correlation between ministry and theology.

Methods can only show us how to do ministry. It is the purpose of theological reflection to give us the courage to know and to say that our ministry is Christ's ministry. The renewal of one's theology through the rediscovery of the reality of Christ's presence and power in ministry will reduce debilitating stress and restore the joy and hopefulness of ministry.

With elegant form and eloquent style, Graham Buxton weaves the theme of participation in Christ's ongoing ministry through each chapter. He begins with God's ministry through Christ toward the world and ends with Christ's ministry though the people of God in the world. The author's exegesis of God's contemporary work through the presence and power of the Spirit in the context of ministry provides a hermeneutic of Christ as incarnate Word and the Scriptures as inspired and infallible Word. Even as Barth turned scholastic theology on its head by insisting that God's being is revealed in God's act, this book turns revelation theology on its side, drawing ecclesial form into incarnational function.

I would be pleased to have it available for students preparing for ministry as well as for Doctor of Ministry students engaged in ministry. Dealing with such issues as the nature of the church, the calling to the vocation of ministry, the missionary character of the sacraments, the therapeutic grace of pastoral counselling and the liberation of both women and men as leader-servants, the book also provides a compendium on pastoral theology. The final chapter could well be read first for those already engaged in pastoral ministry. For burdens need to be lifted from heavy hearts before entering into the dance!

Ray S. Anderson
Professor of Theology and Ministry
Fuller Theological Seminary, Pasadena, CA 91101, USA

Acknowledgments

It is a privilege for authors to acknowledge those who have had a formative influence upon their work, and it is customary to add a rider acknowledging that such people are too numerous to identify by name, with an apology if some names have not been mentioned. I am happy to subscribe to both conventions! *Dancing in the Dark* represents the fruit of nearly thirty years of Christian life and ministry, so it is appropriate to mention by name those whose lives have had a lasting impact upon me, as well as those who have more directly contributed to the writing and publication of this book.

My first pastor, Harry Cooke, instilled in me a love for God, and a desire to involve the local church with the surrounding community. During my ten years at St Matthias Church in Leeds in the north of England, a church which opened me up to charismatic renewal (with all its joys and pains), my commitment to incarnational ministry was forged. Harry also bequeathed to me an appreciation of honesty, perseverance and a sense of humour in pastoral ministry. His gentle and compassionate ministry has been an inspiration to me.

I would also like to acknowledge the influence of countless numbers of people not only at St Matthias, but also at St John's, West Ealing, and St Paul's, South Harrow (both in London), and Coromandel Valley Uniting Church in Adelaide, South Australia. Amongst these people I learned what it means to belong to a community of faith. Looking back over the years, I realize how much I have received from people who have been willing to open up their lives to one another.

At St John's College, Nottingham, where I studied theology

in preparation for ordination within the Anglican church, my doctrine lecturer, Tom Smail, introduced me to Trinitarian theology, and encouraged me to keep on wrestling with theological issues as I continued into ministry. I am indebted to him for his Christological insights, as well as for his pastoral wisdom. In particular, he helped me to understand the grace of a God who works in and for us in the midst of our struggling humanity.

At Tabor College, Adelaide, others have helped to shape my theology of grace, particularly my colleague and friend, David McGregor. I am grateful to faculty and students, especially those who participated in my exploratory Theologies of Ministry classes, with whom I have shared many of the ideas presented in this book. Their insights and comments did not go unnoticed! Baxter Kruger's visits to Tabor College in recent years were timely, not only in enriching my appreciation of the Trinity, but also because he reinforced in my thinking the metaphor of dance as an expression of the joy and fullness of life which we are privileged to share with the Trinitarian God of grace.

As I wrestled with the ideas contained within this book, I corresponded with Gary Deddo in the United States, who encouraged me to persevere with the manuscript. I would like to take this opportunity to acknowledge his contribution in helping me to re-shape the text along the theme of participation. Ray Anderson's writings have been formative in my own theological understanding of Christian ministry and have helped me over the years to interpret ministry within a robust Christological and incarnational framework. I am grateful for his endorsement of the book and for contributing a foreword.

I would also like to thank Pieter Kwant for his faith in the original manuscript, and Paternoster Publishing for their expertise and skill in steering the manuscript into its finished form. My editor, James Croft, contributed many lucid insights which have made this a more readable text. Jill Morris and Peter Little were helpful and encouraging throughout the production stage, and I greatly appreciated the co-operation and support of Jonathan Francis in the final marketing stages of the process.

My wife, Gill, has been an invaluable support to me throughout the writing of this book, and her perceptive reading of the manuscript brought to light important changes which have made the text easier to read. Gill and my three children, David, Rachel and Joanna, have provided for me an environment within which writing this book has been a joy and a pleasure. I dedicate it to them with my love.

May 2001
Adelaide, South Australia

Introduction

An Invitation to Participate in the Dance

Blessed are those whose strength is in you,
who have set their hearts on pilgrimage.
Psalm 84:5

In Psalm 84 we are reminded that life is a journey, a travelling through a progression of stages of understanding, of mystery, and of experience. For the psalmist, the pilgrimage carries with it the promise of drawing closer to God along the way. In this book I adopt the metaphor of journeying with God as a secondary motif in my exploration of the nature and content of contemporary Christian ministry. However, my primary thesis is that Christian ministry is fundamentally about participation in the ongoing ministry of Christ himself, who invites us into all that he is doing today by the power of the Spirit.

When I began my Christian life at the age of twenty-seven I did not understand that I was beginning a pilgrim walk which would lead me along a path not only of personal spiritual growth, but also of evolving theological understanding. (By 'theological', I simply mean my understanding of the nature and relevance of God.) I thought that once I had grasped the essentials of the Christian faith – the doctrinal core – the challenge was then to live out the doctrine as faithfully as I could. In other words, my theological foundation would serve my ethical and moral life as a Christian. I also absorbed the idea that ministry was all about what I could accomplish for God, given the right training and environment.

In recent years I have come to see that, although there is a necessary connection between faith and lifestyle, it is far too simplistic to assume that we can accumulate a set of doctrines and wrap them up in a neat and tidy package ready for consumption and transmission throughout life. Life has a habit of unravelling the packaging and leaving us with more questions than we had at the beginning of our Christian walk. I often refer in my teaching to a 'God with fuzzy edges' precisely because we cannot encapsulate God in our little boxes, as if he could be tied down to our finite way of thinking. We can neither domesticate God nor fully understand him; theology is all about coming to terms with the mystery of God, and allowing him to *remain* a mystery even as he reveals something of himself to us along the way.

My last ten years as a theological educator have impressed upon me the vital importance of 'doing theology', a term which I will explore more substantially elsewhere in this book. As I have engaged not only in theological reflection, but also in debate and encounter with other Christians, I have discovered the truth of the statement that 'theology was made for human beings, not human beings for theology'.[1] In recent years, I have been challenged as much about what to believe as about how I am to live. Lest some are troubled by this, I want to make it clear from the outset that I am not advocating the wholesale rejection of foundational Christian beliefs; rather, I make a plea here for a willingness to think about what we believe.

Dancing in the Dark is not a systematic treatment of the theology of ministry, although it certainly examines key dimensions of Christian ministry in some depth. I have attempted to write not so much a textbook as a theological investigation into the nature of ministry, with appropriate emphasis on the contemporary cultural climate. I freely acknowledge that in the process I explore themes which have been formative in my own personal journey as a Christian pastor and educator. These themes, notably Trinitarianism, the mission imperative, incarnational theology, the creativity of the Spirit, and community life, are immediately recognizable in some of the section headings in a number of chapters. However, they are also woven throughout the fabric of the text: they are implicit in my understanding of Christian ministry.

In a landmark book written over thirty years ago, Harry Blamires declares that our responsibility as Christians is not to seek a 'Christian line' concerning this or that particular issue; what is needed first of all is 'a Christian dialogue in which a given issue can be expressed and known by the thinking Church. And even then that is not the beginning. For there is something before the Christian dialogue, and that is the Christian mind – a mind trained, informed, equipped to handle data of secular controversy within a framework of reference which is constructed of Christian presuppositions.'[2] The implications of this statement are profound: if the Christian community is to witness effectively to the power of the gospel in a world that is both confused and confusing, it needs to think seriously about the nature of Christian ministry. It simply will not do to assume that our own favourite model of ministry, or the approach which prevails in our own particular church or denomination, should be applied wholesale to any and every situation we encounter.

My exposure to Christian ministry within a wide variety of denominations is evident in the diversity of ministry approaches and models identified and referred to in these chapters. My roots in Anglicanism have been nourished not only by my charismatic experience, but also by my involvement in a multidenominational Christian education centre. Over many years I have been privileged to enjoy a richness of input in my theological journey, during which I have been challenged and changed. I hope those who read this book will be similarly encouraged to explore the nature of Christian ministry in a spirit of openness and inquiry.

In this book we shall discover afresh the importance of responding sensitively to the context in which we are living and working: it is not our task within the Christian church to export a particular ministry style into whatever environment we face. Rather we are called at all times to respond to the voice of the Spirit, whose prerogative it is to open our eyes to 'the heartbreaking brutality and the equally heartbreaking beauty of the world'.[3]

More than that, it is the Spirit of God who is already at work in the world, touching lives, revealing the life of God in situations of distress and hopelessness, *in the fulfilment of whose agenda we are invited to participate*. Caught up in the love of the Trinity, we are privileged to dance with God in the darkness of his world: hence the title of this book. Christian ministry has, as its starting point, God himself. In fact, we are unable to develop sound theological foundations for ministry until we have critically examined God's ministry in the world. What God has done incarnationally in Christ is the starting point for our theology: ministry thus precedes theology.

So a clear Trinitarian framework is established for our understanding of ministry. If we define all ministry as God's activity in the world to reconcile those whom he loves to himself, then it has already become evident that both Spirit and Son serve the mission of the Father. The three persons of the Trinity are caught up in glorious unity in their love for and work in the world. This interpretation of ministry will undergird much of what I have to say about the nature of the church. In recent years, the concept of 'community' has been proposed as that which most appropriately describes the essence of the Christian church.[4] I shall argue that the social community of the Trinity is a necessary way into understanding the dynamic reality of the church, which has been called into being as the expression of the life of God on earth.

In Chapter One, I offer a Trinitarian framework for ministry, and introduce the Greek word *perichoresis* as a way into understanding the social community of the Trinity. Jürgen Moltmann suggests that this word 'grasps the circulatory character of the eternal divine life ... The Father exists in the Son, the Son in the Father, and both of them in the Spirit, just as the Spirit exists in both the Father and the Son. By virtue of their eternal love they live in one another to such an extent, and dwell in one another to such an extent, that they are one. *It is a process of most perfect and intense empathy.*'[5] Such perichoretic empathy enables the threeness of the Trinity to be expressed without violating the oneness.

In this book I suggest that the metaphor of 'dance' expresses the energy and life which is implicit in this intensely empathetic 'circulation' of the eternal divine life. Though we may dance alone, that is not the kind of dancing envisaged here. Here we are thinking of dance as an exuberant, communal activity. We dance with others, not apart from them. Similarly, though each person within the Trinity is distinctive, they are at the same time bound together in a rhythmic pulse of dynamic life.

To have our eyes opened by the Spirit is – de facto – to be drawn into this perichoretic dance of Trinitarian life, which is both immediate in its availability to us and a promise of richer things to come. Some may be hesitant to step onto the dance floor, but soon that hesitation is transfigured into an eagerness to participate in what Moltmann has described as an 'unconditional Yes to life'. One evening he was reading a passage from Augustine's *Confessions* which led him to respond: 'When I love God I love the beauty of bodies, the rhythm of movements, the shining of eyes, the feelings, the scents, the sounds of all this protean creation. When I love you, my God, I want to embrace it all, for I love you with all my senses in the creations of your love.'[6] Is this not the language of dancing? The Spirit of God calls us into a sensual symphony of life, a dance of praise to our Creator, who alone can meet our deepest longings.

The ministry of Christ in the world, on behalf of the Father, in the power of the Spirit, is continued by the church in ways that not only reflect the truth of the gospel as it has been handed down to us over the past two millennia, but which also relate to the many unique and varied contexts and cultures in contemporary society. Two words which I find helpful in describing my understanding of Christian ministry are *faithfulness* and *relevance*; these are the two essential requirements that govern the ministry of the church, whether in far-flung corners of the globe or in the immediate neighbourhood. Our ministry needs to reflect the ministry of Christ in the world: 'As the Father has sent me, I am sending you,' said Jesus to his disciples, as he breathed on them the empowering Holy Spirit (Jn. 20:21). We dare not lose our centre in the unchanging Word of God. However, at the same time, we dare not lose touch with the world that Christ came to save.

Christian ministry has to do with contextualizing the truth of God in an accessible and relevant way. Herein lies the inevitable tension implicit in all ministry, for the possibility of a dilution or loss of the Christian message in specific contexts is very real as we seek to be those who live in the world without being contaminated by the values of a world that is hostile to the purity and promise of the gospel. As we develop these thoughts in the pages that follow, we shall consider the importance of understanding the different world-views which inform how people live and behave in society. As we look forward to the challenges of the new millennium, in which the future engenders both excitement and apprehension, we will focus especially on the postmodern philosophy of life and examine its implications for Christian ministry.

There are many today who insist that the church needs to change radically if the gospel is to be heard at all by those whose perception of Christianity has been negatively distorted by past experiences, secular stereotypes, and ineffectual ministry. The comedian Lenny Bruce once quipped that 'every day people are straying away from church and going back to God!' Whilst attempting to avoid the trap of unfairly indicting the church, I examine several dimensions of church life in order to direct us to an authentic, vital and dynamic ecclesiology which enables Jesus Christ to be seen as an attractive and compelling alternative to the many philosophies of life currently in vogue.

Part One of *Dancing in the Dark* is therefore a treatise on ministry as participation in the continuing ministry of Christ in the world. Participation as incarnational activity is given Christological emphasis in Chapter One, Trinitarian emphasis in Chapter Two, and contextual emphasis in Chapter Three. Together, these three chapters offer the basis of a liberating theology of ministry which has its source in the gracious ministry of Christ, not in what we do for God. The role of the Spirit is highlighted within this theological perspective.

Part Two – 'Some Implications for Ministry Practice' – is devoted to an in-depth exploration of three specific dimensions of the ministry of the church within the overarching paradigm of participation. As Christians, our journey of faith as a community of believers seeking to make a difference in the world is a calling to participate in the worship, mission, and compassion of Jesus Christ himself. An authentic theology of worship starts with our realization that Christ is our great high priest: in him our imperfect worship is converted by the Spirit into that which is holy and acceptable to the Father. Chapter Four examines the implications of this insight with regard to worship styles, the sacramental life of the church, and the privilege of prayer. The overriding theme that all true worship is a participation in the Son's worship of the Father, who is now our Father, is central to our understanding of what it means to be caught up in the dance of the triune God.

In Chapter Five I adopt a robust pneumatological stance in my presentation of the mission of the church in the world. I argue that participation in the ministry of Christ in the world, which must not be divorced from our worship, opens us up to the creative ministry of the Spirit. Rather than relying upon strategies for mission which may be inappropriate in given contexts, we are invited into the adventurous ministry of the Spirit, a ministry which at times may challenge our preconceived ideas about the way God works in the world!

In Chapter Six I consider the ministry of the church as participation in the compassionate ministry of Christ. In particular, I offer the motif of remembrance as a helpful root metaphor in pastoral ministry: we remember God, each other and others in the world precisely because we have a God who remembers us. Furthermore, to remember that our personal stories are part of the larger story of God who is both Creator and Redeemer is to offer hope and purpose to those who struggle in life. The attention which I give to the power of narrative in one-to-one pastoral counselling ministry reflects this important insight: contemporary emphasis on community must not overshadow concern for the story of the individual in the ministry of the church. Special emphasis is also given to the interpretation of Christian therapy as a 'dance of blessing' in which all are involved, irrespective of their role within the counselling context.

In 1987 the American pastor and theologian Eugene Peterson wrote a book in which he attempted to redefine ministry in terms of keeping communities of sinners attentive to God, rather than pulling in 'customers' in order to build successful churches.[7] He argues that there are three acts which are fundamental to Christian ministry: praying, reading and giving spiritual direction. These acts are quiet, never public, and represent the three angles of a triangle, the lines of which are the more visible acts of preaching, teaching and administration. 'Working the angles is what gives shape to the daily work of pastors and priests. If we get the angles right it is a simple matter to draw in the lines.'[8]

At the end of this book I pick up these important themes of personal spirituality in ministry within the context of self-care and survival. It is so easy for all who are involved in pastoral ministry to allow their lives to be shaped by exterior pressures rather than the interior demands of a loving and ever-present God. Peterson's emphasis needs to be heard in the light of the pragmatism and activism which pervades much of church life today, and which results in hurting and confused people being touched less by the ministry of the Spirit than they are by the frantic efforts of well-meaning but weary pastors.

Part Three addresses these concerns. Two particular temptations face those who are engaged in pastoral ministry: the first is the temptation to rely upon methodology in order to achieve results; the second is the temptation to rely upon personal effort, occasionally to the point of collapsing with exhaustion. There must be a better way! I close with two chapters which advocate participation in and dependence upon Christ in contrast to ministry approaches which rely upon either pragmatic methodology or personal effort.

My own background in marketing and management has given me a particular interest in the relationship between management and ministry. I have already commented upon the dangers of pragmatism, and Chapter Seven examines this critically in the light of the proliferation of books, seminars, and conferences on church growth, church planning, and church management. Tertullian once asked, 'What is there in common between Athens and Jerusalem?', thus establishing a clear distinction, or opposition, between pagan philosophy and Christian revelation. This dichotomy has led some to reject the insights of management theorists and practitioners in Christian ministry. I will argue that this is both hasty and unwise, although I hear those critics who are concerned that we are in danger of burying the gospel message in our pursuit of success and achievement. Ultimately we must insist that any methodology or technique is valid only if it serves the purposes of God, and pastoral ministry is enriched by such approaches only insofar as they keep us focused on God's will and prevent us from being driven by our own ambitions.

Chapter Eight considers the topic of personal spirituality in ministry, drawing together many of the themes which resonate throughout this book. A few years ago a colleague brought back from America a book for me, one chapter of which is entitled 'What does it mean to be incarnational when we are not the Messiah?'[9] The lesson for us to learn in the midst of the enormous pressures to perform or succeed is that we are not the answer to every need – in fact, we are not the answer to *any* need. Christ is. Christian ministry is participating in what God is already doing in Christ in the power of the Spirit.

This insight releases us into a freedom to do only that which God is doing. Believing that truth with all our heart, and living it without fear of the approval or judgment of others, is to minister the gospel in the powerful grace of the triune God. It is to move out of legalism into liberty, and beyond survival to the promise of *revival* in ministry. To be effective in Christian ministry is, in fact, to acknowledge not how spiritual we must be, but how very human we all are, and we are thereby encouraged to embrace our humanness even as Christ embraces us in our weakness so that his power and strength might be revealed through us ... as we dance in the dark with him.

To speak of darkness here is not to propose a dualistic separation between God and his world, as if one were all light and the other all darkness. The world in which we live is a positive and delightful reality which all of God's creatures are privileged to enjoy and appreciate. Later on in this book I affirm some of the riches of God's good creation, and so my notion of darkness needs to be understood in the context of the fundamental Christian truth that unless our eyes are open to the reality of the God who imparts life in all its glorious abundance, then our light is only a partial light, which is as darkness when compared with the glory of the true light of Christ. So Paul reminds the Corinthian Christians that 'The god of this age has blinded the minds of unbelievers, so that they cannot see the light of the gospel of the glory of Christ' (2 Cor. 4:4), and elsewhere declares that 'whenever anyone turns to the Lord, the veil is taken away' (1 Cor. 3:16).

C. S. Lewis conveys this delightfully in the final volume of *The Chronicles of Narnia*, where the company of dwarfs are very much in Narnia, recipients of all the good things that come from the hand of Aslan (a type of Christ) and yet remain prisoners in their own minds, denied the experience of grace because of their own unbelief. So, though actually living in the light of God's goodness, they are in fact in darkness – represented metaphorically by the 'pitch-black, poky, smelly little hole of a Stable' which is all they can see around them.[10] The anguish and frustration of Lucy, one of the children in the story, who asks Aslan to do something for the poor dwarfs so that they too might enjoy the beauty and warmth of the creation around them, highlights the great gulf between the joy of the dance and the lostness of those whose eyes are not yet open. Lucy and all those around her, whose eyes have been opened to the truth and reality of Aslan and the land of Narnia, present us with a parable of Christian ministry. The privilege of Christian ministry is to participate in all that Christ is doing, in the power of the Spirit, to lead those who are in darkness into an awareness of that reality.

Notes

1. John Douglas Hall, *Thinking the Faith* (Minneapolis: Fortress Press, 1991), p. 63.

2. Harry Blamires, *The Christian Mind* (London: SPCK, 1966), p. 4.
3. John V. Taylor, *The Go-Between God: The Holy Spirit and the Christian Mission* (London: SCM Press, 1972), p. 19.
4. See, for example, Stanley J. Grenz, *Theology for the Community of God* (Carlisle: Paternoster Press, 1994), esp. pp. 603–31.
5. Jürgen Moltmann, *The Trinity and the Kingdom of God* (London: SCM Press, 1981), pp. 174–5, my italics.
6. Jürgen Moltmann, *The Source of Life: The Holy Spirit and the Theology of Life* (London: SCM Press, 1997), p. 88.
7. Eugene Peterson, *Working the Angles: The Shape of Pastoral Integrity* (Grand Rapids: Eerdmans, 1987).
8. ibid, p. 4.
9. Charles van Engen and Jude Tiersma (eds.), *God So Loves the City: Seeking a Theology for Urban Mission* (Monrovia CA: MARC, 1994) pp. 7–25.
10. See C. S. Lewis, *The Last Battle* (London: Collins, 1980), esp. pp. 145–57.

Part One

A Theological Paradigm for Ministry

Chapter One

Participating in the Ministry of Christ

'... I am in my Father, and you are in me,
and I am in you.'
John 14:20

From time to time I ask those who are involved in the ministry of the church to define what they mean by the word 'ministry'. Because they are actively involved in serving people both within and outside the congregational life of the community of faith, their responses tend towards a description of specific, visible pastoral functions, especially preaching, teaching, pastoral care, and evangelism.

I recently invited a group of students to list a number of key words which were helpful in their own understanding of Christian ministry from a theological perspective. The majority put forward terms which relate closely to the familiar pastoral triad of *kērygma, koinōnia,* and *diakonia,* which speak of the outward, observable expression of the life of the church in proclamation, fellowship, and service. Their perception of ministry was governed by what they encountered and experienced as participant members of local congregations. One or two suggested worship, not in the inclusive sense of our total orientation towards God, but in the more limited sense of a series of actions which bind believers together in their corporate identity as the people of God: so prayer, sacramental acts, singing and various liturgical rites might be included within the broad rubric of worship.[1]

In recognition of the multi-faceted nature of ministry, one student volunteered 'diversity', and this too must be acknowledged as an essential dimension of Christian ministry. In my introductory comments, I suggested that ministry is God's activity in the world to reconcile those whom he loves to himself. There is no one way in which this happens, because God in his wisdom comes to each of us in our own personal struggles and longings, and sovereignly touches our lives as we journey through life. By his Spirit, he opens our eyes to his infinite grace and mercy, drawing us into his embrace in ways that enable us to respond according to where we are on our own personal faith-journey.

A careful reading of the New Testament demonstrates the glorious variety in God's dealings with those whom he calls to life in him. That is why we need to be wary of pragmatic solutions and techniques which offer the hope of success in ministry. It is as foolish to promise church growth and healthy, vital congregational life through the strategic application of 'tried and proven methods' as it is to suggest that certain evangelistic formulae will guarantee personal conversions to Christ. The central thesis of this book is that no aspect of the pastoral ministry of the church is exempt from the radical insight that pragmatism must be eschewed in favour of participation in the life and ministry of the triune God of grace in our midst. I am not implying here that we must throw all ministry principles out of the window, for though methods cannot of themselves bring in the kingdom, it may well be found that the kingdom can usefully bring in methods 'as appropriate means to accomplish the work of the kingdom'.[2]

The Christological basis of ministry

The characteristic features of Christian ministry suggested by my students are all vital components of the active life of the church, and we shall be giving some of them due attention in this book. However, they fail to do justice to ministry as that which finds its source and purpose in the will of God. In short, they do not get us to the real heart of the matter. Thomas Oden points us to the centre of ministry by reminding us that this centre is 'Christ's own ministry for and through us, embodied in distortable ways through our language, through the work of our hands and quietly through our bodily presence'.[3]

The major limitation of the typical functional terminology proposed is that it focuses primarily on practical actions without offering us any insight into the essentially revelatory and Christological basis of Christian ministry. It is not the task of the church to decide how and when to make God known: it is the privilege and responsibility of those who confess Christ to discern the will of the Father, and in obedience to respond to the Spirit who ever seeks to glorify Christ in the world. So ministry is not what *we* do, but is 'determined and set forth by God's own ministry of revelation and reconciliation in the world, beginning with Israel and culminating in Jesus Christ and the Church'.[4]

The implications of this are profound, for to view ministry in this light is to emphasize the crucial relationship between the ministry of Christ and the ministry of the church. This is what I mean by describing the ministry of the church as Christological. Any local church which attempts to influence and persuade without reference to Christ ceases to be a part of the true church of God. Once the head is severed from the body, the life of the body is extinguished. When the Spirit was poured out on all flesh at Pentecost, the commission given to Jesus' followers to 'make disciples of all nations' (Mt. 28:19) was authenticated. The ascended and exalted Christ was, as it were, back in business again, continuing his work through his disciples.

Bromiley articulates the Christological basis for ministry well:

Christians may press others with cogent arguments, move them by eloquent addresses, manipulate them by clever techniques, influence them by efficient organization, capture them by attractive personality, but they cannot alone do the one thing that finally counts: i.e. give the inner enlightenment and bring about the inner conversion that mean eternal salvation. God uses their ministry as a means to this end, but the power of Christian evangelism and edification is the power of the Word's own ministry by the Spirit and in high-priestly intercession.[5]

Furthermore, the present ministry of Christ in the world may be described as revelatory, for human attempts to minister Christ fail to reveal God in his saving grace. Truly we may say with Barth that 'it is not [Christ] that needs proclamation, but proclamation that needs him ... He makes himself its origin and object.'[6] Only Christ in the power of the Spirit is able to make God known to us, to reveal God as he truly is. And when we are confronted with God as he truly is, that revelation in itself effects reconciliation. All we can do is to be willing participants in God's self-revelation. That is our privilege and our calling as co-workers with Christ in his ongoing ministry in the world.

A Trinitarian framework

Our present discussion leads us into a brief consideration of Trinitarian theology as we acknowledge the essential inter-dependence between Father, Son and Spirit in the ministry of the church. As Christians, birthed anew by the Pentecostal Spirit of mission and power, we are equipped and called to participate in the continuing ministry of Christ in the world. We are given power not only to live as adopted sons and daughters within the family of God our Father, but also to serve a broken world as the Spirit opens our eyes and energizes our lives. Our ministry in the world in the power of the Spirit is predicated on the ministry of the incarnate Christ under the power of the same Spirit. Therefore, it is only in terms of the relationship between Son and Spirit, and the subsequent relationship between the Spirit and ourselves, that we will rightly understand Christian ministry. Later on in this chapter we will consider in greater detail the role of the Spirit in the ministry of Christ and in the experiences of the early church as paradigmatic for contemporary Christian ministry.

A Trinitarian framework for ministry leads us into an appreciation of the historic ministries of Christ and the Spirit in the outworking of God's redemptive purposes for humankind. Orthodox Trinitarian theology reminds us that we cannot separate Father, Son, and Spirit in the mission of God in the world. All three are intimately involved in each other in perfect union and harmony, rejoicing in one another, and ever seeking to express outwardly the love that both defines them and binds them together in a relationship of mutual indwelling (expressed by the Greek word *perichoresis*); similarly, all three are united in divine love for all people.

This love may be described as an intense longing within the heart of the Trinity for human beings to be reconciled to God. Just as the Father longs for all to be brought back home – 'He is patient with you, not wanting anyone to perish' (2 Pet. 3:9) – so there is an echo of that desire deep in the heart of both the Son and the Spirit. All three rejoice not only in each other, as they celebrate the glory of divine life within the Godhead, but also in the homecoming of all who, like the wayward son in the parable in Luke 15, realize how lost they really are and who seek a place back in the family home.

We must not picture the Father as a lonely figure up in heaven, trying to work out some plan of rescue for his rebellious creatures. In a delightfully fresh little book, Baxter Kruger invites us to liken the relationships within the triune God to three books who read each other. 'If you take three books and put them together, they remain three books no matter how hard you press them together! You can stack them on top of each other and place a ten-ton stone on them, but they will remain three books. But what if the books managed to read each other so thoroughly and perfectly that they all began to say the same thing in their own way?'[7] We cannot fully comprehend the completeness and intimacy implicit in such a communion, primarily because, at the human level, we rarely experience it in our own lives.

Yet there are times when we glimpse such a fellowship of love, and the emotion is overwhelming. Lovers who are caught up in joyous delight in each other reflect the love that I am seeking to convey here. At times, in our worship of God, we may be 'lost in wonder, love and praise', as the hymn writer expresses it, to the point where we sense that we have been drawn into the very dance of God himself. We need to articulate more clearly here our theology of worship, as the Spirit draws us into the perichoretic life of the Trinity. In a later chapter, we will interpret the worship of the church as participation by the Spirit in the Son's worship and communion with the Father; we will discover how liberating this insight is for those who are weary of trying to 'whip up' worship, which so often reflects human striving to manipulate God to do what we want him to do (as if that were at all possible!).

It is important to note that we are already as Christians participating in the life of God through the ministry of the Spirit who 'delights in the loving relationships of the divine dance and exults in the self-emptying love that binds Father and Son'.[8] Moreover, the Spirit 'delights to introduce creatures to union with God, the dance of the Trinity and the sabbath play of new creation'.[9] So Father, Son, and Spirit are united in their longing to see all humanity forever caught up in the joy of divine love. That is their passion, their goal in history. It is a passion in which we are invited to participate, dancing with God in a world that has lost its way. So our focus on participation in the ministry of Christ will lead us to consider not only the worship life of the church, but also its ongoing concern for others in terms of mission and compassion.

Not only do the three persons of the Trinity desire our adoption into the life of the Godhead (Eph. 1:5); they are each involved in the outworking of the divine mystery. In systematic theology, we are accustomed to identifying the elements of God's action in Christ in history as distinct, even separate, events. So we develop a doctrine of the incarnation, a doctrine of the atonement, a doctrine of the ascension, and so on. However, it is far more appropriate to view the various dimensions of the Christological event as interconnected aspects of one multi-faceted jewel, from the incarnation through to the *parousia* (the return of Christ), in which all three members of the Trinity are intimately and necessarily involved.

This overarching framework for understanding God's redemptive work, in which the community of the Trinity takes an active part in the economy of salvation, is helpful in thinking about the nature of the church's ministry. Not only are we alerted to the importance of sourcing all ministry in God himself, but we are encouraged to interpret ministry as that which flows out of the corporate life of the church. Outmoded concepts of ministry, which ascribe responsibility for the various dimensions of church life to only a few people (the 'ministers') are therefore replaced by an understanding of the ministry of the community of God's people which reflects the communal life of the Trinity.

Incarnation and servanthood

In our discussion of the Trinity we alluded to the incarnation of Christ. It is rewarding to reflect not only on the Christological and Trinitarian basis for ministry but also on the significance of the incarnation for all that the church is called to be and do. Our discussion will focus on the mission orientation of the church, predicated on the mission of the Son who came to earth in obedience to the Father. However, we should note that 'the prime purpose of the incarnation, in the love of God, is to lift us up into a life of communion, of participation in the very triune life of God.'[10]

Incarnational theology firstly has to do with God's deepest desire in relation to humanity, which is to renew his image in us. In his treatise, *De Incarnatione Verbi Dei*, the early church father Athanasius argued that no one could do this save God alone: 'Therefore He assumed a human body, in order that in it death might once for all be destroyed, and that men might be renewed according to the Image.'[11] So when Christ died, he took all humanity into his death, and in his resurrection, all humanity is lifted up with him. This is what Athanasius describes as 'the good pleasure of God', so enabling us to participate in the gift of life in the Spirit, redeemed and made new by the grace of God, and free to share in the fullness of life and ministry within the community of the triune God.

The implications of this are vast. Now seated with Christ in the heavenly realms (Eph. 2:6), we interpret all ministry from a new vantage point. More significantly, however, all ministry finds its source in our relationship with the triune God. God's very life has entered us in such a way that, renewed in his image, we are privileged to engage, not in our own ministry for God, but in God's ministry for us and for the world. This is true empowerment in ministry – to know that ministry does not depend upon our own efforts, but originates in the heart of God. It is within this understanding of the theology of incarnation that we consider the nature of God's love in Christ in coming amongst sinful humanity in redeeming grace.

In a discussion on the phenomenology of love, W. H. Vanstone, an English parish priest, argues that Christ's self-emptying (*kenōsis*) in his incarnation, far from impairing the fullness of his revelation of God, contains the very heart and substance of that revelation, which is of a kenotic God who is ever self-giving in authentic love.[12] This love is at once limitless, precarious (in that it does not force itself on another), and vulnerable. The servant heart of God is immediately evident in this understanding of kenotic Christology, which speaks of the God who stoops down from on high to take his place among sinful human beings.

Vanstone has touched upon something which is at the heart of the incarnational theology of such writers as P. T. Forsyth,[13] namely the way of love as the motive for *kenōsis*. God is not separated from his creation, uninterested and uninvolved. It is a mark of his great love, and of his freedom too, that he has chosen a relationship with human beings that is given its fullest expression in the incarnation (and ultimate suffering) of his Son. It is far more helpful to interpret the incarnation as a positive filling (*plerōsis*) of manhood, rather than a negative emptying (*kenōsis*) of Godhood. So we might follow Irenaeus's suggestion that Christ filled the manhood with as much of the Godhead as he was able to bear, in the same way that a skilled carpenter, working with the grain and capacities of the wood in his hands, exploits them to the full as a craftsman in woodcarving.

A careful exegesis of Philippians 2:7 suggests that servanthood and suffering are closely connected with the concept of *kenōsis*. We could say that Christ's glory, the glory of his pre-existent oneness with the Father, was concealed in 'the form of a servant' which he took when he assumed our nature, a *kenōsis* which led ultimately to the obedience of the cross. The linguistic connections between the Greek word meaning 'to empty' and the Semitic original can be traced to Isaiah 53:12: 'He poured out his soul to death.'[14] This insight has important implications for the ministry of the church, reflected in Paul's words in Philippians 2:5 that self-sacrificing humility should mark the lives of Christ's followers.

Jesus' own words in John 13:14–15 highlight the servant nature of Christian ministry, modelling the *diakonia* implicit in his washing of the disciples' feet: 'Now that I, your Lord and Teacher, have washed your feet, you also should wash one another's feet. I have set you an example that you should do as I have done for you.'[15] All ministry is diaconal, whether it is the bold kerygmatic proclamation that summons people into a new state of being in Christ, or the more silent, yet equally powerful, kenotic community of the faithful, sacrificing and suffering in and for the world.

Our understanding of incarnation leads us to a view of ministry which focuses on the church as a servant people ready to listen to and identify with the world in its diversity and pluralism. The model for such ministry is, as we have emphasized, the ministry of Christ, the incarnate *Logos*, the Word made flesh, who fulfilled in attitude and action the messianic mission implicit in Isaiah's 'servant songs'. It is a mission of justice, salvation and restoration for the peoples of *all* nations – an inclusiveness picked up in Simeon's hymn of praise in Luke 2:29–32 as he held the Christ-child in his arms. In other words, God became involved with the whole world in Christ. He is not a God who switched on the lights and then stood back to admire his creation, a deistic God who wound up the clock and is now watching us from a distance as the years tick by. He became involved at the most personal level possible, and he became involved with us all.

The God who has come to us, who has entered our lives and simultaneously drawn us into his life – 'I am in my Father, and you are in me, and I am in you' (Jn. 14:20) – is our model for ministry. Marion Ganey, a Christian who made the villagers of Fiji amongst whom he worked feel that he believed in them because of his empathetic respect for them, once wrote: 'You will never do very much for people until you realise in your whole heart and soul that you are not doing them a favour by being with them. They do us a favour by permitting us to enter their lives; we are their servants, not their bosses.'[16] Here was a man who understood the nature of incarnational, servant ministry. Ganey immersed himself in the Fijian culture, determined to understand the villagers who were so different from himself.

At this point, we need to distinguish between responding to Christ as our model for ministry and participating in Christ's continuing ministry in and for the world. To use the language of 'model', helpful though it may be, is to risk the danger of straying into territory occupied by liberal theology's advocacy of Jesus as our 'moral example', and no more. In the early part of the twentieth century, P. T. Forsyth, amongst others, challenged subjective interpretations of the incarnation and atonement of Christ, insisting that on the cross a *work* was accomplished, effecting the transformation of humanity. The objective work of Christ in his incarnation demands an interpretation of ministry as more than something we pattern after Christ, as if he were external to us. It is precisely because we are in Christ, transformed by his grace into his new humanity, and privileged to share in the life of the triune God, that Christian ministry must be expressed in terms of participation rather than pattern.

Incarnational theology reminds us that we participate in Christ as we participate in the world, sharing in the particularities of local contexts. In a study of local church ministry, the Australian theologian Denham Grierson examines the characteristic features of local congregations, arguing that each faith-community is unique in its history and identity. 'Naming' those characteristics (signs of meaning in the local context) will help to determine purpose and direction in the church's ministry in the community, and, to aid the process, Grierson proposes a simple sequential model: *understanding → accepting → loving*.

Grierson's framework is incarnational, earthing pastoral ministry in the actualities of congregational life. This focus on understanding others is central to his model of ministry, which is presented as a framework within which a faith community can discern openings for ministry. Only in understanding a given local context is it possible to avoid 'the dogmatism that teaches us nothing and the scepticism that does not promise us anything'.[17] Such understanding enables us to accept and love others more readily, thus creating ministry opportunities as we share more significantly in their lives. To Grierson's framework I would add 'listening' as a necessary first stage: we will never understand others until we are willing first to listen to them.

The American missiologist Charles Kraft confesses to fears of slipping out of theological conservatism into liberalism in his early missionary endeavours, fears fuelled by opening the door to new contextual interpretations of the gospel. Later, he realized that to be contextual (a concept which I will examine fully in a later chapter) was a methodological rather than a theological modification, requiring him 'to quest continually after new truths even at the expense of previously held understandings'. He saw himself increasingly as an 'open' conservative, 'open to learning things from people of a different culture concerning what biblical Christianity should look like in their culture'.[18]

This methodological transformation is central to my understanding of ministry, for it represents a shift away from a propositional, dogmatic approach to one that has its roots in a willingness to learn from others. Instead of telling others, I listen to them. If those of us who claim to be the Christian church are to minister effectively the gospel of Christ in the world, we need to understand why people think and act the way they do. In a later chapter, I argue that Christian ministry demands a willingness to engage in 'paradigm shifts'[19] in order to interact creatively with people whose perceptions of reality may be very different from our own. In other words, we need to be willing to see things differently. By 'engagement' I am not suggesting any abandonment of the Christian world-view, but rather a commitment to genuinely listen to those who think and act very differently from ourselves. This implies more than just passive acknowledgment: it is active involvement.

Now this can create considerable tension amongst those Christians who are understandably motivated by a desire to see God as the source and author of all ministry. To focus initially on the recipients of ministry rather than on the one in whom all ministry originates may be regarded by some as a retrograde step, an approach which runs the risk of responding to the needs of people rather than to the initiative of God. I understand that fear, and I intend to address it throughout this book, particularly in my discussion of contextualization in ministry. It is sufficient to emphasize here that we need to avoid putting a wedge between an approach to ministry that starts with God's agenda and an approach that starts with people's needs. I will argue later that in the actual practice of ministry it does not really matter too much where we start: what is more important is where we end up, and the journey we are willing to travel along the way.

Ministry as divine revelation

Earlier in this chapter I referred to the dangers of pragmatic methodologies in the practice of Christian ministry. I would like to pick up this theme again in the context of ministry as divine revelation rather than human initiative. How do we respond to those who insist that the church should take every opportunity to introduce as many programmes, strategies, and techniques as are needed in order to facilitate its own health and growth? More extended treatment of this issue – a particularly modern one in the light of the success-orientation that has seduced much of the Christian community in recent years – can be found at the end of this book. However, our current concern with the essential nature of ministry encourages a preview of the topic.

The matter may be rephrased as follows: how can we distinguish between the worldly and the spiritual in the way we go about ministry? Besides raising the thorny issue of a sacred-secular dichotomy, there are many obvious parallels in other dimensions of Christian life. In soteriology, do we hold the Calvinist line (which emphasizes the sovereignty of God) or follow the Arminian perspective (which gives weight to human response) in the effecting of personal salvation? What are the roles of grace and faith in the rite of baptism? When someone comes for counselling, how legitimate is it to introduce psychological insights drawn from the secular world? What is our theology of revival in relation to human actions designed to hasten a visitation from God? It will be readily seen that these questions contain an implicit 'either-or' response, and I suggest that we would be well advised to consider our answers carefully.

As in so many areas of the Christian life, we may not be able to respond in as black or white a way as some would like. There are many 'grey areas' that confront us as Christians, both ethical and doctrinal, several of which we address in this book. At times we find ourselves oscillating between conflicting perspectives on an issue, unable to find any satisfactory middle ground (at least, not for very long!). For example, I often find myself swinging between Calvinism and Arminianism in my theology of salvation, particularly when I am engaged in meaningful conversation with someone about becoming a Christian.

Having been trained in my early adult life in the discipline of management, and having taught management theories and skills at university level, I struggled with the problem of reconciling spirituality and pragmatism when I became a Christian. I have been greatly helped by the insights of Ray Anderson, who makes an important distinction between methodology and 'preparing the way' in the practice of Christian ministry. Drawing from Bonhoeffer, he approves of any strategies which prepare the way for the kingdom of God, for they are dependent upon an awareness of the future *as God has revealed it.* Any methods which serve this goal are acceptable, for methods are neutral in themselves.

Anderson continues his argument by directing us to the eschatological purposes of God. He describes the future, theologically, as 'both a purpose and a promise that has come to the present, rather than being extrapolated out of the present'.[20] He employs Latin terminology to clarify his point. Rather than operating under the concept of *futurum*, which emphasizes that which arises out of the present, those who are engaged in ministry need to focus on *adventus* (which translates the Greek *parousia*), which has to do with that which comes into the present out of the future. In *adventus* – which corresponds to God's future, yet to be revealed and outside human control or manipulation – the present apprehends the future in terms of that which is yet to be or come, and asks what yet can be done to bring that future into reality. So the controlling factor is God's revelation of his will. The ministry of the church is concerned with discerning that will and entering into the stream of God's gracious working – in partnership with him – such that God's future comes into being in its time.

Without falling into the trap of rejecting judicious planning, Anderson proposes a model of ministry which leans heavily towards what we might call the prophetic as a response to the pragmatism of 'what works' which prevails in many Christian communities. His discussion brings into sharp focus the need to acknowledge the sovereignty of the Holy Spirit who brings into being what, humanly speaking, is impossible, and who exposes the shallowness of the merely human. We are confronted with an eschatologically-determined theology of ministry which has its roots in the revealed will of God. It is a sad fact that too many Christian leaders find themselves so embroiled in the day-to-day demands of ministry that they fail to take time out to discern 'God's future'. Many mistakenly interpret what they are currently involved in as the will of God without reference to the wider, eschatological purpose and promise of God for their church or organization.

The significance of all this for Christian ministry is immense. We are called to enter into what God is doing, imaginatively and creatively working in co-operation with the Spirit as he accomplishes the will of the Lord through us. We must ask the 'who' and 'what' questions before attempting to tackle the 'how' – before engaging in appropriate programmes or methodologies.

For example, rather than assuming that I ought to put into motion a strategy for attracting young people to my church, perhaps on the rather flimsy basis that every local church should have a strong contingent of youth within its ranks, I am encouraged to seek God for his purposes for the Christian community of which I am a part. God's will may or may not include a significant programme for youth ministry: he may have other goals of which I am currently unaware. God has a habit of surprising us at times, leading us into areas of ministry that relate to his own reconciliation purposes for the church and the neighbourhood. Discernment of those purposes rightly leads to a consideration of the most appropriate means of accomplishing God's ends.

We recognize, then, a creative tension between promise and plan in the practice of ministry. All who are called to serve within the life of the community of faith are invited not just to reflect upon God's promise for the future, but to actively enter into the realization of that promise through careful, wise planning. This will be the subject of a later chapter.

In her discussion of ministry in urban areas, Jude Tiersma, who has spent part of her life in a Hispanic immigrant neighbourhood in central Los Angeles, likewise emphasizes ministry as participation in what God is doing: 'We do not bring God's reign into the city. God is already there. He invites us to join him in his activity.'[21] Mother Teresa insisted that she was never called by God to serve the poor, only to follow Jesus. These insights are liberating, and represent a dynamic for ministry that centres on responsive obedience to the Father's will, rather than prior concentration on a clearly marked out strategy for action.

The ministries of Paul and Barnabas

Beyond this dynamic tension between what we may call mystery and methodology, we may identify another characteristic of ministry which has to do with our participation in God's purposes. I recall many years ago a speaker making a distinction between what he called a 'task-person' and a 'people-person'. A task-person is someone whose primary vision has to do with getting something done. Motivated by action and achievement, such people are often visionaries who think in terms of goals and the strategies necessary to accomplish them. Whilst not dismissive of pastoral concerns, they tend to relegate them in their order of priorities. A people-person, however, is inspired by a desire to come alongside others in order to encourage and assist them in their personal lives. Their primary goal is to serve others with compassion and mercy, seeking to identify with them in their struggles and joys.

We might suggest the apostle Paul as someone who fits into the category of a task-person, a man who was convinced that 'he was a key figure of eschatological significance, a key agent in the progress of salvation history, a chosen instrument in the Lord's hands to bring Gentiles into the obedience of faith as a necessary preparation for the ultimate salvation of all Israel and the consummation of God's redeeming purpose for the world.'[22] It is evident from the New Testament accounts of his ministry that he was also a man of prayer who held others dear to his heart; nevertheless it is his missionary zeal that commends him most powerfully to us.

In contrast to Paul we have Barnabas, whose life marks him out as a people-person. His nickname, 'son of encouragement', suggests his character. A brief survey of his appearances in the book of Acts reinforces the impression that he was highly regarded and appreciated as a caring and considerate disciple. He is singled out in Acts 4:36–37 for his generosity in giving; he gave the newly-converted Paul the benefit of the doubt when the other disciples remained suspicious (Acts 9:26–28); and he is portrayed as a man of integrity who was trusted to check out reports that Gentiles were becoming Christians at Antioch. Upon finding that it was indeed so, he then invited Paul to take over the reins of leadership there (Acts 11:22–26). To know when to withdraw as well as when to get involved is a vital lesson to learn in ministry, as we shall emphasize in our final chapter.

In no time at all 'Barnabas and Paul' became 'Paul and Barnabas' (Acts 13:42–46), causing someone to comment that 'I would rather have a little of Barnabas's grace than all of Paul's genius!' Barnabas had his faults (see, for example, Acts 15:36–41 and Gal. 2:11–13) but the overriding impression from the biblical account is that he was a man with a gracious and gentle heart, concerned above all for the welfare of others.

The 'task versus people' distinction is helpful in appreciating Christian ministry as that which seeks to keep foremost in our minds the eschatological purposes of God (as in the case of Paul) whilst simultaneously attending to the ever-present needs of both the community of faith and the wider public. Doubtless Paul and Barnabas each shared something of the dominant passion of the other, and we should expect the ministry of the local church to reflect both characteristics in its engagement with the world. We need to be those who listen attentively to the voice of the Spirit in order to 'keep on track' in our ministry in the world; but we need also to be those who listen compassionately to those amongst whom God has called us.

The Spirit in the ministry of Christ

In our discussion of Trinitarian theology, we observed that Father, Son, and Spirit are all caught up in unending unity in the outworking of the divine redemptive purpose for humanity – our adoption into the life of the Godhead. The incarnation has been the touchstone for our understanding of God's ministry in the world on behalf of human beings, and explicit attention has been given to Christ as the 'Word made flesh'. Our references to the Spirit so far have focused primarily on the community of the Trinity and the Spirit's action in disclosing to us the purposes of God for Christian ministry. We now need to turn our attention more specifically to the person and work of the Holy Spirit in Christian ministry.

This chapter has presented the case for the closest possible relationship between the ministry of Christ and the ministry of the church through the motif of participation. Accordingly, the starting point in our interpretation of the Spirit's role in Christian ministry is the relationship between Christ and the Spirit in the mission of the Son. This is an aspect of incarnational theology that has been overlooked in many systematic theologies, which tend to place Jesus in a superior role to the Spirit in this regard. This imbalance needs to be corrected, for 'it was anointing by the Spirit that made Jesus "Christ" ... and it was the anointing that made him effective in history as the absolute Saviour.'[23] PINNOCK

Old Testament prophecy about the coming of the Messiah made explicit mention of the Holy Spirit in the inauguration of a new age (see, for example, Is. 44:1–3 and Ezek. 37:12–14). When John the Baptist arrived on the scene of history to prepare the way for Jesus' coming, he announced, amongst other things, that the Messiah would usher in the outpouring of the Holy Spirit. John's appearance after four hundred years of apparent silence marked the renewal of the presence of the prophetic Spirit amongst God's people. The ministries of Jesus and the Spirit are inextricably interwoven.

As we introduce into the picture the church, empowered at Pentecost to continue the ministry of the Son, we recognize three distinct, yet related aspects of the relationship between Christ and the Spirit. The first has to do with the incarnation: the Spirit incarnated the Son in the world in the womb of Mary. The Spirit remained with Jesus throughout his ministry, encouraging and enabling him at all times. Secondly, without getting caught up in the theological debate about whether the Spirit proceeded from the Father, the Son, or both (the *filioque* controversy), we have sufficient support from Acts 2:33 to maintain that the Son was very much involved in the outpouring of the Spirit upon the world at Pentecost.[24] The third dimension of their relationship has to do with the present-day ministry of the church: in his ministry in and through the Christian community, the Spirit mediates the life of the Son as the church recapitulates his life in the world.

Another way of expressing this is to affirm that the activity of the Spirit cannot be divorced from the activity of the Son in the ministry of God in and for the world. The biblical record is quite explicit about this. The Spirit, as we have seen, overshadowed Mary as she conceived the Christ-child in her womb. He was active at the baptism of Jesus, descending upon him as a dove, empowering him for his mission on earth. The Spirit led Jesus

into the wilderness, and strengthened him in times of temptation
as he prepared for his ministry. The gospels record that Jesus,
upon returning from the desert, commenced his ministry in
Galilee in the power of the Spirit: there, in the synagogue at
Nazareth, he read from the scroll of Isaiah words which he
attributed to himself, thus claiming that he was the promised
Messiah, upon whom the Spirit rested. Those words proved true
throughout his ministry, as he spoke with authority, in such a
way that many were amazed at his teaching, and as he demonstrated through signs and wonders that the kingdom of God had
come in his person.

In our understanding of Jesus' ministry we must be careful, as
we have already said, not to separate incarnation and atonement: they are two aspects of the multi-faceted Christological
event, and both involve the presence and activity of the Spirit. In
the atonement, suffering was welcomed into the life of the
Trinity, so that 'what happens at Golgotha reaches into the innermost depths of the Godhead, putting its impress on the Trinitarian life in eternity.'[25]

Theologians are divided in their interpretation of the relationship between the three members of the Godhead at the moment
of Jesus' death on the cross: did the Father 'turn his back' on his
Son as he drank the cup to the full, or did he behold him in the
agony of suffering his Son's dying? We cannot know, though we
may struggle with the notion of the ever-loving Father closing his
eyes as his beloved Son hung on the cross. Whatever our interpretation, we might suggest that the Spirit has a mediating role in
the mystery of the atonement, such that 'the common sacrifice of
the Father and the Son comes about through the Holy Spirit, who
joins and unites the Son in his forsakenness with the Father.'[26]

Of course, the story does not end there, and the Spirit's role is
evident not only in the resurrection of Jesus from the dead, but
also in his ascension. In his exalted state in heaven, the Son has
divine authority to pour out the Spirit, the promise of the Father,
in order that the ministry of the Son may continue through those
whom the Spirit calls into life. Throughout this book, we shall
observe how vital the Spirit is in the ministry of the church, as

indicated by Jesus' words to his disciples in the upper room immediately before his death. Not only does he underscore the relational privilege of being united with him in his own union with the Father, but he reminds them of their need to be utterly dependent upon the Spirit, who will be to them both truth and teacher, the one who will bring comfort and conviction. And, supremely, 'he will bring glory to me by taking from what is mine and making it known to you' (Jn. 16:15).

It is clear from the preceding discussion that the ministry of the church in the world is a continuation of the ministry of Christ. In the same way that Jesus did only that which he saw his Father doing (Jn. 5:19), the church is given the gift of the Spirit to do only that which is in the Father's heart, neither more nor less. We recognize, then, that Word and Spirit are given explicit prominence in our understanding of Christian ministry, not just the proclaimed word, nor even the written word, but the Word of God himself.

HAND + GLOVE (WORD + SPIRIT)

But bereft of the Spirit, that Word has no power. It is like a glove reaching out to grasp an object – in itself, it is useless for the task. But thrust a hand into that glove, a hand that is vibrant and alive and that fills every part of that glove, and it is a very different story. In the same way that Jesus was filled with the Holy Spirit in order to fulfil his divine mission, so we too, as the church of God, need that same empowering, that same awareness of our divine identity that Jesus knew as the beloved Son of his Father. We need both Word and Spirit, and must never be satisfied with less. It is not a question of one or the other: the church needs both evangelical conviction and charismatic power. Any theology of ministry which sells the church short on either fails to articulate the mission of the Son in his love for the world.

Before examining further the relationship between the Spirit and the church in ministry (a theme which will also occupy part of the next chapter), we need to consider more critically the nature of Jesus' relationship with the Spirit in his own ministry. In his important study of unity and diversity within the New Testament, Dunn identifies four main strands of Christianity: Orthodoxy, Catholicism, Protestantism, and what he calls

'Enthusiastic Christianity'.[27] He defines this last strand, or stream, in terms of the 'immediacy of experience', often expressed in a vigorous way, as distinct from the ordered structure of liturgy and ministry. Arguing that the earliest form of Christianity reflected a strong bias towards enthusiasm, he asks if Jesus himself stood within that stream. Was he an 'enthusiast' and, if so, what sort of 'enthusiast'? His study is highly suggestive for us today in our understanding of the nature of Christian ministry, and the role of the Spirit in the outworking of that ministry.

Citing Jesus' visionary, or 'ecstatic', experiences, the many miracles he performed, and his inspired prophetic utterances, Dunn concludes that Jesus certainly ministered in a way that approximates to the enthusiastic stream. He was different, however, from those who depend on such experiences for their 'spiritual sustenance and sense of direction'.[28] What marked Jesus out as utterly unique was his consciousness of his unique relationship with his Father, and 'his own consciousness and conviction that the eschatological Spirit of God had anointed him',[29] as evidenced by his authoritative declaration in the synagogue at Nazareth as he read out the prophecy from Isaiah 61:1–2.

These distinctive features in the ministry of Jesus lead Dunn to label him as a 'charismatic' rather than an 'enthusiast', in the sense that his Spirit-experiences were rooted in a profound awareness of his messianic identity. He knew who he was and why he had come into the world as the incarnate Word. Rather than relying upon superficial evidences of the Spirit in ministry, Jesus was motivated by a deep Trinitarian consciousness. His whole ministry was directed towards Calvary in fulfilment of the Father's will under the anointing of the eschatological Spirit. This emphasis on Jesus as the suffering Messiah is given explicit treatment in the Gospel of Mark, which is in sharp contrast to the more obviously enthusiastic content in Luke. We may applaud Luke for encouraging us into a needed awareness of the visible manifestations of the Spirit, but we need to hear the restraint of Mark, whose portrait of Jesus is altogether more sober and challenging.

The Spirit and the ministry of the church

These thoughts are relevant for the contemporary church in its
mission to mediate the ministry of Jesus in the world. To be a
'charismatic' Christian is to be immersed in the grace of God,
aware of his Fatherhood in our lives, and mindful that we too are
privileged to participate in the Son's ministry in the world. Not
only mindful, of course, but actually and visibly living out that
participation in the power of the same Spirit who anointed Jesus
for his own ministry. To be a charismatic Christian is to experience at the deepest levels of our being that same intimate *Abba*-
consciousness that inspired and encouraged Jesus.

This is perhaps the most profound statement that we can
make about Christian ministry, for it is only when we truly discover who we are as sons and daughters of our Father in heaven
that we will be motivated to live our lives as authentic and joyful
'eye-witnesses of his majesty' (2 Pet. 1:16). What a contrast to
the burdens too frequently placed upon Christians to commit
themselves 100 per cent to do the will of God in their lives! A
friend of mine once referred to 'the bondage of oughtage and
mustery'! In other words, 'Now you are a Christian, you ought
to do this … you must do that …' Jesus knew none of that: his
ministry flowed out of a self-awareness that was affirmed both
privately – 'You are my Son, whom I love' (Lk. 3:22) – and pub-
licly – 'This is my Son, whom I love' (Mt. 3:17) at his baptism. It
is when I know what God has done for me that I will be motivated most effectively to serve him: the indicative of what God
has done precedes and enables the imperative of what I am called
to do. Experiencing the truth of Jesus' words that 'you are in me'
precedes the empowering truth that 'I am in you' (Jn. 14:20).
Being comes before doing; relationship anticipates service. When
we reverse the order, ministry suffers. This will be the subject of
our final chapter.

Our participation in the triune life of God is, then, our
impulse for ministry. And that ministry may take us with our
Lord where we would not choose to venture. Peter, the metaphorical foundation stone of the new Christian community, was

led where he did not want to go (Jn. 21:18), and so it often is for the contemporary church in its calling to witness to Christ in the world. It is in this sense that the church is called into being as an eschatological community, a phrase which we will unwrap in the next chapter. This also has something to do with being a pilgrim people. Though centred in the stillness of God's heart, which is our security and our peace, our ultimate experience of *shalom*, we are yet called to be a people who are on the move, ever responsive to the Spirit's leading, as we seek to co-operate with God in the unfolding of his future. And the way of discipleship cannot be divorced from the experience of suffering if our ministry is to recapitulate the ministry of Jesus.

Our understanding of Jesus' experience of the Spirit, therefore, reinforces our earlier insights regarding kenotic Christology and incarnational ministry. The Spirit is the one who not only invites us to participate in the exhilarating dance of the Trinity; he also invites us to take the light of that life into a suffering, cruel, and confused world. Mother Teresa was once asked how she could stay so radiant and positive in the midst of the poverty and disease surrounding her in Calcutta. 'I want them to remember joy at the end of their life,' she replied, 'and I want them to know that they are loved.' Here is darkness in all its ugliness and pain. The blindness of those whose eyes are closed to the beauty of Christ has given rise to unimaginable suffering in the world. This darkness takes us beyond the darkness of unbelief and entraps countless people in misery and torment. Unbelief has its consequences, and these are seen not only in the slums of Calcutta but wherever love, compassion, and the beauty of Christ have been replaced by selfishness, hardness of heart and personal ambition. How are those whose eyes have been opened by the Spirit to respond to the pain and the cruelty around them? The answer given to us by Mother Teresa is that they are privileged to play out the divine dance of love in this darkness, for there the life of the Trinitarian God transforms and transfigures. 'Spirit brings us into intimacy with God, not to foster mystical rapture as an end in itself but to sensitize us to the will of God. Spirit wants us to follow Jesus and embody the kingdom in our lives and relationships.'[30] So it was for Mother Teresa: her ministry was rooted in a deep and abiding relationship with Jesus. To be 'in Christ' is also to be Christ in the world.

But what does it mean to be Christ in the world in a corporate, communal sense? Here we may point to a tension which was present in the developing ministry of the early church. Jesus' experience of the Spirit was vibrant and spontaneous, and his ministry evolved amongst a group of disciples who, though specifically called, were not subject to any real structural organization. The disciples were followers of Jesus, a man whose charismatic personality and miraculous deeds both attracted and astounded them. He was a remarkable person in whom was demonstrated the reality of the kingdom of God. They were an assortment of disparate individuals, bound by a common call, who followed their Master in ways that reflected their personalities.

FULL OF GRACE

The tension we may discern here is that between kingdom and church in our interpretation of ministry. As the early church expanded it had to come to terms with the problems of growth. Inevitably this led to the development of different patterns of organization, which in itself is not to be condemned. After all, institutional form 'is part of the givenness of social existence; groups spontaneously create structures to govern their life together and further their purposes.'[31] Those interested in ecclesiology have rightly noted the many different forms of organization which emerged as the church sought to accommodate growth and protect itself from heresy.[32]

Furthermore, it is apparent that the early church displayed what Käsemann has described as a multiplicity of confessions as the Christian community grappled with articulating their faith in a wide variety of settings. This variability in the New Testament *kērygma* 'is an expression of the fact that in primitive Christianity a wealth of different confessions were already in existence, constantly replacing each other, combining with each other and undergoing mutual delimitation.'[33] It is misguided to insist upon a single confessional theology within the early church.

Likewise, there is no *a priori* reason to argue for a single model of church to suit all contexts: organizational variety should not be rejected in favour of a specific pattern, least of all a 'New Testament pattern'. The way the early Christians organized themselves evolved as a response to the social and religious realities of the day. All aspects of ministry – including church government – should be flexible enough to adapt to the unique social and cultural environment of the day. However, organizational flexibility is a very far cry from the rigidity and suffocating hierarchy that afflicts some parts of the contemporary church. Whenever the kingdom imperative of following the person of Christ is replaced by an insistence on responding to the demands of the church as an institution, Christ's ministry is in danger of being stifled.

Authentic Christian ministry must steer away from conventional approaches and models that have as their *raison d'être* the survival of the church. The gospel does not serve the church; the church is called into being to serve the gospel. All ministry is sourced in the gospel of forgiveness and freedom for all humanity, and wherever the Spirit leads the Christian community to bring that into being, there the joy of discipleship is expressed. It may involve a way of following that is at odds with 'accepted church ministry'. There are many stories of people who have been turned down by missionary organizations because they 'failed to meet the required standards' or who struggled in their relationship with the authorities, but who went on to serve the Lord in fruitful ways. Amongst them we could cite Amy Carmichael and the Dohnavur Fellowship in South India, Jackie Pullinger's remarkable ministry in the 'walled city' in Hong Kong, and Bruce Olson's courageous perseverance amongst the Motilone Indians of the Colombian jungle.

In the same way, ministry amongst those closer at home demands a willingness to be flexible and open to the unpredictability of the Spirit, not only in how we structure ourselves, but also in the way we interpret the gospel such that it becomes accessible to those who would otherwise be passed by. An extended quote from John Taylor puts the case admirably:

Our theology would improve if we thought more of the church being given to the Spirit than of the Spirit being given to the church. For if we phrase it in the second way, although it is the New Testament way, we are in danger of perpetuating the irreverence of picturing God's Spirit as a grant of superhuman power or guidance, like a fairy sword or magic mirror to equip us for our adventures ... [T]he promised power from on high is not of that kind at all ... [T]he primary effect of the Pentecostal experience was to fuse the individuals of that company into a fellowship which in the same moment was caught up into the life of the risen Lord. In a new awareness of him and of one another they burst into praise, and the world came running for an explanation. In other words, the gift of the Holy Spirit in the fellowship of the church first enables Christians to *be*, and only as a consequence of that sends them to do and to speak.[34]

When we put our focus on the church being given to the Spirit, we acknowledge that it is not for us to ask the Spirit to bless our plans. Rather, we acknowledge the sovereignty of the personal, divine Spirit, who enables us to understand what God is doing in his world, and then graciously invites us into that work. Taylor's emphasis on the 'beingness' of Christians reminds us, too, that when the church is given to the Spirit, Christians are caught up in the life of the Trinitarian God, who is 'God-in-community'. As the church lives out the life of 'God-in-community', mission and ministry become the inevitable outflow of that life.

Notes

1. See, on this, Grenz, *Theology for the Community of God*, pp. 632–64.
2. Ray S. Anderson, *Minding God's Business* (Grand Rapids: Eerdmans, 1986), p. 46.
3. Thomas Oden, *Pastoral Theology: Essentials of Ministry* (San Francisco: Harper & Row, 1983), p. 3.
4. Ray S. Anderson, 'A Theology for Ministry' in Ray S. Anderson (ed.) *Theological Foundations for Ministry* (Edinburgh: T & T Clark Ltd, 1979), p. 7.

5. Geoffrey W. Bromiley, 'The Ministry of the Word of God' in Christian D. Kettler and Todd H. Speidell (eds.), *Incarnational Ministry: The Presence of Christ in Church, Society and Family* (Colorado Springs: Helmers & Howard, 1990), p. 84.

6. Karl Barth, *Church Dogmatics*, IV/1 (Edinburgh: T & T Clark Ltd, 1956), p. 227.

7. C. Baxter Kruger, *Home* (Jackson MS: Perichoresis Press, 1996), p. 8.

8. Clark H. Pinnock, *Flame of Love: A Theology of the Holy Spirit* (Downers Grove: IVP, 1996), p. 39.

9. ibid.

10. James B. Torrance, *Worship, Community and the Triune God of Grace* (Downers Grove: IVP, 1996), p. 32.

11. *St Athanasius on the Incarnation*, translated and edited by a religious of C.S.M.V. (Crestwood: St Vladimir's Orthodox Seminary, 1993), p. 41.

12. W. H. Vanstone, *Love's Endeavour, Love's Expense: The Response of Being to the Love of God* (London: Darton, Longman & Todd, 1977), pp. 39–54.

13. See, for example, P. T. Forsyth, *The Person and Place of Jesus Christ* (London: Congregational Union, 1909), pp. 293–357.

14. R. P. Martin, 'Kenosis' in J.D. Douglas (ed.), *The Illustrated Bible Dictionary*, Part 2 (Leicester: IVP, 1980), p. 848.

15. For a valuable discussion of the servant dimension in pastoral ministry, see Earl E. Shelp and Ronald H. Sutherland (eds.), *The Pastor as Servant* (New York: Pilgrim, 1986); Ronald E. Osborn, *In Christ's Place* (St Louis: Bethany, 1967).

16. In Gerald Arbuckle, *Earthing the Gospel* (Homebush NSW: St Paul Publications, 1990), p. 218.

17. Denham Grierson, *Transforming a People of God* (Melbourne: JBCE, 1984), p. 11.

18. Charles H. Kraft, *Christianity in Culture* (Maryknoll NY: Orbis, 1979), p. 8.

19. See Thomas Kuhn, *The Structure of Scientific Revolutions* (Chicago: University of Chicago Press, 1962).

20. Anderson, *Minding God's Business*, p. 48.

21. van Engen and Tiersma (eds.), *God So Loves the City*, p. 15.

22. F. F. Bruce, *Paul: Apostle of the Free Spirit* (Exeter: Paternoster Press, 1977), p. 146.

23. Pinnock, *Flame of Love*, p. 80.

24. See Tom Smail, *The Giving Gift* (London: Darton, Longman & Todd, 1988), pp. 116–43.
25. Moltmann, *The Trinity and the Kingdom of God*, p. 81.
26. ibid. p. 83
27. James D. G. Dunn, *Unity and Diversity in the New Testament* (London: SCM Press, 1977), pp. 174–202.
28. ibid. p. 178.
29. ibid. p. 189.
30. Pinnock, *Flame of Love*, p. 144.
31. Kevin Giles, *What on Earth is the Church?: A Biblical and Theological Inquiry* (North Blackburn VIC: Dove, 1995), p. 187.
32. For an excellent discussion of church growth in the New Testament see Eduard Schweizer, *Church Order in the New Testament* (London: SCM Press, 1961). For a descriptive analysis of alternative forms of church government, see Millard J. Erickson, *Christian Theology* (Grand Rapids: Baker Books, 1983), pp. 1070–87; and Grenz, *Theology for the Community of God*, pp. 714–25.
33. Ernst Käsemann, 'The Canon of the New Testament and the Unity of the Church' in *Essays on New Testament Themes*, trans. W.J. Montague (London: SCM Press, 1964), pp. 103–4.
34. Taylor, *The Go-Between God*, pp. 133–4.

Chapter Two

The Church – Participating in the Community Life of God

And in him you too are being built together to become a
dwelling in which God lives by his Spirit.
Ephesians 2:20–22

The contributions of Trinitarian theology to an understanding of
the nature of Christian ministry, as developed in the last chapter,
are helpful as we formulate a robust theology of the church
(ecclesiology). Typically, ecclesiologies have been articulated
with reference to the biblical material or to the unfolding shape
of the church over the centuries. Patterns of church life as suggested by scripture and/or history are then given fresh interpretation in the light of contemporary situations. For example, both
scripture and history testify to the centrality of the Lord's Supper,
or Eucharist, in the worshipping life of the church: accordingly,
this sacrament plays a vital role in exploring how Christians
today express their common life together. Similarly, much has
been written about the governmental structures of the church as
evidenced in the New Testament epistles, and interpreted (not
without dispute!) within the various denominations over time:
attention is naturally given to their implications for the regula-
tion of church life today.

But neither scriptural texts *per se* nor a survey of the history of
the church are satisfactory foundations for a true systematic theology of the church. They may be useful in a descriptive sense,
but they do not direct us in any immediate sense to the *essence* of
the church. In this chapter, I argue that a Trinitarian perspective

offers a richer and more profound interpretation of the nature of
the church than do traditional approaches. As in the last chapter,
our approach leads us away from empirical definitions of church
to one that is grounded in the very being of God. Our primary
concern in this chapter is not with the church's relationship with
a changing world – that comes later – but with a theology of the
church that has its roots in the unchanging nature of God. We are
concerned therefore with internal realities rather than external
forms. It is only when we have got the first right that we can
usefully address the second: we need, therefore, a theologically
rigorous framework within which to evaluate alternative forms
of church life.

Archbishop William Temple's oft-quoted saying that the
church is the only society on earth that exists for the sake of those
who do not belong to it is helpful in directing us towards the
mission orientation of the church. The twentieth-century theologian Emil Brunner commented, in like manner, that the church
exists by mission as fire exists by burning. Vital though these
observations are, however, they fail to define the 'beingness' of
the church, its existential reality. They tell us what the church is
called to do, rather than what the church in actuality *is*.

To speak in terms of mission as its primary orientation is to
locate the church on earth as a temporal reality, whereas the
church needs to be defined primarily and essentially in terms of
its relationship to God. Only then can we begin to speak of the
purpose of the church in its outward orientation. Paul writes in
Ephesians 2:6 that 'God raised us up with Christ and seated us
with him in the heavenly realms in Christ Jesus.' Our discussion
in the last chapter reminds us of the amazing truth that Christians are those who have been caught up in the divine dance of
the Trinity. In love, God has called the church into being, so that
it exists for him before it exists for other people.

Grasped by this glorious truth, we discover a way of life that is
centred in the grace of God, rather than human effort. The Christian church has its starting place in the very life of the triune God,
in which our participation in the divine community of Being
takes precedence over all that we are privileged to do as partners

in the divine mission in and for the world: so it is being before doing that gives 'church' its primary orientation. This understanding of church releases us into a freedom of being that draws from the freedom that is in God himself. Before we take these thoughts further, we need to consider some of the more traditional interpretations of the nature of the church. Whilst not dismissing their value, we shall recognize their limitations in the light of all that we have discussed so far.

Traditional interpretations of church

It is quite clear that any thought of the church as a physical structure of bricks and mortar does a gross injustice to the biblical picture. Jesus declared that he was going to build his church (*ekklēsia*) on the rock of Peter (Mt. 16:18). The notion of *ekklēsia* in biblical times conveyed the idea of any gathering or assembly of people, and here Jesus is adopting a common secular term and investing it with Christological significance. He is almost certainly referring to the earthly representation of the church in this passage, in which the man Peter, for all his weaknesses and human frailty, is appointed to continue the ministry of Christ; this is a ministry in which the other disciples, and the subsequent community of the faithful, participate. Notice too that just as the ministry of the Christian community is Jesus' ministry, so also the church, established by Jesus, is *his* church: 'I will build my church.'

Nor is the church to be identified with denominational labels. When I became a Christian, I was asked on many occasions which 'church' I belonged to, with the expectation that I would respond in denominational language. In my early days, I did just that, replying that I belonged to the Church of England. Although denominations may play a positive part in the life of the wider Christian community, espousing the sort of diversity which we acknowledged in our brief discussion of New Testament ecclesiology in Chapter One, they do not get us very far in our understanding of the word 'church'. We need to probe more deeply.

Another common understanding of the church, held by many who have little contact with Christianity, is the view that the church is identical with professional Christian ministry. When I was accepted as a candidate for the ordained ministry, one or two of my friends and family observed that I was now 'going into the church'! They failed completely to appreciate that my incorporation into the church took place when I was 'baptized by one Spirit into one body' at conversion. For them, as for many people today, 'church' carried a sense of professionalism and clerical status. Nothing could be further from the truth.

Having dispensed with the more popular misconceptions, we now turn to a number of different traditional approaches to ecclesiology. Though not exhaustive, the three I discuss here are representative of conventional interpretations. I have labelled them the 'classical-dogmatic' approach, the 'paradigmatic' approach and the 'biblical-metaphorical' approach'. The 'classical-dogmatic' approach explores the key attributes of the church in terms of its commonly identified internal and external characteristics. Typically, these are expressed in terms of the distinctive 'marks' of the authentic church – one, holy, catholic, and apostolic; the distinction between the 'visible' and 'invisible' church; the differentiation between the local occurrence of the church and its universal expression; the difference between the church and the kingdom; and the relationship between Israel and the New Testament church.

The 'paradigmatic' approach draws upon analogies, or models, of the church, reflecting particular theological typologies. Typological analysis is a traditional methodology for synthesizing and categorizing a range of metaphysical concepts, and can be traced to the earliest Greek philosophers. One of the most helpful studies in this area is the work of the Catholic theologian Avery Dulles[1], who initially proposed five models of the church – institution, mystical communion, sacrament, herald, and servant – to which he added a sixth, 'community of disciples', a variant of the communion model and one which offers, in his view, potential as a basis for a comprehensive ecclesiology.

Although Dulles' models are only partly metaphorical in the sense that they reflect various analogies employed in the Bible (for example, the communion model draws from such biblical images as the body of Christ and the flock of sheep), they are not as explicit as the metaphors which are familiar to many Christians today. Rather, they draw from different 'root metaphors' which undergird each specific model. The herald model, for example, is a kerygmatic ecclesiology, which relies on proclamation of the Word of God and faith as a response to the gospel. The institutional model highlights authority and hierarchy and may at times tend towards triumphalism: school and army are its chief root metaphors. Dulles defends his ecclesiological approach because of its scope in 'exploring the basic models of the Church that have arisen in history, as a result of the differing points of view or horizons of believers and theologians of different ages and cultures'.[2]

The 'biblical-metaphorical' approach is more clear-cut. There are many different, though complementary, images used in the Bible to describe the nature of the church. We will find ourselves referring to a number of them throughout this book. They are helpful in presenting us with a comprehensive picture of the church. So the church is variously described as the people of God, the body of Christ, God's temple or building in which the Spirit dwells, God's family or household, the bride of Christ who is destined to become the wife of the Lamb, an army, a lampstand, a flock of sheep, God's vineyard, and a field. Taken together, they represent a kaleidoscopic picture of the one, true church of God. They provide us with a rich tapestry of the life of the church and give us important insights into the way church members are meant to relate to God, to one another and to those outside ecclesial boundaries.

It is not my intention to examine in depth each of these three traditional approaches to ecclesiology.[3] However, each approach contains insights which are important in articulating a theology of the church which is based on what I have called the 'internal realities' of our life in God. My framework is Trinitarian, and specifically derives from the first three biblical metaphors mentioned above. These are 'the people of God', 'the body of Christ'

and 'the temple of the Holy Spirit'. As we expand our theme we
will identify other important motifs which lie at the very heart of
the church's identity, notably the themes of covenant, community, and mission. We will examine the theme of mission in
greater depth in Chapter Three.

Covenant points us back to God's eternal purposes in choosing a people for himself; community describes the present, existential reality of social relationships, which have their origin in
the concept of *imago Dei* (human beings created in the image of
God); and mission points us forward to participation in God's
eschatological purpose 'to bring all things in heaven and on earth
together under one head, even Christ' (Eph. 1:10).

There is a dynamic dimension to an ecclesiology which inte-
grates past, present, and future in this way: contemporary
church life is thus anchored in the richness of God's eternal purposes and motivated by the thrill of participating in God's future
brought into the present. We discover that by grace we are drawn
into the progressive unfolding of God's purposes throughout the
ages. Released from the pressures to develop strategies in order
to get results, especially instant ones, we discover a new freedom
to participate in all that God is doing according to *his* timetable,
not ours. Our perspective shifts from a narrow focus on the
present to a healthier incorporation into the continuing flow
of God's gracious work in history. We actually participate in
Heilsgeschichte, God's saving history! This is the joy not only of
life in God but also of all Christian ministry.

Theologians have found it helpful to distinguish between
static and dynamic approaches to ecclesiology. Static theories
consider the nature of the church and focus on what the church is
in its essence; dynamic approaches are more concerned with the
life that flows outward from the church, so emphasizing what
the church does. There need be no opposition between the two,
for just as God does what he does because he is who he is, so it is
for the church. There is a movement in God which beckons the
church ever forward and ever onward.

The dynamic nature of the church is explored by Jürgen
Moltmann in terms of 'openness': 'It is open for God, open for

men and open for the future of both God and men. The church atrophies when it surrenders any one of these opennesses and closes itself up against God, men or the future.'[4] Developing his theme, Moltmann argues that the church needs to take seriously its responsibilities to change. This change, however, is not the result of 'adroit adaptation' – which may be none other than external manipulation – but rather derives from what he calls an 'inner unrest' implicit in the nature of the church, ruled by Christ crucified and empowered by the Spirit.

What Moltmann is saying to us here is of crucial importance in our understanding of the dynamics of church life. Insisting on a doctrine of the church which is at the same time both Christologically faithful and relevant to the world, he challenges the church 'to think radically about its origins, to lay hold decisively on its charge, and to return to Christ's future from its now flawed and dying form'.[5] His argument leads him to propose four dimensions of the church today – the church of Christ, the missionary church, the ecumenical church, and the political church. These four dimensions are important in responding to his challenge to think radically about the origins of the church. We begin by taking a brief look at God's relationship with his people through the lens of covenantal theology.

The people of God

The idea of covenant is central in God's dealings with human beings. In our world today, we are accustomed to negotiating agreements through contracts, which specify the conditions binding two or more parties together. Such contracts always contain clauses which define the limits of the commitments entered into by the signatories. Similarly, nations enter into political and economic treaties to protect their own interests on the world stage. It is inappropriate to describe such contracts and treaties as covenants, since they involve parties who, as it were, come to the table on an equal footing.

The distinctive feature of God's covenantal action is his free love in entering into a committed relationship with his people. There is neither negotiation, nor any 'small print' at the bottom of the page. The idea of covenant carries with it both promise and expectation, and can be summed up in the biblical word 'grace'. Referring to God's historic covenant with Abraham, Paul reminds us that 'God in his grace gave it to Abraham through a promise' (Gal. 3:18).

By grace God called a people into being as his own chosen people, and poured out his love and favour upon them. Grace is God taking the initiative, and throughout the Bible we encounter a God who again and again made the first move in restoring his people back to himself whenever they went astray. The prophet Hosea reminds us of the deep compassion of a God who is bound by covenantal love despite the faithlessness of his people: 'I will not carry out my fierce anger, nor will I turn and devastate Ephraim. For I am God, and not man – the Holy One among you' (Hos. 11:9). It is precisely because God is who he is – divine and not human – that we can speak here of covenantal love, or *hesed*, a Hebrew word that conveys a steadfast lovingkindness and loyalty that flows out of the heart.

God is unchanging throughout history in his nature and purposes, and the concept of covenant links the Old Testament to the New: 'I will put my law in their minds and write it on their hearts. I will be their God, and they will be my people,' declares the Lord through the prophet Jeremiah (Jer. 31:33). This promise was fulfilled in Jesus, whom the author of Hebrews describes as 'the mediator of a new covenant'. Through the one Christo-logical event, culminating in Christ's crucifixion, resurrection, and ascension, God's saving grace was universalized for all people for all time. The 'people of God' no longer find unique identity in the nation of Israel, but, through the inclusive, multi-cultural miracle of Pentecost, the Spirit was poured out on *all flesh*.

It is therefore appropriate to suggest a continuity between the Old Testament nation of Israel and the New Testament church. In the Greek translation of the Old Testament, the Septuagint, *ekklēsia* translates the Hebrew *qahal*, which comes from the root word meaning to summon, thus referring to those who respond to the Lord's call. Torrance suggests three phases or stages in the life of the church: preparatory, new, and eternal. He describes the Israelites under the old covenant as 'the Church of God in its preparatory form in the tension and struggle of expectation, unable to be yet what it was destined to be when incarnation and reconciliation were fulfilled'. He likens them to an expectant mother, 'waiting for its new birth in the resurrection and its universalization at Pentecost'.[6] It is incorrect to speak of the church as successor to Israel, however significant Israel may be in the consummation of God's eschatological purposes: rather, Israel is now embraced within the church as the one true people of God.

The 'people of God' motif points us towards the glorious richness of humanity caught up in God's redemptive purposes. In one of his visions on the island of Patmos, the apostle John was taken into the throne-room of heaven, where he heard the four living creatures and twenty-four elders proclaiming in song the worthiness of the Lamb 'who purchased men for God from every tribe and language and people and nation' (Rev. 5:9). I often recall an incident that took place when I was leading a group of Christians in worship in the Garden Tomb complex in Jerusalem. Just as we were beginning to sing, a Russian group burst forth in praise, immediately followed elsewhere in the garden by a party of French Christians. At the same time I heard strains of singing in one or two other languages, and nearby an American began to speak words of encouragement and hope to those gathered around him.

For a moment we were spellbound by the wonder of it all, and the verse from Revelation quoted above took on special significance for us, as we anticipated all that God has in store for us. I realized afresh the meaning of church as participation in the community life of God. Gathered in that place we were defined neither by the structures that reflected our denominational loyalties, nor by the strategies that characterized our interpretations of Christian ministry. Quite simply we were enjoying the richness of our collective communion with God as the Spirit led us all into a deeper experience of the inclusive love of God.

It is important to remember that, although God's inclusive love for all people finds its most complete and explicit expression under the new covenant, his covenantal grace has always embraced his whole creation. Through his covenant with Abraham, God promises to bless all peoples on earth, reflecting the divine benediction in Genesis 1:28. When we speak of the people of God, therefore, we imply diversity. In my early days as a Christian I well remember thinking, 'What on earth do I have in common with all these people?' Little did I appreciate at the time the rich blessings of belonging to such a diverse congregation of people. Over the years I have discovered that the maxim 'variety is the spice of life' is richly applicable to church life!

Variety is a feature not only within local churches, but, even more so, within the wider community of God's people, often referred to as the 'universal' or 'catholic' church. The universal church designates the worldwide fellowship of believers, as distinct from local assemblies, whereas catholicity conveys inclusiveness, an openness to all peoples irrespective of race, sex, colour, and background. This ecumenical perspective, of course, is a challenge to fundamentalist Christian groups and all denominational groupings, where there is the ever-present danger of erecting man-made boundaries restricting member-ship. There is no room for discrimination in God's church – God has no favourites, and neither should we.

In his discussion of the ecumenical nature of the church, Moltmann comments that 'the parochial barriers begin to crumble whenever a church recognizes itself in the other churches in the world and sees itself as being a member of the one church of Christ.'[7] Moltmann's ecumenical perspective is helpful in drawing not from the 'negative consensus' of comparative ecclesiology but from the positive common ground of Christol-ogy. In reality, what binds communities of the faithful together is a common allegiance to Jesus Christ as Lord, not doctrine and tradition. This echoes our comments in Chapter One about the relational identity of a diverse group of disciples, whose centre was found in the person of Jesus rather than a set of propositions.

The body of Christ   UNITY

If the term 'the people of God' suggests diversity, the idea of unity is conveyed in the metaphor of the church as 'the body of Christ'. The following personal experience introduces us to this vital theme of unity in the midst of diversity. In a recent meeting of church leaders I received what others acknowledged as a prophetic vision. As we were singing together, I was led by the Spirit into a house with several storeys, and I recognized a number of different rooms – a kitchen, a bedroom, a study, a family room. I was taken into each room, where people were engaged in particular activities. In the kitchen, food was being prepared, and the invitation was given to 'Come into the kitchen – we've got some good food for you. The door's wide open.' In each of the other rooms the scene was similarly busy with people. In the bedroom, the bed was being made and the encouragement was to enter and enjoy the intimacy and closeness that a bedroom offers; the study was lined with books, and people were being invited in to read from the shelves of the library; and so it was in every room. The door was left open and others were being called to 'Come into my room ...' Then I heard very distinctly what I believed to be the voice of God: 'When you begin to walk in each other's rooms, then will I come and visit your house. You do not know when I will come, but it will be as you are willing to walk through your own doors and into the rooms of others.'

It was clear to all of us gathered in that room that Christ was amongst us, but in parabolic fashion we were reminded of the urgency to 'make every effort to keep the unity of the Spirit' (Eph. 4:3). Just as the river in Ezekiel's vision flows from the one source in the sanctuary, so the church derives its existence from the one Christological source. The river widens and deepens, but never splits off into different streams; likewise, the church is created as one body with Christ as its head, ever widening and deepening as more are drawn in by the grace of God, yet never dividing: 'Christians are one body not because they meet together, but because of divine initiative.'[8]

This is the mystery of the 'one, holy, catholic, and apostolic church'. It is a mystery to be appropriated as well as apprehended. Unity is not just a gift of the Spirit – it is the Spirit's goal to make that unity a reality on earth as it is in heaven, and Christians are exhorted to participate in the realization of that goal. Participation in the community life of God, therefore, is not something that just happens to us: we are urged to make that participation actual as we co-operate with God and his saving grace in our lives. Thus Paul exhorts the Philippians to 'continue to work out your salvation with fear and trembling, for it is God who works in you to will and to act according to his good purpose' (Phil. 2:12–13).

Linguistically, the phrase 'body of Christ' may be interpreted literally or metaphorically. Theologically, however, it is difficult to sustain the idea of a literal body of Christ on earth, as some have maintained. Christ, who is the head of the body (Col. 1:18), is at the same time the one, indivisible glorified Christ in heaven (Acts 2:32–33). Furthermore, given Paul's extensive use of metaphors to describe the nature of the church – one of which is the body of Christ, a peculiarly Pauline term – we are wiser to interpret the phrase as a rich and powerful metaphor, reflecting the reality of the church as the 'one new man' in Christ (Eph. 2:15).

This new corporate identity in Christ is given explicit treatment by Paul in 1 Corinthians. Written to correct congregational licence, division and the abuse of God's gifts, this letter reminds the Christians at Corinth of their spiritual unity in Christ. The apostle emphasizes that this unity derives from their incorporation into Christ as a result of the action of the Spirit in their lives: 'For we were all baptized by one Spirit into one body – whether Jews or Greeks, slaves or free – and we were all given the one Spirit to drink' (1 Cor. 12:13). The 'body of Christ' image is therefore a powerful reminder of the transformation that takes place through baptism of those who now belong to Christ.

We could express this unity in a number of ways. Firstly, Paul's 'new man' language in Ephesians 2 directs us back to the physical body of Christ on the cross: through his death and resurrection Christ has reconciled all people to God. By tying our new identity to the one body on the cross Paul is emphasizing the reality that, as Christians, we are ontologically one in the same way that Christ's physical body is indivisibly one. At the same time we are reminded of the fact that, through baptism, we participate in his death and resurrection. In the first Adam, we are all united in sin; by faith expressed in baptism we 'reign in life through the one man, Jesus Christ' (Rom. 5:17), the second Adam.

Secondly, Christians are one not only because of their spiritual union with Christ, but also by virtue of their adoption into filial relationship to God (Eph. 1:5). This echoes the 'people of God' motif, but takes us further: Christians are those who, by adoption, have received all the family privileges ascribed to Jesus as 'natural son'. 'Both the one who makes men holy and those who are made holy are of the same family. So Jesus is not ashamed to call them brothers' (Heb. 2:11).

The most intimate expression of this family relationship shared with Jesus is the affectionate *Abba*-cry which the Spirit enables in all who believe, assuring them of their status as children of God. To know that God has called us by name is to be released into a relationship in which we are free in the Spirit to call God our Father. All this, of course, is rich Trinitarian theology and Paul's frequent references to the Spirit in his discussion of the body of Christ throughout his epistles should not escape us here. Body and Spirit intertwine continuously in Paul's theology of the church, for there can be no church unless the Spirit brings it to life. This is an important theme which we will pick up later on in this chapter.

Thirdly, Paul's allusion to one family becomes more pronounced in his development of the body metaphor and his insistence on mutual life expressed in responsible relationships. One passage of Scripture which draws this out most helpfully is Ephesians 4:1–16. In the first six verses, Paul spells out the fact of our unity as Christians, and follows this immediately by a call to mutual service, through which that unity becomes, at least in part, a reality in our life together. The results of this unity are then developed by Paul in terms of maturity, which has to do with Christlike character, 'the whole measure of the fullness of Christ'.

In Paul's exposition, paralleling his amusing elaboration of Christians as members of the human body in 1 Corinthians 12, we are alerted to the supremacy of love as we honour one another and seek to lift each other up. In the same way that the human body consists of interdependent members, each needing the other if the body is to function healthily, the body of Christ consists of those who not only acknowledge their need of one another, but who are willing to 'make every effort to keep the unity of the Spirit through the bond of peace' (Eph. 4:3).

The image we have here is that of 'community'. Drawn into community with the triune God, participating in his life as a gift of grace, Christians are those who at the same time have been drawn into community with each other. It is theologically inconsistent to argue for one without the other: 'We were fashioned by a God whose deepest joy is connection with himself, a God who created us to enjoy the pleasure he enjoys by connecting supremely with him *but also with each other*.'[9]

Our world today is a world in which individualism is encouraged to the point where we lose touch with each other. Loneliness is experienced as much in the clamour of city life as in the open spaces of empty countryside vacated by those who seek fulfilment in the urban sprawl. To meet the deep needs of the human soul to belong, town planners construct shopping 'villages' and residential housing estates, complete with community centres. Voluntary associations have been set up to bring people together, whilst technological innovations such as the Internet have created a false sense of belonging to a 'global village'. However, we cannot create community in the fullest sense of that word, for true community is a gift of God which has its source in his own being. Only as we connect with God do we discover the real joys of community life.

Our attempts to recreate community, however noble the motive, are a shadow, a pale reflection of the true experience of community that awaits all those whom the Spirit leads into 'the dance of God'. Moltmann bemoans the fact that although the church has sung its shared experiences of God ever since the Middle Ages, it has not danced them with the effervescent joy which we see even today in some religious groups. This 'impoverishment of body language' causes him to ask: 'How can the body be a "temple of the Holy Spirit" if it is frozen into rigidity and is not permitted to move any more? People who are moved by God's Spirit move themselves, and people who experience grace move gracefully.'[10] The dance of life into which the Spirit leads us is the communal dance of the beloved of God. Just as the three persons of the Trinity interact with creative and recreative energy, ever gracious in their perichoretic dance of life, so all who are caught up in this life engage in the same liberating dance in the power of the Spirit. With this in mind, we turn now to the 'temple of the Spirit' metaphor as it applies to the church.

The temple of the Spirit

In Chapter One we alluded to the Spirit's role in the ministry of the church, emphasizing the activity of the Spirit in enabling the Christian community to co-operate with God in the unfolding of his purposes in the world. However, we also stressed that our participation in the life of the triune God is our impulse for ministry. The temple motif is helpful in interpreting this further. In its original meaning, this word refers to physical buildings erected for the worship of deities; therefore temples were regarded as dwelling places for national and local gods. As a centre of worship, the temple therefore represented an important unifying ingredient in the life of a nation or group of people. In the Old Testament, the Israelites were instructed to build a mobile tabernacle as a dwelling place for God, superseded by the construction of a permanent temple in Jerusalem by Solomon. The post-exilic community rebuilt the temple, which stood for nearly five hundred years, succeeded by Herod's temple, which was destroyed by the Romans in AD 70.

The temple, therefore, signifies the unity of God's people. Under the new covenant, the physical temple is reinterpreted spiritually: 'Consequently, you are no longer foreigners and aliens, but fellow-citizens with God's people and members of

God's household, built on the foundation of the apostles and
prophets, with Christ Jesus himself as the chief cornerstone. In
him the whole building is joined together and rises to become a
holy temple in the Lord. And in him you too are being built
together to become a dwelling in which God lives by his Spirit'
(Eph. 2:20–22).

The action of the Spirit in creating a new temple is reminiscent of the promise in Ezekiel 37:26–27 of a sanctuary, or dwelling place, amongst the restored community of Israel, brought
back to life as the *rûaḥ* of God is breathed into the dry bones of
Israel. This is given new covenant significance by Paul in his
rebuke of those who were yoking themselves to false teachers in
idolatrous worship: 'For we are the temple of the living God'
(2 Cor. 6:14–16).

The temple metaphor also has eschatological significance in
its identification with heaven. The psalmist speaks of the Lord
who is in his holy temple, which is his heavenly throne (Ps. 11:4),
and the writer to the Hebrews describes the sanctuary as 'a copy
and shadow of what is in heaven' (Heb. 8:5). The presence of
God's glory in heaven is such that there is no need for a temple
other than the Lord God Almighty and the Lamb, who are its
temple (Rev. 21:22). The concept of the temple permeates the
whole Bible: it is a metaphor which is flexibly interpreted to
express God's relationship with his people both on earth and in
heaven.

And the constituent membership of this new temple is, as we
have noted on a number of occasions, richly diverse, embracing
all people. In proclaiming the inclusiveness of the gospel, Jesus
offered his listeners a glimpse of the eschatological community,
united under his shepherding care: 'I have other sheep that are
not of this sheep pen. I must bring them also. They too will listen
to my voice, and there shall be one flock and one shepherd' (Jn.
10:16). At Pentecost, the Spirit of God was poured out on *all
flesh*, on sons and daughters, on men and women, on young and
old. So all have been baptized by one Spirit into the one body,
irrespective of race, gender or culture, just as all are welcomed by
the Father and all included in the saving action of the Son on the

cross. The characteristic action of the Holy Spirit, therefore, has to do with both <u>unity and diversity</u>, providing us with a metaphor, 'the temple of the Spirit', which expresses the ontological reality of the church in terms of unity-in-diversity.

However, the Spirit is not only resident in this new temple of believers – he is president too! This 'presidency' may be interpreted in terms of creative energy: 'the Holy Spirit in the church is the Spirit not of repetition but of creativity.'[11] The Spirit takes that which is of Christ and applies it imaginatively and with fresh relevance to both the church and the world. He enlivens the community of faith, leading it out of the sterility of dead tradition and opening it up to the new wine of the gospel. The Spirit not only affirms the historic norms of the Christian faith; he seeks to bring those norms to life in contextually relevant and inspiring ways, so that faithfulness and relevance characterize the ministry of the church. In subsequent chapters we will explore specific aspects of that ministry, suggesting how the church can respond to the creative impetus of the Spirit, both in its internal life and in its mission in the world.

Our discussion here would not be complete without reference to some of the more general ways in which the Spirit 'constitutes' the church. There are a number of directions we can usefully explore. Firstly, the Spirit, who sanctifies the individual believer, is also at work in the Christian community, encouraging change and growth into the likeness of Christ. In the New Testament, Paul reminds the Christians to whom he was writing that they have been called into relationship with one another: so he exhorts them to 'teach and admonish one another with all wisdom' (Col. 3:16), considering how they may 'spur one another on towards love and good deeds' (Heb. 10:24).

<u>Paul's vision of community</u> was of groups of people living <u>transparently before one another</u>, and though we may not be our brother's keeper, we are certainly our brother's brother! This must not be imposed in any authoritarian way; as with all that the Spirit seeks to do in the church, encouragement to personal and corporate holiness is <u>'something we accept freely</u>, because we take part in its very emergence'.[12] In our call to live ethically

in the church and in the world, we actually need one another because we are created for relationship and can only realize our full humanity as we participate in community life with God and with each other.

This communal life in the Spirit is what Anderson calls a 'lived transcendence', which assumes a number of forms: the life of a kenotic and 'ek-static' community; a reality of life in solidarity with the world; and an eschatological life in God.[13] Taking the first two, he argues that the Spirit is continuously at work re-forming us into the *real* form of our intrinsic nature as the image of God. Kenotic community is not something we strive to achieve, it is the goal of our existence as we receive one another in love. If *kenōsis* relates to our movement towards one another in communion with the incarnate Word, then *ekstasis* designates our movement towards transcendent life in the Spirit. In essence, life in the Spirit has both horizontal and vertical reality, and the two must never stand in opposition to each other. The challenge to the church is to be open to the Spirit so that its ministry is not characterized by an unreal dichotomy between the 'sacred' and the 'secular'.

Such openness demands sensitivity and boldness as we respond to the creative initiatives of the Spirit, for 'the wind blows wherever it pleases' (Jn. 3:8): at times the Spirit may lead us along unlikely paths and into unpredictable places. Chapter Five illustrates some of the improbable ways in which the Spirit works in order to reconcile to the Father those who are caught up in false or destructive systems of belief and behaviour. To participate in the life of God is to be willing to embrace (or to be embraced by!) the unpredictability of the Spirit and to thrill to the divine adventure!

In a stimulating discussion of the impulse towards adventure which is God's gift to human beings, Paul Tournier reminds us that the word 'enthusiasm' literally means 'feeling God within oneself'. To be filled with the Spirit is to be enthusiastic! (Notice the difference in meaning to that employed by Dunn, to which we referred in Chapter One.) Specifically, it is to be an adventurous person, willing to embark on risky and perhaps dangerous pursuits. Tournier suggests that all of us are endowed with this spirit of adventure because we are all made in the image of an adventurous God. This instinct 'may be cloaked, smothered, and repressed, but it never disappears from the human personality. The timidest pen-pushing clerk will disclose under psychoanalysis, and particularly in the analysis of his dreams, a secret nostalgia for the adventure which he has sacrificed to security.'[14]

The motif of journey relates to the concept of adventure. The church which sees itself as an institution, rightly conforming to the historic deposit of faith, but lacking the vitality of the Spirit who brings that faith to dynamic life, is a church that has sacrificed adventure to security. But a church that is willing to plunge into that which the Spirit is doing enters into the adventure of God, who in fresh and creative ways guides the Christian community on a journey that is characterized by a robust tension between faithfulness to the gospel of Christ and relevance to the world that Christ came to save.

Participation in community

The concept of community is such an important theological concept that we need to give it fuller attention. The word, as we have already seen, reflects God's dealings with his people throughout history in his desire to shape them into a faith-community. Though God loves each person as a unique expression of his creative urge, his Spirit is ever at work to weave his people into a rich tapestry of life and light, reflecting his glory. The Greek word which captures the essence of God's invitation to share in his Trinitarian life is *koinōnia*, which is best translated 'participation'. We now need to explain this word more fully in the context of the church.

The idea implicit here is not that of belonging to a church, or sharing together in some form of overt Christian activity, but of being incorporated into a dynamic and relational organism, which has its origin in the Trinitarian life of God himself. Of Dulles' earlier-quoted ecclesiological models, that of 'mystical communion' comes closest to expressing the *koinōnia*-life of the gospel. One of the most central elements of the life of the faith-community – the sacrament of holy communion, or Eucharist – powerfully conveys this notion of mystery as believers gather together to celebrate their life in God in the power of the Spirit.

However, we need to be careful that we are not carried away by too much talk of transcendent mystery. The church is also flesh and blood here on earth, and we know only too well the reality of our creaturely existence. The Hebrew understanding of our humanity is far more robust and earthy than some Christian interpretations, which often tend towards a dualistic contrast between spirit and matter. In early Christianity, the church at Corinth, for example, came under the influence of Greek thought, and failed to appreciate that human beings are created as part of nature, formed from the dust of the ground (Gen. 2:7). Believing all matter to be evil, they espoused a bizarre pre-gnostic philosophy offering release from the evil material environment into a higher spiritual plane. Paul, whose feet were firmly on the ground, needed to remind them that the idea of community as participation in mystery must never overshadow the biblical call for people to act responsibly in the world that God has created, living in ethical relationship with one another.

In order to understand this more clearly, we need to consider the meaning and significance of *imago Dei* – humanity created in the image of God. Whilst acknowledging traditional interpretations of this concept, notably the structural and functional aspects of human existence,[15] our focus will be on the relational dimension. As we proceed we will discover how the *koinōnia*-fellowship of the church assumes sacramental reality on earth.

In his book, *Imaging God*, the Canadian theologian Douglas John Hall discusses at length what he means by 'the ontology of communion'. He states his position in the form of a theorem or axiom: 'the basic ontological category of the tradition of Jerusalem is not, as with Athens, that of "being" as such, but *being with*. Or, as an equation: Being=Being-With.'[16] What Hall and others advocate is an interpretation of *imago Dei* which takes into account the theological fact that human beings are created for relationship. This may be expressed three-dimensionally: the relationships between human beings and God; the relationships amongst human beings; and the relationships that human beings have with God's creation, or nature.

In the first place, human beings desire to relate to God, even though they may not appreciate that longing for what it truly is. Augustine's words in his *Confessions* sum this up most famously: 'You have made us for yourself, and our hearts are restless until they rest in you.' Deep inside every human being there is a longing to relate to someone 'other'; but fallen humanity is resolute in its endeavour to satisfy this longing in ways that leave God out of the picture.

However, this Augustinian 'longing for Jerusalem' is not a complete statement of *imago Dei* as a relational concept. In the creation story, God declares that 'It is not good for the man to be alone. I will make a helper suitable for him' (Gen. 2:18) – and so a companion was given to man, female complementing male. In a clear exegesis of Genesis 1:26–27, Karl Barth argues that this complementarity, or juxtaposition, between male and female lies at the heart of *imago Dei*. He cites the work of the Jewish scholar Martin Buber,[17] who distinguished between the impersonality of *I-It* relations (such as a person's relationship with an inanimate object, though a human being may also be treated as an '*It*') and the mutual, two-way character of personal *I-Thou* relationships, fulfilled most completely in the marriage relationship. Buber's philosophical treatise not only affirmed the personhood of God as the one, eternal, and unalterable 'Thou', but maintained that the essence of human personality is summed up in terms of *I-Thou*. This entails activity on both sides, in which both parties are free to either disclose themselves or withdraw. Characteristic of such a relationship is the involvement of the total person: at its highest level, *I-Thou* involves all of me and all of you, intellectually, emotionally, volitionally. Mutuality, liberty and totality are therefore the defining features of *I-Thou* knowledge.

For Buber, to be human is to participate in the richness of reciprocal relationships. Experientially, we actually discover who we are in the context of an extensive network of intricate relationships: I am, for example, a husband to my wife, a father to my children, a colleague in my place of work, a neighbour to those who live around me ... a brother in the community of God's family, and a son of my Father in heaven. It is a liberating truth to know to whom I belong, for then I begin to discover who I am. Logically, our emphasis on God as a Trinitarian being drives us to this conclusion: to be made in the image of a relational God-in-community is to be invested with the same capacity for relatedness, representing the very essence of our being. The German philosopher Georg Hegel once remarked that to be a person is to be in self-dedication to another.

However, human relatedness is not just a theological proposition derived from our understanding of God as Trinity. The pages of the Old Testament are filled with stories which describe God's relationship with his people, and the way these people related to one another. As stories, they function powerfully as 'right brain ways of communicating profound truths about life'.[18] As the father of three children, one of my enduring memories is the joy I experienced as I read to each of them in turn the celebrated *Chronicles of Narnia* by C. S. Lewis. Having read them over and over again, I can say with conviction that they are stories that speak not only to the child but also to the adult. They contain truths that are timeless, and uniquely encapsulate the gospel message in a way that communicates powerfully to those who are drawn into the tales of dwarfs and talking animals, of adventures on high seas, of magic and deep mystery, of ordinary children caught up in a world not their own, of evil spells and strong enchantments, of a lion, a witch, and a wardrobe.

Stories, then, are about relationships, not propositions. And that, of course, is their power. They teach us implicitly and vicariously by drawing us in so that we become part of the stories themselves. Storytelling, however, is a lost art, just as the experience of genuine community has disappeared from the lives of many people today. Stories also remind us about values for living. Sidney observes how glad people are 'to hear the tales of Hercules, Achilles, Cyrus and Aeneas; and, hearing them, must needs hear the right description of wisdom, valour and justice;

which, if they had been barely, that is to say philosophically, set out, they would swear they be brought to school again.'[19]

Jesus knew the importance of stories when he spoke in parabolic style about publicans and Pharisees, Samaritans and Jews, farmers and shepherds, rich fools and poor beggars. Here are real people, whose stories reflect the vitality and power of a given, historical community, bearing the marks of its culture and persisting over the generations as a part of its tradition. Discard the social framework, the cultural context, the history and tradition of a community, and the unique environment within which friendships and loyalties – and hostility and revenge! – take place, and we are left with abstract principles which have no flesh and blood.

Stories work because they embody the life of a community. Biblical narrative is at heart 'a contextualization of the life of Israel (Old Testament), of Jesus (the Gospels) or of the early church (Acts) for the later community of God'.[20] Thus we are encouraged to receive the story of God's people as our story. In its telling and re-telling – in which our stories are also woven into the eternal story – we learn truths about ourselves and God, about relationships and life, and, uniquely for Christians, about life within the community of faith that is the church.

The third dimension in a relational interpretation of *imago Dei* – that of our relationship with nature – is not immediately germane to our theme of community, though it is one that cannot be ignored. Just as we find our identity in the context of a myriad of human relationships, we are also 'creatures of nature' in a far more profound way than many of us realize. Psalm 8 may remind us that God has placed us as rulers over nature, but our exploitation of the planet suggests that it is more appropriate to replace the 'technological' model of human beings *above* nature with one that recognizes that we are created to live *within* the natural order. In turning away from our Creator, we have arrogated ourselves above nature, denying the symbiotic relationship that exists between all living things. Hall's 'ontology of communion' recognizes the essential interrelatedness of all three elements of our 'being-with', so much so that 'human spirituality is cheapened when it fastens on the divine in such a way as to exclude nature and even history from the realm of transcendent wonder.'[21]

The motif of community, therefore, is a profoundly theological one. We have traced its source to the Trinitarian life of the Godhead, which is the prototype for the life of the church on earth: it follows that the defining characteristic of human community as God intended it to be is love. Here we are talking about a quality of love that starts from within the life of the community as the result of each member's personal communion with God. The following illustration may help. Imagine a circle, similar to the wheel of a bicycle, around the rim of which individual people are situated. As each person moves along a spoke towards the hub of the wheel, there is a growing closeness between them. So it is in community: as we seek to draw close to God in our own personal Christian walk, we discover that Christian community becomes more of a reality. That which God has given to us as gift becomes real amongst us. The actuality of community life is not something that we have to engineer or manipulate, though it certainly demands our co-operation and energies.

When we realize the beautiful truth that our love for God has this capacity to radiate out to embrace others, we are released into a new freedom to love. We no longer strive to love, but rest in the love that is in God himself. When we truly come to know this God who is pure love, and begin to rejoice in his gracious acceptance of us, we discover that we can accept others, however different they may be from us. Writing of this love that flows from the heart, Jean Vanier observes that 'the more impossible it is in human terms, the more of a sign it is that their love comes from God and that Jesus is living.'[22]

However, this must not be interpreted as a recipe for passivity in community. Far from it: we are called to vibrant participation in the Christian life. This begins in the heart, for 'a community is only a community when the majority of its members is making the transition from "the community for myself" to "myself for the community".'[23] In our contemporary western society, marked not only by individualism and narcissism but also by

increasing social mobility, there is a danger that the deep longings in the human heart to belong will be translated into selfish
interpretations of 'community for myself'. The challenge facing
the Christian community is how to organize itself in such a way
as to be not only attractive to those who belong but also an
authentic reflection of the life of God, and therefore attractive to
those as yet outside its boundaries.

Perhaps we need to go back to the New Testament for an
answer. We have already noted that the ministry of Jesus was
characterized by an unstructured discipleship: those who travelled with him in his three years of itinerant ministry were bound
not by organizational form but by charismatic call. Probing
further, we discover that the early Christians spent time together
in small groups, sharing their lives in such a radical way that the
world beat a path to their door (Acts 2:42–47; 4:32–33).

Robert Banks echoes the plea of many biblical and systematic
theologians today for the establishment of more organic,
familial, ecclesial groups within the existing congregational
structure.[24] This two-tiered model of church adopts a 'bottom-
up' philosophy, rather than a 'top-down' one: in other words,
the *ecclesiolae* (little churches within a church) are the foundational building blocks of the congregation, rather than representing microcosms of an already existing macro-organism. The
benefits of such an approach over current models based upon
small groups within the church organization are their flexibility
and inclusiveness.

On the one hand, the larger congregational assembly provides the opportunity for the whole faith-community to gather
for combined celebration and witness, and may also act as a
safeguard against any potential drift towards heresy or manipu-
lative leadership within small self-contained *ecclesiolae*. On the
other hand, the small size of *ecclesiolae* offers those who attend
opportunities to share more freely and deeply than is possible in
the church at large. The unstructured nature of *ecclesiolae*
invites a varied and spontaneous participation, uncluttered by
such potential stumbling blocks as 'conditions of membership'
and 'commitment classes'. In practice, many Christians discover

that the charismatic gifts of the Spirit – notably the *charismata* that Paul discusses in his Corinthian correspondence – flow more liberally in smaller groups, encouraging those who seek to grow in this area to venture out beyond the confines of the group. Such groups may also be more effective in reaching out to the neighbourhood, engaging in compassionate service as they identify with specific social welfare needs in the local community.

Increasingly, in many parts of the world, groups of Christians are exploring ways in which their life in God can be more fully and creatively expressed, a life of worship in which they can also get in closer touch with their God-given humanness. In our examination of contextualization in ministry in the next chapter we will be looking at one or two examples of Christians meeting together in this sort of way. The Spirit, who is infinitely creative, desires to lead Christians into imaginative and relevant expressions of community life, attractive to those who are victims of our fragmented society. There are many social networks with which Christians could identify in order to connect more relevantly to the outside world; in the workplace and the university, in the local pub, or shopping centre. These and other networks represent fruitful launching pads for creative incarnational ministry in contemporary society.

We now consider the *modus operandi* of the three persons of the Trinity in fostering and facilitating the type of community we have been discussing. Because they are ontologically a 'community of being', we should expect each of them to be involved 'economically' in the expression of their shared life through the community of faith. The doctrine of 'appropriation' in Trinitarian theology asserts that each member of the Trinity participates in a specific activity of God within time and space, without violating their essential oneness. One way of looking at this is to suggest that it is appropriate to think of the Father as the one who *embraces* such community, the Son as the one who *establishes* it, and the Spirit as the one who *enlivens* it. At the same time, we must be careful not to be too dogmatic, and limit each member of the Godhead to one specific role only: the richness of their perichoretic life together is such that we may reasonably attribute concern and activity to each member in all three areas.

The grace of God has to do with his extravagant love, a love that is both unconditional and fiercely true to the divine nature. As we suggested earlier, it is a love that takes the initiative in blessing others, always reaching out in welcoming embrace. The parable of the prodigal son in Luke 15 speaks so completely of this grace that some commentators have suggested that it is more appropriate to call it the parable of the gracious father. It is a story of a human father's unimaginable generosity and love as he embraces his wayward son, showering him not only with forgiveness for the past but also with a new freedom to enjoy the future. It is a story too of the father's embrace of the elder brother, whose life, though exemplary on the outside, betrays a total misunderstanding of grace. 'All these years I've been slaving for you and never disobeyed your orders' (Lk. 15:29) are not the words of a free child but of a person bound by legalistic self-righteousness. Yet the father gazes upon him with equal tenderness: 'My son, you are always with me, and everything I have is yours' (Lk. 15:31).

There is no favouritism in the grace of God, for it is a quality that finds its source in the unchanging nature of the God who cannot be false to himself. His longing for all people is expressed in his forbearance, 'not wanting anyone to perish, but everyone to come to repentance' (2 Pet. 3:9). In the same way that the father in the parable treats his two sons with equal affection, so the Father of all creation reaches out in love to every person without discrimination, seeking to draw each one into 'the dance of God'.

While the prodigal son is still a long way off, the father in the parable is filled with compassion and *unquestioningly* accepts him back into the heart of the family. That is grace: extravagant and unquestioning love. There is a story – which has its parallels all over the world – of a dishevelled tramp who decided to make his way back home after a life of thieving and imprisonment. As a young man, he had found life at home rather drab; he accumulated debts, stole from his parents to settle his accounts, and left home without saying goodbye. Now he was overcome by an urge to see them again. He wrote to them, asking them to leave a white handkerchief in the window of his old bedroom if they were willing to have him back. Hesitantly he made his way to his parents' home: in amazement, he found himself staring at a house festooned with white sheets, pillow cases, towels, table cloths, handkerchiefs and table napkins, with white muslin curtains trailing across the roof from the attic window![25]

This modern-day parable speaks to us of a God who willingly embraces vulnerability by opening his heart to all people. The tramp could not miss the extravagant display of white linen that beckoned him through the open front door. God's arms have always been open wide in welcome, ready to embrace all who would come to him. Though he called into being the nation of Israel which was distinct in identity from the surrounding nations, all individual foreigners were to be treated in a way that reflected his own grace. In Leviticus 19:34 God declared to his people through his prophet Moses that 'the alien living with you must be treated as one of your native-born'. The all-inclusive, embracing love of God is given even more radical expression when the Lord pronounces his temple as 'a house of prayer for all nations' (Is. 56:7). This is a theme picked up in the New Testament by James, whose letter encourages Christians to eschew all forms of favouritism: the extravagant grace of God finds expression in the royal law of love, turning the world's values upside down as the disadvantaged and poor are embraced by the community of faith.

The community of which we speak here is, as we discussed in the last chapter, Christologically determined. There are certain features of the nature and life of the church which are unalterable, normatively and historically established by Christ in his ministry on earth. For example, we are not free to dispense with the commandment to love one another as Christ has loved us. This new ethic of love 'is not an arbitrary fiat of omnipotence but rests upon a new gift. It is the love of Christ which constitutes the new community.'[26] Modelling its life on the life of Christ, the church community is called into a love that is at the same time both rich in *koinōnia*-fellowship and sacrificial in its kenotic identification with the world.

The Greek Orthodox theologian John Zizioulas expresses this 'provocation to our freedom' in terms of 'institution', using the word in the sense of that which is presented to us as a *fait accompli*.[27] Further examples of the givenness of that which has been handed down authoritatively to us include the sacrament of the Eucharist and the injunction to participate in the mission of the Son in the world. Again, the church does not have the freedom to negotiate on these. They represent aspects of the life of the church which derive from the authority of Christ; he is the head of the body, and as such he has rightful dominion over its life. Over the past two millennia the Christian community has engaged in energetic, and at times virulent, debate as to what is or is not normative. This has often centred on ecclesiological issues rather than disputes over the doctrinal core of the Christian faith: the nature of church government, in particular, has been a continual source of friction, at times leading to schisms and the establishment of different denominations.

Despite the many disagreements which have plagued the life of the church, the historic formularies that have been handed down through the centuries, enshrined in the creeds of the early church and reinterpreted more or less faithfully in a wide array of denominational statements, represent 'the good deposit' of the gospel that Paul writes about in 2 Timothy 1:14. It is in this sense that we affirm that the Son establishes the church: the community of believers are those who are called the body of *Christ*, in whom they are united ontologically, and in whose ministry they participate by virtue of their adherence to his authority as head.

However, Zizioulas takes us beyond that which has been instituted by Christ, arguing that the vitality of the church is dependent upon the creative ministry of the Holy Spirit, who 'constitutes' the church. Pneumatology actually conditions the ontology of Christ and his church because the Holy Spirit is both the Spirit of communion and the eschatological Spirit who points us beyond history. Both of these ingredients, communion and eschatology, are expressions of the nature of the church. The

72 *Dancing in the Dark*

Spirit constitutes the church as communion in the sense that, as the Spirit of *koinōnia*, he transcends all distinctions and not only enables the church to come alive but actually causes it to come into existence: so 'pneumatology does not refer to the well-being but to the very being of the church.'[28]

So the Holy Spirit operates within the dialectic of the now and not yet, liberating the church from a preoccupation with history and directing it to the future – this is the eschatological perspective. It is this perspective that challenges the contemporary church to view its life as an adventure of faith, a participation in the active life of God in the world. It is to this dimension of the ministry of the church that we now turn.

Notes

1. Avery Dulles, *Models of the Church: A Critical Assessment of the Church in all its Aspects*, expanded edn. (Dublin: Gill & Macmillan, 1988).
2. ibid, p. 190; see also Avery Dulles, *The Craft of Theology: From Symbol to System* (New York: Crossroad, 1996), pp. 41–52.
3. For a more comprehensive treatment of the 'classical-dogmatic' and 'biblical-metaphorical' approaches to ecclesiology, see Kevin Giles, *What on Earth is the Church?*; Edmund P. Clowney, *The Church* (Leicester: IVP, 1995); David Watson, *I Believe in the Church* (London: Hodder & Stoughton, 1978).
4. Jürgen Moltmann, *The Church in the Power of the Spirit* (London: SCM Press, 1977), p. 2.
5. ibid, p. 2.
6. See Thomas F. Torrance, *Theology in Reconstruction* (London: SCM Press, 1965), pp.192–208.
7. Moltmann, *The Church in the Power of the Spirit*, p. 11.
8. Giles, *What on Earth is the Church?*, p. 103.
9. Italics mine – Larry Crabb, *Connecting* (Nashville: Word, 1977), p. 55.
10. Moltmann, *The Source of Life*, p. 131.
11. Smail, *The Giving Gift*, p. 193.
12. John D. Zizioulas, *Being as Communion: Studies in Personhood and the Church* (Crestwood NY: St Vladimir's Seminary Press, 1985), p. 140.

13. Ray S. Anderson, *Historical Transcendence and the Reality of God* (London: Geoffrey Chapman, 1975), pp. 227–51.

14. Paul Tournier, *The Adventure of Living* (Crowborough: Highland Books, 1983), p. 5.

15. See, for example, A. A. Hoekema, *Created in God's Image* (Grand Rapids: Baker, 1983), pp. 66–101.

16. Douglas John Hall, *Imaging God* (Grand Rapids: Eerdmans, 1986), p. 116.

17. Martin Buber, *I and Thou*, tr. Ronald Gregor-Smith (New York: Charles Scribner's Sons, 1958).

18. Howard Clinebell, *Basic Types of Pastoral Care and Counselling*, rev. edn. (Nashville: Abingdon, 1984), p. 51.

19. Sir Philip Sidney, 'An Apology for Poetry' in Edmund D. Jones (ed.), *English Critical Essays* (London: Oxford University Press, 1922), p. 23.

20. Grant R. Osborne, *The Hermeneutical Spiral: A Comprehensive Introduction to Biblical Interpretation* (Downers Grove: IVP, 1991), p. 171.

21. Hall, *Imaging God*, p. 138.

22. Jean Vanier, *Community and Growth* (Homebush NSW: Society of St Paul, 1979), p. 34.

23. ibid, p. 22.

24. See Robert Banks, *The Quest for Community in Church and World Today* (Zadok Paper S81, Winter 1996).

25. For the full story, see Patricia St John, *Would You Believe It?* (Basingstoke: Pickering & Inglis, 1983), pp. 9–11.

26. Lesslie Newbigin, *The Light Has Come: An Exposition of the Fourth Gospel* (Edinburgh: Handsel Press, 1982), p. 176.

27. Zizioulas, *Being as Communion*, p. 140.

28. ibid, p. 132.

Chapter Three

Contextualization – Participating in the World

*... men of Issachar, who understood the times
and knew what Israel should do.*
1 Chronicles 12:32

The Christian God is both transcendent and immanent: he is the supreme, absolute Other, who is beyond the world, and yet also the God who is ever present in the world. As sovereign and all-sufficient, he is not a deistic god who created the world and established its operating mechanisms, only to depart from the scene as an 'absent landlord'. To continue the metaphor, he ensures that our habitation is structurally in order and is continually present to provide for us and sustain us, his special creatures.

In other words, God is involved with his world, intimately and constantly. This is the God we proclaim as Christians, the God who has come to us in the person of Jesus Christ, and who comes to us still in the power of his Spirit, revealing Christ to us as Saviour and Lord. This is the gospel the world needs to hear, the gospel which affirms that we are special objects of God's love, and that deep inside each one of us is an aching void that only God can fill. In this chapter we affirm that the Christian community of faith is privileged not only to participate in the community life of the triune God, but also to participate in the life of the world that God has created for himself. In fact, to participate in God's perichoretic life is to participate in his mission in and for the world: the two cannot be separated.

In his discussion of theological method – how we approach Christian theology as a discipline in order to better interpret, communicate, and apply it – Douglas John Hall contrasts the methods of two great twentieth-century theologians, Karl Barth and Paul Tillich.[1] Barth emphasizes the Word of God as that which addresses the human condition because it is final truth that comes to us as revelation. Any condescension towards a world that is fallen creates the possibility of a message distorted by contact with sinful humanity. This 'positivism of revelation', a phrase coined by Dietrich Bonhoeffer,[2] emerged out of a deep concern to reaffirm the gospel in a world that was confused and in crisis between two world wars. Barthian methodology understandably – perhaps necessarily, given the historical context – insisted upon 'the dissociation of the Christian message from the aspirations, mores, wisdom and (especially!) religion of its culture'.[3]

Tillich's methodology has its source in the human predicament – what he calls the conflicts of our existential situation – and proceeds to 'the positive or constructive exposition of the meaning of the Christian message pertinent to that aspect of reality'.[4] Tillich refers to this as 'the method of correlation' because it connects the theological tradition with the issues and concerns within the unique context or situation encountered. The starting point for Tillich in his theological method is therefore the world rather than (for Barth) the Word. The issue, as Hall rightly points out, is one of continuity versus discontinuity. For Tillich, theology reflects the existential nature of our beingness in continuity with the beingness of God, with the result that his theology lacks the prophetic cutting edge typical of Barth.

Barth's approach acknowledges the reality of the discontinuity between God and human beings: 'For I am God, and not man, the Holy One among you' (Hos. 11:9). In his insistence upon the sovereignty of the Spirit, who alone interprets the will of God in the world, Barth stands against any theological position which has its origin in corrupt human nature. We must be careful, however, not to minimize his recognition of the need to keep in close touch with the realities of the human condition – so we hold a Bible in one hand and a newspaper in the other!

Ironically, Barth's theological method was shaped and conditioned by the exigencies of his day. In particular, his confessional approach challenged the subjectivism of the nineteenth-century German theologian Friedrich Schleiermacher. Furthermore, his rejection of the theology of his liberal teachers was provoked by their endorsement of German imperialist policy at the onset of the First World War. Faced with these two situational realities, Barth espoused a kerygmatic theology of Word and Spirit which was 'from above' rather than 'from below'.

The issue of contextualization in both theology and ministry has much to do with the tension which exists between Barthian and Tillichian theological method. The poet Alexander Pope once penned these words: 'Know then thyself, presume not God to scan; the proper study of mankind is man.' Although we are no longer living in the Enlightenment period in which Pope wrote, the spirit of his age pervades today's culture. The growing interest in spirituality and the supernatural should not deceive us into thinking that we, as a species, are no longer infatuated with ourselves and our own ability to put the world right. Liberal theology's emphasis on human experience at the expense of supernatural revelation as the basis for truth and knowledge – and therefore ethics – is very much alive in contemporary western society and threatens to undermine the efforts of those who seek to direct people back to the reality of a God who is outside time and space and yet intimately involved in the lives of those whom he has created in love.

The gospel, therefore, straddles the twin themes of transcendence and immanence. With Barth, we declare that the Christian message has its source in the unchanging nature of God, who is final truth, and which has no need of any human instrument to be effective in the world. Through the prophet Isaiah, God declares that his word 'will not return to me empty, but will accomplish what I desire and achieve the purpose for which I sent it' (Is. 55:10).

But it is also a message which needs to be *heard* by those to whom it is sent, heard in a language which they can understand, and presented in a way that acknowledges the uniqueness of each specific and concrete time-and-place context. This lies at the heart of the church's participation in the world. Each Christian community is a localized congregation of believers called together because of their common allegiance to Christ and their participation in the gracious life of the Trinity. They do not live in isolation from the world, but in critical solidarity with their neighbours, both near and distant, as Barth insists.[5] This contextual dimension reflects Tillich's 'method of correlation', but needs to be modified to <u>avoid the relativistic</u> tendency of Tillichian theology, which <u>allows culture rather than the gospel</u> to be the controlling element in theological method.

Engaging in paradigm shifts

So we need to acknowledge the importance of being aware of other people's contexts in the practice of Christian ministry. An <u>underlying thesis of this book is that in o<u>rder to incarnate effec</u></u>   *THESIS*
tively the gospel of Christ through the ministry of the church, we need to understand why people think and act the way they do. Christian ministry demands a willingness to engage in paradigm shifts in order to interact creatively with people whose perceptions of reality may be very different from our own.

In a seminal study within the field of the philosophy of science, Thomas Kuhn observed that people 'whose research is based on shared paradigms are committed to the same rules and standards for scientific practice'.[6] Arguing that scientific progress has historically depended upon the successive transition from one paradigm to another via 'revolution', Kuhn introduced the concept of 'paradigm shift', which we may define as a change in the way in which we perceive reality.

Just as a scientist, operating within a particular paradigm, develops research-based theories which are consistent with that paradigm, so we may propose a Christian way of doing things which adheres to precepts and theories consistent with a particular theological paradigm.[7] But when a scientist is confronted with a different paradigm, a different *perception* of scientific reality – such as those put forward by Copernicus, Newton or Einstein – a choice has to be made: to adjust to the new paradigm and creatively engage with it, or to ignore it and forfeit the new insights afforded by the offer of that paradigm shift.

So it is with Christian ministry: the challenge facing the faith-community is to be willing to relinquish styles of ministry which are incompatible with the unique features of a given contextual setting: 'Everything must be geared to the concrete realities of time-and-place; everything must serve the *here and now* beloved by God.'[8] To ignore the particularities of specific contexts is to misunderstand the real meaning of participation in the world, for participation has to do with *partaking* of the very nature and being of something or someone else. It is to be conscious of and open to surrounding realities.

Paul Hiebert suggests that the western world-view has a blindspot that makes it difficult for many western missionaries and pastors to understand, let alone answer, problems related to spirits, ancestors, and astrology.[9] This blindspot, claims Hiebert, arose as the result of the secularization of science and the mystification of religion. The Enlightenment era witnessed the growing acceptance of a Platonic dualism which separated science and religion, divorcing the empirical world of our senses from the transcendent world of religious faith. Hiebert's 'excluded middle' brought the two together, recognizing the supernatural working of God in human history, a God who acts in power in the lives of individuals and nations *today*.[10]

It is in this sense that those involved in Christian ministry may need to engage in paradigm shifts in order to interact effectively with those whose lives are governed by a different understanding of reality. In other contexts, all that may be necessary is a sympathetic understanding of what others believe as a 'way into' an effective presentation of the gospel. At times, this may be an extremely difficult task: for example, for a westerner to understand the eastern way of thinking, a vast communication gap needs to be bridged. 'Cyclical history, paths that cross, doctrines that disagree, evil that is good, knowledge that is ignorance, time that is eternal, reality that is unreal – all these are the shifting, paradoxical – even contradictory – masks that veil the One.'[11]

Similarly, many Christians are overwhelmed by the challenge of penetrating the mysteries of New Age or comprehending postmodernist thought-systems. However, to sidestep the task of engaging with these contemporary cultural paradigms is to forego the opportunity of creative ministry amongst those who may otherwise never hear the gospel in a language they can understand. With Paul, the Christian faith-community is summoned to become 'a slave to everyone, to win as many as possible' (1 Cor. 9:19).

Faithfulness and relevance

If servanthood is one of the primary defining characteristics of Christian ministry, mission is the central outward orientation of the church: 'called out of the world, the community is genuinely called into it.'[12] In his own methodological transformation, Charles Kraft began to listen with new ears to those who came from a different culture rather than dictate to them: 'I began to ask questions concerning their problems rather than simply state solutions to them.'[13] This raises the all-important question, suggested by Robert Schreiter in his discussion of faith and cultures: 'Where is the appropriate place to begin: with the gospel message or with the culture?'[14]

The question may be rephrased: where does the task of mission begin? With the given truths laid down in Scripture, or with the particular social, ethnic or cultural environment within which people live today? Do we go out into the world, armed with the unchangeable propositions of 'Holy Writ', ready to confront the godlessness of this age with the Word of God, which is 'sharper than any double-edged sword' (Heb. 4:12)? Or do we immerse ourselves in the lives of those whom we seek to influence, entering as fully as possible into their contexts, identifying with their problems, their struggles, and their longings?

This question has to do with *faithfulness* and *relevance*, two essential requirements that govern the ministry of the church if it is truly to reflect the ministry of Christ in the world. The danger, of course, is that we can so emphasize one part of the mission equation that we fail to communicate effectively to people either the liberating message of the gospel or in ways that relate to them where they are. Faithfulness to the gospel and relevance to the community are both necessary dimensions of authentic Christian mission.

In his ministry on earth, Jesus called people to repent of their self-centred ways and to embrace the kingdom of God, personified in himself. As the Word made flesh, he was uncompromising in his radical pronouncements. Many people felt uncomfortable in his presence. Yet, equally, others felt wonderfully comforted, accepted and restored because he gave of himself to them. As the Word made flesh, he entered into the pain and reality of ordinary human experiences, mixing with outcasts, prostitutes and all manner of needy people. In doing so, he continually crossed the accepted boundaries of his day.

Jerome Neyrey quotes the groundbreaking work of Mary Douglas, who observed that 'the image of society has form; it has external boundaries, margins, internal structure.'[15] Developing this concept of 'boundary', Neyrey suggests that throughout his ministry Jesus was continually crossing the boundaries of his day, contacting 'unclean' people, relating to women, travelling in Gentile territory, disregarding dietary restrictions, healing on the Sabbath and disrupting the temple system.[16] In a word, he participated in the lives of those amongst whom he travelled.

However, to 'pass over into the feelings and perspectives of persons'[17] must not be interpreted as capitulating to the culture. Richard Niebuhr observes that 'in his single-minded direction towards God, Christ leads men away from the temporality and pluralism of culture. In its concern for the conservation of the many values of the past, culture rejects the Christ who bids men rely on grace.'[18]

The possibility of a dilution and loss of the Christian message in any given cultural context is a real one. In his classic study of his ministry among the Masai of East Africa, Vincent Donovan critiques mission approaches for failing to be faithful to the gospel: the gospel was 'lost' in the missionaries' involvement in the lives of the people. Being 'contextual' had occurred at a price. However, it was not true contextual ministry: 'The church was the receptacle of salvation and the cultures and nations of the world were the ones to whom salvation was to be doled out by the church.'[19] What Donovan realized was lacking was a theology of mission that emerged from the context, a theology 'growing out of the life and the experience of the pagan peoples of the savannahs of East Africa'.[20]

Likewise Douglas John Hall critiques the North American theological scene, arguing that there has been a failure to develop an authentic North American theology; instead, he claims, theology has capitulated to the culture. He quotes the work of Ernest Becker in some detail, noting his incisive comment that 'If traditional culture is discredited as heroics, then the church that supports the culture automatically discredits itself. If the church on the other hand chooses to insist on its own special heroics, it might find that in crucial ways it must work against the culture, recruit youth to be anti-heroes to the ways of life of the society they live in.'[21]

For Hall, the church's task in North America is to offer its own special heroics – the triumph of the cross – to a culture which has become imprisoned by a shallow hedonism. But, claims Hall, the church has failed to proclaim a theology of the cross in the midst of the triviality in which North Americans are trapped. Participation has taken place, but at a price which has compromised the gospel. His answer is to invite theology – and here I would add ministry too – to sharpen itself and become more explicit. The link between gospel and culture is then clearly stated in terms of contextualization: 'A truly contextual theology will be a critical theology: for it can serve the biblical God in its social context only by naming the inadequacy and the dangers of the illusion its society tries still to cling to. Its task is not to buttress that illusion but to explore the depths of truth present in our real disillusionment, so that the new metaphysic of hope which may come to be shall be constructed out of God's Word, and not only out of our own desperate need.'[22]

Donovan and Hall share this in common: they believe passionately that the gospel, God's Word, has something of great value to offer people. Its value lies in the <u>theological proposition that human beings are valuable precisely because they are loved by God: they are not loved because they are valuable</u>. <u>God's love is such that it *creates* value;</u> accordingly, the gospel must not be muzzled in the commendable desire to be contextual. However, this is a long way from saying 'We're right and you're wrong!' No Christian is called to be 'a religious huckster who is simply hawking God's word'[23] in order to get decisions for Christ. In fact, if the gospel is all about making *disciples* rather than getting people to make *decisions*, then the sooner we jump on to the contextual bandwagon the better! <u>God is already at work in the most pagan of environments</u>, even before we make our presence felt. <u>Our responsibility is to try and find out 'where the Spirit of God is already disturbing the soul of their humanity so we can begin to dialogue'</u>.[24]

So what is needed in Christian ministry is honest critical, contextual inquiry, not culture-denying but culturally aware. Jesus, the incarnate Word of God, and Paul – like Jesus, the *apostolos* of God – worked *within* their cultural milieus, understanding, interpreting, relating to them; yet they necessarily called people *beyond* their cultural horizons. In a book offering a vision of the people of God as a family standing for sharply focused values in a devalued world, Hauerwas and Willimon express genuine concern about modern translations of the Christian faith in order to make it intelligible to 'modern people'. They are not unsympathetic towards 'theologies of translation' *per se*, but they do challenge what they call a misguided 'theology of translation', giving rise to Tillichian or Bultmannian existentialism or process theology.

Although their interpretation of the contextualization debate may be viewed by some as being rather too exclusive and apologetic, I believe that their defence of the *content* of the gospel needs to be heard: 'In Jesus we meet not a presentation of basic ideas about God, world, and humanity, but an invitation to join up, to become part of a movement, a people. By the very act of our modern theological attempts at translation, we have unconsciously distorted the gospel and transformed it into something it never claimed to be – ideas abstracted from Jesus, rather than Jesus with his people.'[25]

Doing theology and theological reflection

In its incarnational ministry the contemporary church is not only called into 'costly identification with people in their real situations as we see in the earthly ministry of Jesus',[26] but is privileged to invite people to live as 'resident aliens' in the world (to use Hauerwas's and Willimon's phrase), leading them into the liberty of the culture of the kingdom of God. This understanding of contextualization has a lot to do with how we think theologically. All who are engaged in Christian ministry need firstly to understand the context which has shaped their own theological outlook: why do I engage in this particular Christian ministry the way that I do?

This demands honesty in self-examination. My understanding of God arises from my own unique perspective as a white westerner, raised in Europe within the 'baby-boomer' generation, with theological insights drawn from the tradition of European evangelical scholarship. I have been influenced by a particular context which has become very much a part of who I am as a person. Asked a little while ago to identify which theologians have been formative in my own theological journey, I named Martin Luther, Karl Barth, P. T. Forsyth and, more recently, Ray Anderson and Douglas John Hall amongst others. I know nothing of the struggle that many have experienced in their longings for liberation and equality, which has given rise not only to theologies but also to world-views that are liberationist at heart.

My point is a simple one. The context within which we live significantly determines our theological starting point. We are all creatures of history, influenced and moulded by people, events, and ideologies which shape our theological outlook. But, as Hall says, 'conversion to God implies self-knowledge',[27] a process in which we acknowledge ourselves as disciples-in-community who are participants – not just recipients – of the Christian story. It is in this sense that we insist that 'theology was made for human beings, not human beings for theology.'[28]

Neil Darragh suggests that all who are engaged in theological reflection – and, critically, in Christian ministry – need to seek a balance between implicit and explicit theology.[29] He advocates the necessity for all who are engaged in Christian mission of 'doing theology' in context.[30] So we are all theologians, on a journey of discovery (what Hall calls *theologia viatorum*). This is not to argue for a wholesale abandonment of all that our inherited theology contains, but to be willing to expose it to critical analysis, to wrestle with it such that the Eternal-in-Time is not displaced by a preoccupation with the Eternal.[31] Thus Hall affirms the necessity for contextual theology, which, for him, is a tautology.

All theology, all ministry, is an enterprise that involves flesh-and-blood people in given contexts; it is a creative activity, mirroring the creative activity of the Holy Spirit, who is the Spirit of life and movement in a world in which God is continuously and intimately involved. So, as people of the Spirit, as the disciple-community, we are necessarily driven to participation in the world, 'an involvement of the kind that is granted only to those who do *not* know everything in advance'.[32] So Hall eschews 'a fundamentalist treatment of the *Bible* as the locus of once-for-all Truth',[33] and refers to the Spirit who 'will permit us to rest neither in the church nor in doctrinal formulations that know everything ahead of time'.[34]

Doing theology involves us in the ongoing process of theological reflection, and the motif of journey is consistent with the notion of *theologia viatorum*. Not just as a theological educator and as a Christian, but more fundamentally as a human being, I see myself as someone who is on a journey, growing, changing, learning with Christ. Quite simply, I want to learn. The Greek philosopher Socrates once remarked that 'the unexamined life is

a life not worth living.' With this in mind, I want to be continually open to new insights. I value the opportunity to read, particularly authors whose churchmanship and tradition are
different from my own. I also enjoy being with people, engaging
with them in discussion and reflection – both in my pastoral
ministry over the years and in the opportunities to meet with my
peers I have discovered rich insights from others who, like me,
are on the same journey; travelling along different paths,
certainly, but all part of the same faith-community. Ultimately,
however instructive other authors have been, the most important
and significant raw data are people themselves, whose lives
reflect the truths I am learning as I journey with them.

In a fascinating exploration of the limitations of the Socratic
approach to thinking, which seeks to arrive at 'truth' through an
inductive process of questions and statements, Edward de Bono,
the present-day 'guru' of thinking, argues that the western mind
has been squeezed into a straightjacket, locked into a logical
'left-brain' paradigm of thinking.[35] He illustrates his point with a
simple exercise which I have used with students from time to
time, involving a sequence of pieces of card which are presented
one or two at a time. The person receiving these pieces has to
arrange them according to what he or she thinks is 'best' at that
time. The other pieces are offered, to be added to the original
arrangement, and the final piece is given with the invitation to
'complete the square'. Unless the final objective is declared at the
outset, the person attempting the exercise is unlikely to arrange
the pieces satisfactorily at the first attempt.

The implications for the evolution of ideas are spelled out by
de Bono in the form of a fundamental principle: 'In any system in
which information comes in over time and there is a need to
make the best use of it at every moment, there is an absolute need
to be able to go back and to rearrange the components in order to
make the best use of the available information.'[36] Change, therefore, is not just about being willing to move forward, embracing
new ideas: it may be necessary to *move back* to change something which seemed perfectly right in the light of the information
available at the time.

This is a threatening and risky enterprise, but an essential aspect of all theological reflection as it is of all personal growth. De Bono suggests that any new ideas which involve a rearrangement of components should ideally be held 'in parallel' alongside the old idea, so that over time that which is preferable becomes the chosen approach. His methodology invites a spirit of creativity as we are encouraged not just to move forward logically in our thinking, but to be willing to move backwards and to switch between options in order to arrive at the best paradigm to fit the prevailing conditions.

We recognize here an important relationship between our participation in the world and our participation in the community life of God, for each informs and sheds light on the other. As we engage incarnationally in the ministry to which Christ calls us, we discover insights which address both our theological understanding and the nature of our communion with the triune God. And the reverse is also true: our ministry in the world is enhanced by our new theological awareness. So the two cannot be separated.

Stephen Pattison has developed an approach to theological reflection modelled on what he calls 'critical conversation', which has more to do with discovering the right questions than arriving at the right answers.[37] He suggests that success in theological reflection has less to do with academic ability (though this is not to be derided!) than with inventiveness and imagination – a sort of 'right-brain' creativity that seeks to discern what I call 'patterns of truth' within the triad of student presuppositions, Christian tradition, and the appropriate context.

An alternative model has been put forward by David Lyall, whose approach is a classic model of doing theology within a strongly contextual framework, drawing from the work of Edward Farley.[38] It demands that all theological reflection carries with it a necessary freedom either to respond or to stay silent, depending on how one interprets the situation under review. In this respect, it involves a process which has its genesis not in our own 'inherited' theology but in the givenness of the particular issue under examination. Farley's emphasis on history and systems analysis is particularly helpful in the light of temptations to evaluate situations within a *too-localized* time and space framework; we are encouraged to think more widely than we are accustomed to as we interact with those around us.

So the dialectic between gospel and culture is presented here as that which takes place within our own personal faith-journey as we engage in theological reflection. The integrating concept is that of context. God is a God-in-context, who lives and moves amongst his people, whose story is not a story in isolation, but one that interacts with your story and my story. And your story is not my story; my context is not your context. All ministry, all mission, must be founded on this basic premise.

We are all participants in God's story, engaging in *theologia viatorum* as we witness to Christ in the world. And in the process we need to understand our own context and the presuppositions and value judgments that *we* bring to the task of ministry, and we need to understand the contexts of others if we are to learn, grow and experience the richness of engaging compassionately with the world that God loves. But we also need to understand, in a way that informs all that we are and all that we do, that Christ alone is the answer to the pain and confusion of this world. To compromise on that is to lose our moorings and to come well and truly adrift.

My thesis, then, is that authentic Christian ministry demands that we become both servants of the gospel and servants of the community. We are learners, interacting humbly with the Word and with the world, allowing each to enrich the other in our experience of ministry. Perhaps it is not so important where we start in mission as where we end up. There are many advantages in starting with the context: as I argued earlier, we are required to listen in a way that helps us truly to understand what is going on in a person's life. Rather than taking the gospel and trying to work it into the context, it may be far more fruitful to start with the context and work backwards from that to the gospel: what has the gospel to say in this situation or that set of circumstances?

This is not to argue for a model of mission that permits the context to set the agenda for the Christian church: as we have said, the gospel is a proactive and transformative presence in the world. So the challenge is to engage with the world in such a way as to retain both cultural relevance and gospel-faithfulness, without falling into either cultural naivety or dogmatic fundamentalism. Faithfulness to the gospel involves both doctrinal and ethical fidelity, both of which are necessary expressions of Christian witness.

Doctrinal faithfulness refers to adherence to historic biblical truth-statements, whereas ethical faithfulness has to do with personal integrity in living out these truth-statements ('practising what we preach'). In the process, precisely because we are active participants in God's world, our own story and faith-development cannot be divorced from our engagement in ministry. We must change even as we seek change in others – this is *theologia viatorum*. Donovan quotes some advice given to him by a young person in an American university: 'In working with young people in America, do not try to call them back to where they were, and do not try to call them to where you are, as beautiful as that place might seem to you. You must have the courage to go with them to a place that neither you nor they have ever been before.'[39]

The world-view concept

In order to incarnate effectively the gospel of Christ through the ministry of the church in the world, we need to grapple with the issue of diversity in world-views.[40] It is important that we understand and appreciate what people believe about the origin, nature, and destiny of human beings and the cosmos, and where God fits into their perception of reality. These are metaphysical questions which, especially for the Christian, focus on the interplay between philosophy and theology. Here we will explore the world-view concept not only within a philosophical framework; historical and cultural perspectives will also be introduced, since it is helpful to understand how the particular components of a world-view have been shaped.

Our focus will be on societies and cultures whose defining characteristics are essentially of a Christian or secular nature. The complexities of eastern world-views, indigenous religious belief systems, and other non-western philosophies of life are such that we cannot give them adequate treatment in this book. Accordingly, our approach will be slanted towards familiar western world-view categories. Our examination will also identify specific questions to which a well-rounded world-view needs to give basic answers. As we have already argued, Christian ministry demands a willingness to engage in paradigm shifts in order to facilitate meaningful interaction between gospel and culture, which, as we have seen, lies at the very heart of participatory ministry.

Our approach to the task is necessarily multi-disciplinary. Herman Dooyeweerd, the Dutch Christian philosopher, argues that the unifying perspective within one's beliefs, attitudes, and values is an essentially religious one: he contrasts the overt religious stance of a Christian world-view with the quasi-religious nature of scientific humanism – or naturalism – and both unify the believer's life world. In 1961, the United States Supreme Court, in what has come to be known as the Torcasco decision, formally recognized secular humanism as a religion. This adds weight to Hoffeker's view that 'all of life is religion.'[41] The renowned theologian, Albert Schweitzer, regarded the distinction between a religious world-view and a philosophical one as superficial: 'The religious world-view which seeks to comprehend itself in thought becomes philosophical ... On the other hand a philosophical world-view, if it is really profound, assumes a religious character.'[42]

We are confronted here with a fundamental contrast between theistic and atheistic world-views, reminiscent of Augustine's two cities, one peopled by those who are motivated by a love for God, and the other inhabited by lovers of self.[43] A world-view may be defined as 'a set of presuppositions (assumptions which may be true, partially true or entirely false) which we hold (consciously or subconsciously, consistently or inconsistently) about the basic make-up of our world'.[44] 'World-view' is a translation of the German *Weltanschauung*, which Schweitzer defines as the sum total of the thoughts which the community or the individual think about the nature and purpose of the universe and about the place and destiny of mankind within the world.[45] More popularly, world-view has been described as a person's 'ToE', or 'big toe'! – a 'theory of everything'. For Kraft, taking a cultural perspective, it is our 'basic model of reality'.

World-views, as we suggested earlier, can be examined through the lenses of both philosophy and theology. Our basic model of reality is theological precisely because to ask questions about the nature of prime reality or the source of truth and morality is to be confronted by the possible existence of a transcendent being other than ourselves. In his masterly volume, *Does God Exist?*, Hans Küng asks: 'How, then, is the open question of unity and truth, meaning and value, of the whole to be answered? How is a solution to be found for problems of life, of cosmology, of society, of the world?'[46] He then goes on to state that these questions are 'obviously connected with the question of God', a thesis which he develops at different stages throughout his book.

Our world-view is also philosophical because the issues which are addressed are metaphysical in nature. Four areas of metaphysical inquiry may be identified here. They are epistemology, ontology, axiology, and teleology. Epistemology is concerned with the nature and source of truth and the origins of knowledge; ontology addresses the issue of the nature of existence and prime reality; axiology has to do with the study of the theory of values, in which questions of ethics arise; and teleology relates to end purposes, seeking to understand ultimate destinies and final causes.

Truth, existence, values, destiny – these are the fundamental philosophical components of a person's world-view. They form the basic building blocks in our understanding of reality. They address the questions: What is true? What is real? What is right? What is final? These questions probe the very core of our existence as human beings, and govern every dimension of life as it is lived: intellectual, emotional, social, moral, economic, and physical. As human beings, we are motivated by an ever-present, often urgent, need to discover what Aristotle called *summum bonum*, the 'good life'. Accordingly, we may explore the nature of our world-view in terms of our journey in search of this 'good life'.

We are usually unaware of why we interpret our experiences of life as we do: our world-view is largely unconscious, shaped by many factors which have to do with history, culture, education, experience, and personality. This being so, we may confidently claim that many of those who are engaged in Christian ministry are ignorant not only of their own model of reality, but also of those held by others with whom they may be involved. Walsh and Middleton offer some help here in proposing an alternative entry into the world-views of others through the concept of 'faith commitment', which is our response to a similar set of four basic questions: Who am I? Where am I? What's wrong? What is the remedy?[47] These questions represent windows into alternative world-views held by others.

4 QUESTIONS

Historical perspective

Earlier, I referred to the value of an historical approach to the study of world-views. An historically-based evaluation suggests to us that 'there is nothing new under the sun' (Ecc. 1:9). World-views come and go, reappearing in different guises throughout history, so a historical perspective adds important insights into alternative, at times competing, contemporary models of reality. In fact, 'contemporary views have developed only by virtue of the efforts of those who have preceded us. If we see things more clearly than they, that is because we sit on the shoulders of giants of the past. Historical overviews expand our horizons.'[48] We can attempt only a brief historical survey here.

In his important contribution in this area, Hoffeker points out the sharp antithesis between theocentric and anthropocentric world-views, between divine authority and human autonomy. He traces the development of western thought about God and humanity, highlighting major paradigm shifts from the biblical

patriarchal era through to the present day. Three major periods
in history are identified as appropriate in the study of world-
view, which he labels 'antithesis', 'synthesis' and 'post-synthesis':
Hoffeker identifies these periods as the ancient period (2000 BC –
AD 400), the Middle Ages (AD 400–1500) and the modern era
(AD 1500 – present).[49]

The biblical world-view of the early church was primitive in
its formulation, and it was the early fifth-century theologian
Augustine who gave Christian theism its foundational principles. Originally intending to synthesize Greek and biblical
thought, he abandoned the enterprise as he developed his theology of the grace of the triune God and the sinfulness of human
beings. Augustine's world-view was constructed around the
knowledge – and his personal experience – that Christ alone has
'the power to free human beings from savagery and lust'.[50]

In the medieval era Thomas Aquinas sought a synthesis
between the biblical emphasis on revelation and the role of reason
in theology, seeking an all-inclusive world-view. In fourteenth-
and fifteenth-century Europe Renaissance humanism was more
concerned with how ideas were expressed than with their content:
McGrath points out that the humanism of this period was
'essentially a cultural programme, which appealed to classical
antiquity as a model of eloquence'.[51] It is important to recognize
that the scholars, writers and artists of the Renaissance were not
humanists in the modern sense, denying the existence of God;
rather, they sought to reform Christianity by returning to the
original languages of the classical period.

Of all Renaissance humanists, the Dutch scholar Erasmus
articulated the relationship between theology and humanism
most effectively. Rejecting the intellectualism of medieval 'scho-
lasticism', and condemning the superstition and corruption of
the institutional church of his day, he advocated a Christian
humanism rooted in the education of the laity; his published
edition of the Greek New Testament in 1516 was a landmark
contribution in this direction.

However, the re-emergence of classical Greek ideas, combined
with the 'explosive confidence of the human mind, the

celebration of art, morals, thought and life on an eminently human scale'[52] gave rise to what Hoffeker has described as the post-synthetic era. The humanistic ideals of the Renaissance increasingly rejected biblical concepts and values, whilst the Reformation theologians urged a return to biblical principles as the basis of an overall world-view. The battle between theocentrism and anthropocentrism was intense at times as the Renaissance gave way to the scientific rationalism of the Enlightenment and post-Enlightenment romanticism.

Despite the pietism of the seventeenth and eighteenth centuries and the evangelicalism of the Wesleys, Whitefield, and Edwards, secular humanism gained ground at the expense of Judeo-Christian truth-claims and ethics. McGrath observes that 'with this collapse in confidence in universal and necessary criteria of truth, relativism and pluralism have flourished.'[53] The world in which we live today is an intriguing mix of Enlightenment ideals and postmodern experimentation in which 'anything goes', epitomized in the neo-paganism of the New Age movement.

As we begin life in a new millennium, we can look back over the twentieth century and note that 'fundamentalists, feminists, communitarians, evangelicals, liberationists and environmentalists have continued to criticise modern western liberalism, with varying degrees of success.'[54] Of course, the risks inherent in the loss of an overarching philosophy of life may not be as great as those associated with a confusing multitude of belief systems vying with each other for attention and allegiance. In contemporary western culture, 'the present climate of instability and insecurity creates the very real danger of gullibility and, in turn, leaves the way open for a dream run by fundamentalists of all kinds – religious, environmental, political, cultural, astrological and economic.'[55]

Cultural perspective

We observed earlier Kraft's cultural perspective in defining a people's world-view as their 'basic model of reality'. There is a close correlation between culture and the concept of world-view. Hoebel defines culture as 'the integrated system of learned behaviour patterns which are characteristic of the members of a society and which are not the result of biological inheritance'.[56] So culture is a social concept, reflecting patterns and rules which arrive through consensus over a period of time. Along with Kraft, we may describe the world-view of a culture as 'the central control box' of that culture, generating the value system of its members.

In like manner, Walsh and Middleton argue that when we look at culture, we are looking at the pieces of a puzzle: 'We can see the functioning of assorted institutions, like the family, government, schools, cultic institutions (churches, temples, synagogues and so on) and businesses. We can observe different modes of recreation, different sports, transportation and eating habits. Each culture develops a unique artistic and musical life. All these cultural activities are pieces of a puzzle.'[57] But how do these pieces of the puzzle fit together within each social environment? To adopt Walsh and Middleton's phraseology, is there a key to unlock the pattern? This is where world-view comes in: understanding the world-view of a culture provides us with the appropriate 'template', or lens, through which we can interpret the different pieces of the cultural jigsaw.

An example drawn from my own personal experience may help here. When I emigrated with my family to Australia I was aware of the emphasis on sport in my new homeland, but I was not fully prepared for the extent to which it dominated the social life of the nation. Australians are an outdoor people, and there is a spirit of competitiveness which some suggest has a lot to do with their pioneering background. Speaking about his fellow Australians, Banjo Paterson, the famous bushman and balladeer, once declared that 'all men are born free and equal; and each man is entitled to life, liberty and the pursuit of horse-racing'! D.H. Lawrence commented in 1920 that Australians play sport as if their lives depended on it. In his fascinating account of Australian history, *Us Aussies*, Mal Garvin reflects on this sporting fanaticism: 'It seems that from the beginning, the native-born Australians, who were not so keen on abstract thinking and a classical education, found that one way to get the upper hand was through physical ability, and it soon developed that sport was the one area in which Australians could compete with a sense of confidence and self-respect.'[58]

Sport is therefore regarded as the ultimate Australian 'super-religion', perhaps the only thing that many Australians believe in passionately. This is accompanied by a single-minded focus not so much on excelling as on winning. Participation in sport in Australia is facilitated by an organizational infrastructure which encourages people, particularly the young, to gather together in the evenings and at weekends. My growing awareness of and exposure to this central dimension of the Australian world-view has helped me in my understanding, for example, of the difference between the Australian and English attitudes towards sport. English people have their history, their tradition, their centuries of power-broking on the international stage to provide them with a sense of significance and pride: sport has less of a hold on the national psyche. In contrast, the Australian sense of dignity finds its place on the sports field: 'the theory goes that having been robbed of a decent battlefield in our fight for independence, we had to make do with the sporting field.'[59]

The above example helps us to appreciate the relationship between world-view and culture. The distinctive Australian world-view which regards sport and outdoor activities with an almost religious fervour and which has its roots in the search for identity and significance provides us with a way into interpreting many of the pieces of the cultural puzzle, such as family life, leisure activities and economic priorities. In a recent research paper, however, Philip Hughes proposes a more reciprocal relationship between world-view and culture. He argues that 'while changed social conditions have changed the world-view of people, the world-view also changes the way people act. There is a dialectic between social conditions and the assumptions and conceptions by which people live.'[60]

It may be helpful, therefore, to distinguish between the world-view prevailing in a particular culture, which is a unifying concept, and the world-view of individuals within a given culture, which may vary to a greater or lesser extent, but which for each person is given its outline shape by cultural (and usually historical) elements within the society within which he or she lives. Then birth, chance, ability, choice, learning, and so on, give specific content to a person's individual world-view.

For example, in Greek culture scepticism set in as rationalism failed to provide the answers to life that people were looking for. Three competing schools of philosophy – Stoicism, Cynicism, and Epicureanism – emerged as valid expressions of world-view within the culture of the day. In medieval England, peasants and landlords were bound together in the same feudal culture, yet experienced life through very different social and economic lenses. Contemporary white Australian culture is characterized not only by the dominating influence of sport, but by such attributes as egalitarianism, nonconformism, relativism and individualism: yet within such a pluralistic society, different theistic and atheistic philosophies of life co-exist and the quest for personal freedom within an 'open', non-bureaucratic social and political system is as urgent as ever.

Finally, an example relating to the Christian church is suggested by Long and McMurry: 'The more liberal sector of the church ... lacks a paradigm of a "personal devil" and views evil as ignorance or the result of oppressive social structures. Pentecostals, on the other hand, hold to a lively paradigm of a "personal devil". Both the liberal and the Pentecostal worldviews, being western, have an overarching paradigm of the inalienable rights of the individual.'[61] Accordingly, it is arguably simplistic to talk about a Christian world-view, since there are many different expressions of the Christian faith, ranging from a fundamentalist Pentecostalism to an ethics-based liberal theology of the church. Yet, in contrast to the atheistic and pantheistic world-views competing with it, Christian theism holds together well as a world-view: its basic tenets are generally valid across the spectrum of alternative Christian movements, denominations and theologies.

Given the complexity inherent in the world-view concept, it may be reasonably argued that no two world-views are alike. We argued earlier that there is truth in such a statement: world-views are like fingerprints, unique for each individual. Even where cultural norms exercise a strong controlling influence on how people think and behave – as, for example, in many primitive tribal groupings in certain African and South American regions, amongst some aboriginal tribes in Australia, in the materialistic Singaporean economy where the god of mammon is as leaven in cultural dough, or in nations today where militant Islam has become the dominant, all-pervasive ideology – personal world-views may be considerably diffused within a given culture. So the task of classifying world-views is problematic: on what basis, and by what criteria, can such an attempt be made?

Philosophical perspective

We return to the four areas of metaphysical inquiry identified earlier in our search for a solution: epistemology, ontology, axiology, and teleology. Epistemology comprises the systematic study of the nature, sources and validity of knowledge; so epistemological theory is concerned with such questions as how we know what we know, and how we distinguish knowledge from belief, opinion or faith. This leads us to acknowledge the two rival schools of empiricism and rationalism. Whilst there are many different emphases within each school, the distinction between rationalism and empiricism is reasonably clear-cut. Empiricism claims that all ideas and concepts derive from experience and that truth must be established by reference to experience alone. Rationalists, on the other hand, whilst agreeing that many of our ideas come through experience, insist that everything must be filtered through reason: for rationalists, reason is the final arbiter of knowledge.[62]

These two basic philosophical systems appear throughout history in the search for certainty and knowledge. They are discernible in the Renaissance emphasis on human excellence; they surface in Descartes' seventeenth-century insistence on rational deduction as 'the only shovel that can dig down to the bedrock of truth';[63] and they typify many post-Enlightenment philosophies of life right up to the present day. In the seventeenth and eighteenth centuries, the empiricists Locke and Hume and the rationalists Spinoza and Leibniz built upon the foundations of Cartesian rationalism. For example, the British philosopher John Locke (1632–1704) developed the theory that certainty in knowledge is strictly dependent upon the experiences of the five senses.[64] Empirical epistemology is to be seen in such statements as 'I'll need evidence before I believe you' and lies behind many of the sceptical attitudes which have prevailed throughout the ages, from the scepticism of classical Greek thought to modern-day unbelief in a God who cannot be seen, heard, or touched.

It remained for the German philosopher Immanuel Kant (1724–1804) to 'draw together elements of both rationalism and empiricism in a revolutionary synthesis that turned the epistemological world upside down in its search for knowledge'.[65] Kant affirmed the centrality of human beings as the source of knowledge, rejected the objectivism in classical Platonic and Aristotelian rationalism, and prepared the way for the subjectivism so characteristic of modern humanistic world-views. Therefore, in seeking to understand world-views today, it is more helpful to focus on the critical dichotomy between objectivity and subjectivity characteristic of the Enlightenment period, rather than on the classical Greek contrast between rationalism and empiricism.

Both rationalists and empiricists were searching for an answer to the question 'How can I obtain a worthwhile life'? (Aristotles's *summum bonum*). The two philosophical systems they espoused offer 'two entirely opposed views on the origin of our ideas, on the nature of reality, on what is most valuable, i.e. on what is the nature of the good, the right and the beautiful, and, finally, on how to achieve the best life possible'.[66] In the language of metaphysics, these are the concerns of ontology, axiology, and teleology.

These metaphysical concepts have been expressed by James Sire in terms of seven questions to which a well-rounded world-view needs to give basic answers.[67] These questions are:

1. *What is prime reality – the really real?*
2. *What is the nature of external reality, that is, the world around us?*
3. *What is a human being?*
4. *What happens to a person at death?*
5. *Why is it possible to know anything at all?*
6. *How do we know what is right and wrong?*
7. *What is the meaning of human history?*

So, to the contrasting epistemological foundations laid by Plato and Aristotle, Sire adds the primary metaphysical concepts of ontology, axiology, and teleology, and the more specific discipline of philosophical anthropology. His seven questions appear to offer an adequate paradigm in understanding what people believe and their outlook on life.

Sire's philosophical analysis is undertaken within a framework of several world-view categories: Christian theism, deism, naturalism (especially secular humanism and Marxism), nihilism, existentialism (atheistic and theistic), eastern pantheistic monism, and the New Age. Whilst he devotes a chapter in the third edition of his book to postmodernism, he is cautious about cataloguing this approach to life as a world-view, regarding it as a modification of several world-views, notably naturalism, operating within an anarchic perspective. Certainly, postmodernism's rejection of universal, absolute truth and its rejection of God gives it a modernistic flavour, but, as we shall see in Chapter Five, there are significant characteristics of postmodernism which distance it from modernism.

McGrath traces the decline of what he calls the 'modern anti-Christian world-view', labelled 'modernity', to three factors: one, the growing realization that there are no such things as universal rationality and universal morality; two, the horrifying evidence in recent years of the depths to which human beings can go in terms of violence and 'ethnic cleansing', a contradiction of the fundamental tenets of optimistic humanism; and, three, the renewed acceptance of a belief in God.[68] So the door has been opened to new world-views which are liberationist at heart: in

particular, we may cite, with McGrath, feminism, postmodernism, and the New Age movement.

Whilst feminism has to do with what was originally called
'women's liberation', postmodernism represents a liberation
from what we might call 'objective absoluteness'. This creates
opportunities for expressing ourselves within a challenging environment of 'freedom, faith and imagination',[69] but can also lead
to a relativistic arbitrariness bordering on the irrational. The
New Age movement offers the possibility of an experience of
self-liberation, achieved by discovering and worshipping the
'god within'.

New Age is, as Sire helpfully points out, a world-view that
borrows from every major world-view – theism, naturalism and
pantheistic monism – as well as from pagan spiritualities, and is
vulnerable as a world-view in terms of self-deception rather than
self-liberation; 'so long as self alone is king, so long as imagination is presupposed to be reality, so long as seeing is being, the
imagining, seeing self remains securely locked in its private
universe – the only one there is.'[70] This has parallels with the
subjective epistemology of empiricism, unchallengeable by any
objective criteria: therefore, as with postmodernism, the individual becomes the focus of truth. New Age adherents, along with
postmodernists, espouse a relativistic world-view in which what
is true or right is what is true or right for each person, rather than
what is true in any absolute, let alone theological, sense.

We recognize, therefore, a correlation between two present-
day world-views, postmodernism and New Age, which have
similar philosophical and theological foundations. Feminism is
similarly concerned to destabilize fundamentalist positions, in
this case patriarchalism, although, like postmodernism, feminism is only a direct competitor to Christian theism when developed in an extreme form. Both, of course, may be interpreted
within either a theocentric or an anthropocentric framework;
they are significant theologically because they offer important
hermeneutical challenges within historic Christianity, and, in
their more extreme forms, represent world-views which rival
Christian theism. In Chapter Five we illustrate these

hermeneutical implications more clearly by examining in greater detail the opportunities presented to the church by engaging more positively and openly with the postmodern world-view.

We have defined world-view in a way that enables us to understand the notion of participation in the world more clearly. The world in which we live is full of contrast and conflict, and it is unrealistic to articulate a monochrome gospel message in a culturally technicolour world. What is needed is the courage to articulate the gospel in creative and imaginative ways, so that the good news of Jesus Christ can be truly heard by those to whom it is addressed.

The church as contextual community

We have argued that contextualization in Christian ministry implies engagement with the world within the dialectic of gospel-faithfulness and community-relevance. Indeed, the whole church community within a local setting may be encouraged to proclaim the truths of the gospel in a way that helps us to understand the meaning of participation in the world as a creative and innovative enterprise. Michael Frost argues that where creative expression is concerned, 'it is a matter of where and in which way the creative energy is flowing. If it is flowing from culture to the church, forcing the church, like a plasticine model, into different shapes, we have abandoned our distinctiveness. If, on the other hand, the creative energy for connection and reconciliation is flowing from within the church outward to culture, our mandate will remain solid, but its expression can be fresh and dynamic.'[71]

Perhaps it is not as one-way as Frost suggests, for the cultural context may be a rich resource of Spirit-inspired creative ideas for the expression of gospel truth. Christian distinctiveness is more about internal substance than external shape, and the Spirit is at work in the world in surprising and imaginative ways, inviting our participation in his imaginative approaches to make Jesus alive and relevant to those who may otherwise fail to hear the music of the gospel.

One particular cultural phenomenon which has spawned a vast amount of literature is postmodernism. Because of its contemporary significance both philosophically and culturally, we will examine postmodernism from a Christian perspective in Chapter Five, highlighting the opportunities which it presents for the ministry of the church. In its rejection of absolute truth and espousal of relativism, postmodernism contradicts the absolute truth-claims of the gospel; but in its celebration of creative experimentation it invites the Christian community into a dialogue which has for too long been either actively shunned or passively ignored. In the process of dialogue, the church may well be re-shaped (like plasticine), but the substance of the gospel message need not be altered. Sadly, the latter has too often been the case: in its response to the culture, the church has at times changed the content of its message whilst retaining the packaging. Relevance demands a change in the packaging, but not at the expense of the contents.

Consider the following creative attempts to 're-package' church, embracing a desire in each case to relate in an authentic way to different groups of people in contemporary western culture. Each expression of the gospel reflects an understanding of the lifestyles and longings of a range of people, for whom the Christian message needs imaginative contextualization.

'Café Church', Sydney

An Australian couple, Glen and Ruth Powell, are part of a team of young adults at Glebe Uniting Church in Sydney who have developed a concept which they call 'Café Church'.[72] The initiative is based in a building symbolically located in the 'no man's land' between those 'doing it tough' and 'the yuppies'. The church was born out of the realization that for some people – especially 'twenty and thirty somethings' – after-church coffee is one of the most important parts of the service (if not *the* most!). Some of those who attend the mainstream church are honest enough to admit that they go to church services largely out of a sense of duty. The team from Glebe decided to start a service where the coffee part started before church, went all the way through and carried on afterwards. The vision was to establish a 'safe place' where people from all kinds of backgrounds – unorthodox thinkers, artists, non-Christians – could meet to explore their understanding of the Christian faith.

The Glebe Café Church did not begin with one or two people assuming leadership responsibility. Whilst there has always tended to be one person 'carrying the flame', the role has been passed around within a group of people who share a common dream. The church began in 1996 with the purpose of attracting 'ex-church attenders'. Most of the original group had left the church at some stage, so their plan was to try and create a church which they would like to attend, and which would be welcoming to those who had already been exposed to the church culture. In style, Café Church (as its name implies) reflects the café culture in which many people experience much of their relating to one another; so people meet in an environment which closely resembles a café setting. The accent is on creativity: the church is located in a large rectangular hall with a high ceiling and white walls, which once served as a movie theatre: tables and chairs are laid out, allowing people to move around and interact against a background of music and candlelight.

Fellowship is highlighted as much as teaching and worship, with people encouraged to enter into discussion over a wide range of topics, all of which relate to Christian living. Guest speakers present in a conversational rather than sermonic style, generating informal debate at the tables. Christian music from African, South American, Celtic and other backgrounds is favoured at the expense of traditional contemporary praise and worship styles, and where singing takes place it is often *a cappella*. Although Café Church has regular 'biblical conversation' evenings focusing on a portion of Scripture, nobody is coerced into participating. The inclusion of music, slides, drama, poems, paintings, sculpture and dance around various themes, such as prayer, worship, confession, a topical theme or some specific biblical teaching, provides an environment in which no one feels left out, and connects with people who are turned off by

traditional church services. Whilst doctrine is regarded as important, people are the primary concern: 'No legalism, no doctrinal
fascism, just a bunch of sinners relying on grace and trying to
find the truth together ... that's the aim. We're a long way from
it, but that's the target!'

Café Church has been a place where an encouraging number
of believers have reaffirmed their faith and non-believers have
discovered faith, in their own time and in their own ways. It is a
place where it is safe to be honest, where the Spirit can work,
unencumbered by the restraints imposed by an iron-bound order
of service or finishing time. Furthermore, it is a place where those
who are part of the church community feel comfortable inviting
their friends, which suggests that Café Church will continue to
be a place of hope for years to come.

'Communality', Lexington

An inner-city ministry in Lexington in the United States called
'Communality' has created a context in which dramatic change is
taking place in people's lives. Based on the vision of the popular
Australian evangelist and former 'bikie', John Smith, who has
a passion for a 'down-to-earth' Christian presence in society,
the ministry reaches out to the fringes through a Friday night
'Rhythms and Reasons' event, running from eight till late, engaging subjects from the arts to social issues. The atmosphere is open
and free, where musicians often jam for hours, usually provoking
discussion about popular culture. Music represents a powerful
entry-point into people's lives: on one occasion, the music of the
sixties and seventies was revisited, inviting those present to consider the search for meaning conveyed by the music and to reflect
on the Jesus Movement as one response to that search. Another
evening stimulated discussion on environmentalism via the
medium of natural history slides of the Montana Wilderness: the
evening topic was entitled 'Environmental Whackoes and Tree
Huggers or Keepers of God's Cosmos'!

The 'Communality' ministry hinges upon the development of
relationships with those who have been marginalized in society.

Three nights a week a dedicated team of people frequent the streets and bars of downtown Lexington befriending those who feel defeated by life and alienated from the established church. A typical comment heard is 'I really do love Jesus, and I know he loves me, but I can't handle the church. I'm not good enough for them!' The message of grace conveyed in Wesleyan theology has gripped the Lexington team, who grieve at the relative shallowness of many of today's sermons and choruses because of their experience-centred interpretation of the Christian faith. With this in mind, clear exposition of the Bible is given on Sunday nights within the context of deepening relationships. As in Café Church, many lives are being touched with the liberating truth of the gospel enfleshed in the ministry of a caring Christian community.

Mars Hill Church, Seattle

Located in the heart of the University District of Seattle, Mars Hill Church began as an urban church for an emerging postmodern generation.[73] The church was pioneered by three men, Mark Driscoll, who was involved in a church-based college ministry, Mike Gunn, a pastor with a ministry amongst athletes, and Lief Moi, a local radio show host. From its earliest beginnings as a small Bible study group, numbers grew until the official launch of the church in 1996, with attendance levelling off to around a hundred people. An invitation for Mark Driscoll to speak at a national conference on Christian leadership in October 1997 propelled Mars Hill into the national spotlight as a 'model church for emerging ministry paradigms', featured in a wide range of publications. The enormous popularity of the church led to the establishment of a more formal structure in order to distinguish more clearly between those who were committed to Mars Hill as a family and those who attended as 'consumers'.

An old 300-seat theatre was purchased at the end of 1998 as a new home for the church's two evening services. The theatre also hosts a Saturday night 'Street Talk' radio show with live bands, which is broadcast across the United States and affords an

opportunity for people in their teens and twenties to dialogue
about the gospel. About one hundred new people a month visit
Mars Hill, creating the need for new programmes and strategies
to cope with the growth. Mark Driscoll's vision is to plant 1000
churches, and daughter churches are already being planted
through the generous support of those who share the Mars Hill
vision. The concept of community lies at the very heart of the
church, communities that reflect the life of the triune God. The
notion of 'intentional community' is strong: serving one another,
hospitality, sharing meals together, and exercising spiritual gifts
for the common good are highlighted. The emphasis on fellowship, however, has not sidelined the importance of solid preaching; the team at Mars Hill has not fallen into the trap of
underestimating the intelligence of those who are not yet believers and so offers a good hour of challenging biblical teaching,
delivered in a digestible narrative style.

Mars Hill holds to three vital principles of Christian ministry
(all of which are transferable, although they need to be
contextualized in the unique environment served by each local
congregation): a high view of Scripture as an anchor in today's
relativistic age; a strong commitment to community as a reflection of the nature of God as Trinity; and an openness to the
dynamic of the Spirit's working without trying to engineer anything 'supernatural'. Services vary from one week to the next
within a context of worship which is highly eclectic, ranging
from rock to reggae to contemplative. There are also times when
traditional liturgical structure is incorporated into the worship
experience, with candles, silence, and opportunities for reflection and meditation.

'The Other Late Late Service', Adelaide

In Adelaide, South Australia, a group of Christians began to
meet together at the end of 1995, following a visit made by one
of them, Geoff Boyce, to Scotland. The catalyst for their experimental approaches to worship was 'The Late Late Service' in
Glasgow, an attempt by a Christian community to put worship at

the centre of its life in culturally relevant ways. In the early 1980s, a group of young musicians and unemployed people had been asked to run a youth service for the Church of Scotland. They used their experience of club/disco culture as a framework and environment for worship. Back in Adelaide, Geoff Boyce and a few of his friends who were struggling with the contemporary church culture decided to set up a similar 'worship experiment'. This has blossomed out into a monthly series of services called 'The Other Late Late Service' (TOLLS). Included in the programme are such features as a celebratory multi-media event, worship over a meal, a service of silence and contemplation, and a 'nature service' in which participants 'walk through the bush with God'.

What TOLLS is offering is something much more radical than simply getting a good speaker and jazzing up the music. They have discovered that they are attracting people from all ages and backgrounds, though the core group tends to consist of 'thinking evangelicals'. A sense of mission pervades the TOLLS experiment: those who participate see themselves as a provisional community of missionaries, each with their own networks of Christian vocation and ministry. They also regard themselves as a prophetic community, free to explore the questions which many local churches tend to avoid because they are locked into a structure of how things 'ought to be': 'Every congregation already has the freedom of the Spirit to worship in creative and experimental ways – we have claimed that freedom.'

For example, one Christmas, the group wanted to explore the journey of Mary and Joseph to Bethlehem and then to Egypt. After an opening song, they took a hurricane lamp and went out to a nearby paddock, where the message to the shepherds was announced. They moved on to the steps of a nearby pub – which was closed! – placing the figures of a nativity set on the steps, thinking about what it would be like to be an unmarried teenage mother itinerant in a strange town. They then walked to the nearby train station, and, looking at the gleaming tracks, shared with each other significant stories of journey in their own lives. This was turned into prayer for each other and for others known to them. On their way back they got down on their knees in a circle in the middle of another empty paddock and lamented the commercialization of Christmas and their own part in it. Finally, back inside, they took communion, walking in a circle as a reflection of God's provision for them on their own journeying.

The Alpha course

One of the great success stories of the final decade of the second millennium is the Alpha course. Developed from an original training programme at Holy Trinity Church, Brompton (HTB) in London, Alpha is a fifteen-session practical introduction to the Christian faith, based on specially-prepared videotaped talks featuring Nicky Gumbel, who is on the HTB staff. Christian leaders from around the world have heaped praise upon the programme, which leads participants through a clear sequence of topics explaining Christian doctrine and life. Michael Cassidy, the founder of African Enterprise, declared that 'the relaxed, non-threatening but crystal-clear presentations on the tapes could not fail to impact decisively both believer and inquirer alike.'[74] Clifford Longley, the most well-known and respected writer on religious affairs in Britain, devoted one of his columns in the *Daily Telegraph* to Alpha, acknowledging it as 'an unqualified triumph', and adding that 'the reconversion of England … is suddenly almost believable.' Putting the course in its contemporary context, he wrote: 'What is entirely Evangelical about it, but entirely appropriate in this postmodern, post-Diana age, is the emphasis on the person of Jesus and the possibility of a loving relationship with Him.'

Alpha was originally conceived as a teaching course for new Christians, but was very quickly identified as an ideal evangelistic programme. It is also an excellent refresher course for those who need to 'brush up' on the basics of the Christian faith, as well as serving as an appropriate vehicle for welcoming those who are new to the local church. Alpha's appeal is its informality: groups of people meet in homes to share a meal together before watching the video presentation. They are then guided by a trained leadership team through a discussion session, which is open and honest, and in which they are encouraged to 'ask anything'. The small group context facilitates friendship, and the mealtime sharing represents a relaxed environment in which people can to get to know one another and where initial barriers can be broken down. There is a special 'Holy Spirit' weekend, in which the person and work of the Spirit is presented, and participants are encouraged to seek his presence and power in a fresh, personal way. Some churches present the teaching in a central location, dividing the participants into smaller groups for subsequent discussion.

Whatever approach is adopted, the emphasis is on accessible teaching, spiced with humour, and informal, friendly discussion after a shared meal ... and the concept has swept the world, with thousands professing the Christian faith. The programme has proved to be remarkably transferable across cultures, and there are Alpha courses in over seventy countries, from Albania to Zimbabwe. Its contextual significance is that, in many places, it has touched the lives of a biblically illiterate generation with a message that is explained simply and clearly, building on the vital contemporary foundations of friendship and community. In the process, the church community is drawn into active participation in what someone has described as 'cringe-free' evangelism.

In this regard, the Alpha course is similar to the framework adopted by the Willow Creek Christian community in Chicago, where drama and contemporary music are combined with a presentation of the gospel which is both practical and relevant to the 'baby-boomer' search for answers. The Willow Creek promise is to offer 'Christianity without the cringe factor'! Services are therefore designed to be 'seeker-sensitive', an approach which has been criticized by some as being too oriented towards the secular expectations of the unchurched. Where, critics complain, is the mystery of sacramental life, the silence of contemplative worship and the potential for dynamic encounter with the Holy Spirit?

Given the contemporary fascination with spirituality, expressed in the rapid growth of the New Age movement and the revival of primitive faiths such as Celtic spirituality (both pagan and Christian), contextualization of the Christian faith may demand an approach that is sensitive not just to the secular world-view of contemporary seekers, but also to their deeper, spiritual longings. Great wisdom is needed in responding to the unchurched in ways that acknowledge the dictum of the French Jesuit philosopher, Pierre Teilhard de Chardin, who once famously commented that 'we are not human beings having a spiritual experience; we are spiritual beings having a human experience.'

The universality of human spiritual experience implicit in de Chardin's observation alerts us to the danger of treating those who have not opened their lives to the gospel as 'outsiders', as if God looks upon those whom he has created as either 'them' or 'us'. In a number of places the Scriptures testify to the reality that God has no favourites: might we not re-phrase this to say that we are all God's favourites? No one is outside God's favour or beyond his reach. At the same time, however, we must insist with Torrance that there is continuity and discontinuity between the church and the world, signified in baptism,[75] and the existence of that distinction compels the Christian church to participate in the world, proclaiming and living a gospel that is contextualized in imaginative ways inspired and enabled by the Spirit of Christ.

Notes

1. See Hall, *Thinking the Faith*, pp. 349–67.
2. Dietrich Bonhoeffer, *Letters and Papers from Prison* (London: SCM Press, 1953), p. 148.
3. Hall, *Thinking the Faith*, p. 349.
4. ibid, p. 352.
5. Karl Barth, *Church Dogmatics*, III/4 (Edinburgh: T & T Clark, 1961), pp. 285–323.
6. Kuhn, *The Structure of Scientific Revolutions*, p. 11.

7. For a discussion of the possibility of 'scientific revolutions' in theology, see Hans Küng, *Does God Exist?* (London: Collins, 1980), pp. 111–15.

8. Hall, *Thinking the Faith*, p. 367.

9. Paul Hiebert, 'The Flaw of the Excluded Middle' in *Missiology: An International Review,* vol. X, no. 1 (Jan. 1982) pp. 35–47.

10. For an extended discussion of Hiebert's thesis, see John Wimber (with Kevin Springer), *Power Evangelism: Signs and Wonders Today* (London: Hodder & Stoughton, 1985), pp. 74–96. For a helpful introduction to how science and religion relate, see Ian H. Barbour, *When Science Meets Religion* (San Fransisco: Harper Collins, 2000).

11. James W. Sire, *The Universe Next Door* (Downers Grove: IVP, 1997), p. 134.

12. Karl Barth, *Church Dogmatics*, IV/3 (Edinburgh: T & T Clark, 1962), p. 764.

13. Kraft, *Christianity in Culture*, p. 8.

14. Robert J. Schreiter, 'Faith and Cultures: Challenges to a World Church' in *Theological Studies*, 50 (1989), pp. 744–60, in which six models, first suggested by Stephen Bevans, are outlined: transition, anthropological, praxis, synthetic, semiotic, and transcendental.

15. Mary Douglas, *Purity and Danger* (London: Routledge & Kegan Paul, 1966), p. 114.

16. Jerome H. Neyrey, 'The Idea of Purity in Mark's Gospel' in *Semeia*, 35 (1986), pp. 91–124.

17. John S. Dunne, *The Way of All the Earth: Experiments in Truth and Religion* (New York: Macmillan, 1972), p. 53.

18. Richard H. Niebuhr, *Christ and Culture* (New York: Harper & Row, 1951), p. 39.

19. Vincent J. Donovan, *Christianity Rediscovered* (London: SCM Press, 1978), p. 29.

20. ibid, p. 26.

21. Ernest Becker, *The Denial of Death* (New York: The Free Press, 1973), p. 7.

22. Hall, *Thinking the Faith*, p. 195.

23. David Hesselgrave, 'World-view and Contextualization' in Ralph D. Winter and Steven C. Hawthorne (eds.), *Perspectives on the World Christian Movement* (Pasadena: William Carey Library, 1981), p. 403.

24. John Smith, 'More than Babbling Tongues: Engaging the Post-modern World', *On Being* (Sept. 1995), p. 47.

25. Stanley Hauerwas and William H. Willimon, *Resident Aliens: A Provocative Christian Assessment of Culture and Ministry for People Who Know that Something is Wrong* (Nashville: Abingdon Press, 1989), p. 21.

26. Lesslie Newbigin, *The Gospel in a Pluralist Society* (Grand Rapids: Eerdmans, 1989), p. 154.

27. Hall, *Thinking the Faith*, p. 61.

28. ibid., p. 63.

29. Neil Darragh, 'Theology from Elsewhere', *South Pacific Journal of Mission Studies*, 2:1 (1991), pp. 2–8.

30. Neil Darragh, *Doing Theology Ourselves* (Auckland: Accent, 1995).

31. Hall, *Thinking the Faith*, p. 99.

32. ibid., p. 104.

33. ibid., p. 104.

34. ibid., p. 105.

35. Edward de Bono, *Parallel Thinking: From Socratic Thinking to de Bono Thinking* (London: Penguin Books, 1995).

36. ibid, p. 51.

37. Stephen Pattison, 'Some Straw for the Bricks: A Basic Introduction to Theological Reflection', *Contact*, 99 (1989), pp. 2–9.

38. David Lyall, 'Pastoral Action and Theological Reflection', *Contact*, 100 (1989), pp. 3–7.

39. Donovan, *Christianity Rediscovered*, p. vii.

40. The early part of this section draws substantially from Graham Buxton, *Understanding World View for Effective Christian Ministry* (Zadok Paper S84, Spring 1996).

41. W. Andrew Hoffeker (ed.), *Building a Christian World View* (Phillipsburg: Presbyterian & Reformed Publishing Co, 1986) vol. 1, p. 320.

42. Albert Schweitzer, *Civilization and Ethics* (London: Adam & Charles Black, 1949), p. 30.

43. See Augustine, *City of God*, Book XIV, Chapter 28.

44. Sire, *The Universe Next Door*, p. 16.

45. Schweitzer, *Civilization and Ethics*, p. vi.

46. Hans Küng, *Does God Exist?* (London: Collins, 1980), p. 125.

47. Brian J. Walsh and J. Richard Middleton, *The Transforming Vision: Shaping a Christian World View* (Downers Grove: IVP, 1984), p. 35.

48. Hoffeker, *Building a Christian World View*, p. xv.
49. ibid, pp. 3–8.
50. Zeb B. Long and Douglas McMurry, *The Collapse of the Brass Heaven* (Grand Rapids: Baker, 1994), p. 71.
51. Alister E. McGrath, *Christian Theology: An Introduction* (Oxford: Blackwell, 1994), p. 38.
52. Os Guinness, *The Dust of Death* (Leicester: IVP, 1973), p. 5.
53. Alister E. McGrath, *Bridge-Building* (Leicester: IVP, 1992), p. 223.
54. Alton B. Pollard III, 'When World-views Collide: Religion and the Culture of Disbelief', *Theology Today*, 51:4 (Jan. 1995), pp. 583–7, referring to Stephen L. Carter, *The Culture of Disbelief: How American Law and Politics Trivialise Religious Devotion* (New York: Basic Books, 1993).
55. Hugh Mackay, *Reinventing Australia* (Sydney: Harper, 1993), p. 251.
56. Quoted in Kraft, *Christianity in Culture*, p. 46.
57. Walsh and Middleton, *The Transforming Vision*, p. 18.
58. Mal Garvin, *Us Aussies* (Croydon NSW: Hayzon, 1987), p. 122.
59. ibid., p.120.
60. Philip Hughes, *A Maze or a System?* (Kew: Christian Research Association, 1994), p. 13.
61. Long and McMurry, *The Collapse of the Brass Heaven*, p. 28.
62. For a development of this distinction, see Calvin Pinchin, *Issues in Philosophy* (Basingstoke: Macmillan, 1990), pp. 1–6.
63. Long and McMurry, *The Collapse of the Brass Heaven*, p. 76.
64. For a discussion of Locke's views, see G. Vesey and P. Foulkes, *Collins Dictionary of Philosophy* (London: Collins, 1990), pp. 171–4.
65. V. James Mannoia, 'Rationalism and Empiricism' in Hoffeker (ed.), *Building a Christian World View*, p. 274.
66. A. L. Herman, *The Ways of Philosophy* (Atlanta: Scholars Press, 1990), p. 76, in which the author discusses the fundamental distinction between Platonism and Aristotelianism.
67. Sire, *The Universe Next Door*, pp. 17–18.
68. McGrath, *Bridge-Building*, pp. 189–90.
69. Edgar V. McKnight, *Post-Modern Use of the Bible* (Nashville: Abingdon, 1988), p. 1.
70. Sire, *The Universe Next Door*, p. 149.

114   *Dancing in the Dark*

71. Michael Frost, 'Going to Church in the 21st Century', *Zadok Perspectives*, 55 (Summer 1997), pp. 16–18.
72. See Glen Powell and the Café Church Leadership Team, *Café Church*, published by Awakening 2000, 688 Parramatta Road, Croydon, NSW 2132, July 1988.
73. See Mark Driscoll, 'Our History: Seasons of Grace: The Story of Mars Hill' on {http://www.marshillchurch.org/secondarypages/who_we_are/whoweare.htm}.
74. Quoted in the opening pages of Nicky Gumbel, *Telling Others: The Alpha Initiative* (Eastbourne: Kingsway, 1994).
75. James B. Torrance, 'The Place of Jesus Christ in Worship' in Anderson (ed.), *Theological Foundations for Ministry*, p. 365.

Part Two

Some Implications for Ministry Practice

Chapter Four

Participating in the Worship of Christ

*Let us then approach the throne of grace
with confidence ...*
Hebrews 4:16

There is a delightful story of a little girl who was learning to play the piano, and whose musical skills were still very limited. One day she was playing some notes on the keyboard whilst staying with her family in a hotel in Norway. There was little to appreciate in her playing, and several guests found her 'plink ... plonk ... plink ... plonk' intensely annoying. After a while, a man came and sat beside the girl, and started to play alongside her. The result was astounding – wonderful music from the two of them, the little girl playing as before, with the man supplying all the other notes. The man was the girl's father, the nineteenth-century Russian composer Alexander Borodin.

When we speak of participating in the ministry of Christ, we are talking about an engagement between God and ourselves which may be likened to the communion between Borodin and his daughter in that hotel in Norway. In the same way that the great composer welcomed the playing of his little girl, embracing it and transforming it into something beautiful, so Christ receives all that we offer God, in thanksgiving, in worship, and in service, converts it in himself, and presents it as something perfect and wholly acceptable to his Father, who is our Father. This is what the writer of Hebrews conveys in his presentation of Jesus as our great high priest: indeed, in developing a theology of worship we need to consider the implications of Christ's perfect priesthood in contrast to human priesthood.

The theology of the incarnation reminds us that all humanity has been caught up in Christ's ascended and glorified humanity, so making it possible for us to participate by the Spirit in the Son's perfect communion with his Father. This is the gift of God in Christ to all human beings, to which we are invited to respond as free creatures, though even here we may note that our response is not totally our own, but is made possible by the grace of God who, like some divine composer, comes alongside us and releases us into the new music of the gospel! Such are the benefits of what Calvin describes as the 'wondrous exchange': 'Having undertaken our weakness, he has made us strong in his strength. Having submitted to our poverty, he has transferred to us his riches.'[1]

Paul wrote about this exchange effected in the incarnation of Christ in his second letter to the Corinthians: 'For you know the grace of our Lord Jesus Christ, that though he was rich, yet for your sakes he became poor, so that you through his poverty might become rich' (2 Cor. 8:9). Now ascended and seated at the right hand of the Father, the risen Christ, the new man in whom we now live and move and have our being within the Trinitarian life of God, continues to serve us by receiving our imperfect prayer and worship (the faltering, even repetitive and – to human ears – irritating notes on the piano!), translating it into righteous and perfect music. Is this not the meaning of Christ as our intercessor? He is the one true mediator, who has achieved all that was needful to reconcile us to God, and who continues his high-priestly ministry in the service of redeemed humanity: 'Let us then approach the throne of grace with confidence, so that we may receive mercy and find grace to help us in our time of need' (Heb. 4:16).

Worship as communion   God is Subject & Object

Worship, then, has to be understood in the context of our communion with God. The Christian life centres on relationship with

God, from which flows all worship. In its most general sense, worship describes the whole of life: the word derives from the Anglo-Saxon word *weorthscipe*, which has to do with worthiness or respect. To worship someone, or something, is to attribute respect, reverence, worthiness. Technically, there need be no spiritual significance attached to an object of worship, although something which attracts the whole or a large part of our allegiance – money, ambition, acquisition of knowledge – may begin to exert such a hold on us that it may be described as implicitly 'religious' (in the philosophical or sociological sense of the word). In Marxist or Freudian terminology, religious experience derives from personal feelings of alienation and inadequacy, and is therefore highly subjective.

Christian worship, in contrast, is based on the objective reality of a God who is the product neither of self-deception nor of human need. Theologically, Christian worship is grounded in the truth that *God is*: 'I am who I am' (Ex. 3:14) is his declaration, not just to Moses and Israel, but to all humankind. And this God who is declares to all humanity that by his gracious act of love in the incarnate Christ we are included in the life of Father, Son, and Spirit; so worship is participation in the worship that takes place unceasingly within the life of God. Throughout the Old Testament, and particularly in the psalms, worship of God is the primary joy of God's people. Accordingly, when Moses had led the Israelites out of slavery in Egypt, his first responsibility was to lead them in worship (Ex. 3:12). In the New Testament, praise and worship of God is a central reality in the life of the church, anticipating the rapturous exaltation of God in the throne-room of heaven: 'To him who sits on the throne and to the Lamb be praise and honour and glory and power for ever and ever!' (Rev. 5:13)

In Old Testament times, God provided human priests to act as mediators of the old covenant: they led the worship of the Israelites according to the ordinances of God. However, as Hebrews makes clear, their offerings were only a foreshadowing of the one perfect offering of worship that was to come in Jesus Christ, who is now and for all time the one true 'minister' (*leitourgos*) of the sanctuary (Heb. 8:2), and who alone leads the people of God in their worship.

But the wonder of the incarnation is that the one who now leads the church in its worship is the *man* Jesus Christ, in whom we now live as those who have been redeemed and made holy. He has become for us, writes Paul, 'wisdom from God – that is, our righteousness, holiness and redemption' (1 Cor. 1:30). In his representative ministry, he stands on both sides, on the side of human beings and on the side of God. In his redemptive work on the cross, as both man and God, he accomplished the salvation of the whole world. And in his exalted and ascended position, he continues to stand on both sides, gathering up all that we offer and redeeming it, cleansing it, and perfecting it as an acceptable offering in the presence of the Father. God does not look at our imperfections in worship, for what he receives is not our worship in isolation from his Son, but worship which is gathered up and converted in him. This is the glory of our new life in Christ. This is the gracious ministry of the Spirit, who dwells within us and incorporates us into the life of the triune God.

As a reflection of the communal life of God, in which we are now privileged to participate as redeemed humanity, Christian worship involves both human and divine action. We shall look at this in the next section when we consider worship in terms of response. Beyond this, we may note that God is both the object and the subject of true worship. This follows from our preceding argument. As the object of Christian worship, we acknowledge God as Creator and Redeemer, and draw near to him, offering him our 'worthship'. He alone is worthy of our praise, as countless numbers have testified throughout the ages in hymns and spiritual songs. So we offer the sacrifice of praise.

But the one who leads us in our worship is none other than the Lord himself: 'God, Father, Son and Holy Ghost, is both the subject and the object of Christian worship, He who serves and is served by the cult, He who commands and He who welcomes the service, He who speaks and He who listens, He whom we implore and He who grants our requests.'[2] James Torrance invites us to liken this double movement of grace to a hug: as we approach people to embrace them, we simultaneously draw them to ourselves in order to complete the hug.[3] This is the language of communion, the most intimate and intense communion imaginable, leading us to consider worship not only as our response to God, but also, even more wonderfully, as God's gift of response to us.

As we develop this theme, we shall discover how liberating this insight is. For worship then becomes a gift of grace rather than something we do in order to bring God close to us. Within the communion of the triune God, we are drawn by the Spirit into the perfect communion of Father, Son, and Spirit. Paul reminds us in Romans 8:26–27 that in our feeble and uncertain praying, we are given the help of the Spirit, who 'himself intercedes for us with groans that words cannot express'. So the Holy Spirit, who knows the will of the Father and who knows our weaknesses, makes perfect our response to the Father, interceding on our behalf.

Worship as response

Three elements of worship are discernible in Psalm 95: the psalm opens with an exhortation to rejoice; this is followed by the invitation to bow in reverence before the Lord; finally, recognition of the Lord as creator and redeemer leads to the climax, which Kidner defines as a call to response.[4] It would be a mistake, however, to attribute the idea of response to only the last part of the psalm, for the elements of praise and thanksgiving are dimensions of response too. So we respond not only in the way in which we live out our lives in the world, but also in our engagement with God when we have exchanged our working clothes for festal attire, as Barth picturesquely describes it.

All of life, then, is response, and all of life is worship too; so we may define worship in terms of response. Paul tells us in Romans 12:1 that we are to offer our bodies as living sacrifices, holy and pleasing to God; and this, he goes on to say, is our 'spiritual act of worship'. So our work in the world is worship too, for

is not our labour a participation in the goodness of God's creation (see Gen. 2:15)? Certainly, the intrusion of sin means that
our participation is not as productive or rewarding as it should
be, nor is work given its true meaning in the contemporary
world. But God's intention is that we should enjoy the fullness of
all that he has created: 'In creating man God completes his activity and in obedience to God man continues God's creativity.'[5]
This is the background for our theology of work.

As co-workers with God in his world we give expression to
what it means to be made in his image, relating symbiotically
with the created order, a theme we explored briefly in Chapter
Two. Suggestively, von Allmen proposes that the worship of the
church is 'the floodgate through which pass the praises offered
by the world'.[6] Time and again the psalmist reminds us that the
heavens proclaim the wonders of the Lord, that all creation
bursts forth in declaring the greatness of his name, whether
mountains or trees, cattle or wild animals. So worship brings the
church into solidarity with the world.

Our discussion of worship as that which relates the church to
the world highlights the response of obedience. But this is not the
dutiful obedience of slave to master – worship is the joyful
response of those who have been embraced by the Lord of life,
and who have discovered the privilege of sharing with God in his
love for the world. Entering into the mission and compassion of
Christ for the world will occupy the next two chapters, and so we
will not dwell on these themes here. However, we do well to note
that to penetrate the heart of God in communion with him is to
be grasped by his utter other-centredness. Thus worship as our
participation in the life of God in the world takes the form of
obedient other-centredness, not dutiful self-effort. Faith thus
arises in our hearts as the gift of God, who enables our response
by the inspiration and strengthening of his Spirit.

But let us put on our festal attire again, and consider the
nature of worship as it pertains to the intimate gathering of the
faith-community. In many contemporary churches, the theme of
obedience in worship is lacking: emphasis is placed on the *experience* of worship rather than obedience to God. We should not

dismiss experience, of course, for God discloses himself in the joys and sorrows which define our existential relationship with him. Indeed, simply to bask in the love of God, held in his arms and resting in his sufficiency, is a marvellous gift of grace. Often, that is response enough and all that God would have us be and do.

However, the prophet Micah reminds us that response also involves obedience to the will of God: 'He has showed you, O man, what is good. And what does the Lord require of you? To act justly, to love mercy and to walk humbly with your God' (Mich. 6:8). When our hearts are set to obey God, we are in an attitude of worship. Worship, in essence, is neither singing nor music – they are artistic representations of the true worship that describes the actuality of a relationship with God. At times, Christians are guilty of trying to manipulate God through offers of 'surrender' or 'lifting up holy hands', or by exhortations to 'shout to the Lord', as if these overtures could convince God to do more for us – a form of 'works theology' for worship. We do not call out to God or bow down before him in order to gain a response from him: we do these things because God is already amongst us and has already acted on our behalf.

Our response, although it also involves our human will, is better interpreted as our participation in the power of the Spirit in the worship that characterizes the eternal life of the Trinity. Caught up in the life of God, we experience this joy as a gift of the Spirit. However, the graciousness of God is such that he responds to our longings and to our delight in him in the same way that I as a human father respond to my children's appreciation of my presence in their lives. As I write, I have just enjoyed another birthday in my life; on such occasions, the way my children express their gratitude to me for all that I have been to them and done for them causes me to want to offer more of myself to them.

I was leading worship in my local church recently and we were singing a song by Lenny Le Blanc, the first two lines of which are: 'There is none like you, no one else can touch my heart like you do.' We were singing these words to God; as we did so, I sensed the Lord speaking to me, helping me to see that he was singing

RECIPROCAL

these words to me! I was immediately overwhelmed by an intense love and warmth, and tears filled my eyes. I understood at that moment that worship was reciprocal, not just a one-way transaction, as if God were the audience, from whom I was seeking to evoke a response.

There are some who interpret worship in theatrical terms, the actors being the members of the congregation, with God as the audience, and the minister as the (on-stage) prompter.[7] However, such a model fails to recognize the mutuality of worship, which finds its source in the love-relationship between God and his people. We do not have to perform before God in order to evoke his pleasure and applause. Nor is he a God who is present 'at a distance' from the gathered people, waiting to be called down to be with them: he is already amongst them. God cannot and will not be conjured up as if he were at the disposal of the church.

This relates to our understanding of the 'calling down' of the Holy Spirit, the *epiklēsis*, which first became evident in the liturgies of the third-century church. Christians are often confused as to how the gathered community can call down the Spirit if he is already amongst them. Many great hymns testify to a lively expectation amongst God's people of the coming of the Holy Spirit, as if he were absent from their midst. John Leach, an English pastor and worship leader, finds it helpful to speak in terms of invitation and enabling: 'God loves to be with his people; the problem is that all too often we simply don't allow him to be with us because we clutter our attention with so many other things. God is there; we just don't notice. At times he will sovereignly intervene and make his presence felt as he grabs our attention, but most often he waits to be given our attention.'[8] This insight directs us to the notion of remembrance. When the faith-community gathers together, God most certainly remembers his people ... but are they mindful of him? Perhaps some attempts at worship stumble precisely because God has been forgotten. The invitation 'Come, Holy Spirit' indicates a desire for God to make his actual presence more real, more manifest: he is remembered.

Perhaps, with Leach, we could define worship as 'responding to God in order to have more of God to respond to',[9] a cyclical pattern which is discernible, for example, in Solomon's dedication of the temple in Jerusalem in 2 Chronicles 5–7. Musicians and singers combine with the prayers of the people, and the *shekinah* glory of the Lord fills the temple, giving rise to further prayer and praise ... and so the cycle goes on.[10] But note that God is not *coerced* into response; the process is interactive, in which the relationship between God and his people is expressed in terms of mutual delight and remembrance.

This interactive feature of worship is evident in the experience of the early Christian church, faced with persecution from the Jewish authorities in the wake of the initial Pentecostal outpouring of the Spirit. It is notable that Peter and John's experience of being threatened was not confined to the two of them alone; it was promptly owned by all the other believers: 'On their release, Peter and John went back to their own people and reported all that the chief priests and elders had said to them. When they heard this, they raised their voices together in prayer to God' (Acts 4:23–24). The communal significance of Peter and John's experience amongst the ruling religious hierarchy is explored by Richards and Hoeldtke, who point out that 'coming to know God the Father ... involves a process in which we speak and listen to each other. The Father speaks to us about Himself; we respond and together speak to Him.'[11]

Of course, this example of event-motivated response should not override our earlier affirmation that the response of worship is primarily relational in its orientation. We worship the Lord not only because of what he has done, and continues to do in our lives, but because of who he is. This we discover as we participate by the power of the Spirit in the life of the triune God of grace.

'Yes' and 'Amen'

There is an amusing little story of a lively old Pentecostal man who was so animated in the midst of the congregation at worship that he burst out fervently: 'O God, what a wonderful time of worship this evening! But, Lord, you should have been here last night – it was even better then!' The story is doubtless apocryphal, but behind the old man's words there is the disturbing suggestion that when Christians gather together, their worship is not necessarily related to God's presence. Such an idea, of course, is foreign to the understanding of worship that I have presented in this chapter.

In fact, we must insist that the worship of God's people is completely dependent upon the perfect worship offered by the Son to the Father in the power of the Spirit. This can be developed further with reference to Jesus' high priestly role in heaven on our behalf. At the beginning of this chapter I highlighted the significance of Christ's perfect priesthood in contrast to the imperfect priesthood of those who led the tabernacle worship under the old covenant. The epistle to the Hebrews is the most helpful New Testament book in formulating an acceptable theology of worship. There the writer spells out the superiority of Christ's fully effective priesthood over the limited priesthood of human intermediaries. Hebrews 9 draws out this distinction quite clearly in the context of worship: the sin-offerings in the tabernacle worship were unable to cleanse the conscience; this could only be accomplished by the blood of Christ, whose once and for all offering of himself has opened the way for us to now 'draw near to God with a sincere heart in full assurance of faith' (Heb. 10:22).

This is the gospel of grace. Jesus Christ is the mediator of a new and better covenant, foreshadowed by the Levitical priesthood. His perfect sacrifice means that he has now entered heaven on our behalf as a man for all humanity, '*now to appear for us in God's presence*' (Heb. 9:24). He has done what we cannot do, what no human being could ever have done, and, as our faithful high priest in heaven, his perfect and acceptable ministry continues on our behalf. He is our advocate, our intercessor, forever receiving our imperfect worship, concentrating it in himself and presenting it as a fragrant offering to the Father.

Only Christ, the unblemished Lamb, was able to respond with a 'Yes' to the Father's perfect will. As all around him deserted him in Gethsemane, only Christ remained to say 'Yes' to the Father. At Golgotha, it was Christ, and Christ alone, who accomplished the salvation of the whole world as he 'humbled himself and became obedient to death – even death on a cross!' (Phil. 2:8). In kenotic love he gave himself as a self-offering on behalf of all humanity.

The power of Jesus' 'Yes' to the Father lies in the power of his blood shed on the cross: it is the power to purify, not outwardly (as in the tabernacle worship of the old covenant) but inwardly. So the conscience is cleansed, setting people free to serve the living God, which is our acceptable worship. 'The blood of goats and bulls and the ashes of a heifer sprinkled on those who are ceremonially unclean sanctify them so that they are outwardly clean. How much more, then, will the blood of Christ, who through the eternal Spirit offered himself unblemished to God, cleanse our consciences from acts that lead to death, so that we may serve the living God' (Heb. 9:13–14). Notice how thoroughly Trinitarian this is, and notice too that humanity is caught up in the Son's life of worship within the community of the Trinity.

In the light of this, and recognizing the inadequacy of our own worship – for who amongst us can offer to the Father the perfect response of the Son? – we acknowledge that our response can never be the perfect 'Yes', but is a responsive 'Amen' to Christ's 'Yes'. The Hebrew word *amen* literally means 'surely' and conveys the idea of confirmation of a covenant. It acknowledges the faithfulness and truth of that which has been declared or accomplished: 'so be it.' Doxologically, the people of God utter their 'Amen' to the perfect response of Christ, in recognition that in him alone are God and humanity brought near to each other: 'For no matter how many promises God has made, they are "Yes" in Christ. And so through him the "Amen" is spoken by us to the glory of God' (2 Cor. 1:20).

Who enables us to respond in this way? Is it not the Spirit, who in his intercessory ministry enables us to pray the prayers of Jesus, who re-presents Christ to us in the mystery of the Eucharist, who points us back to Christ's baptism which is our baptism

– 'We were therefore buried with him through baptism into death in order that, just as Christ was raised from the dead through the glory of the Father, we too may live a new life' (Rom. 6:4) – and who baptizes us into the body of Christ as one worshipping community, attentive to the word of God mediated through confession and proclamation?

Later on in this chapter we shall give attention to these dimensions of worship, and observe that they all find their completion in the perfect response of the Son to the Father. The Spirit takes our imperfect worship – our prayers, our Eucharistic thanksgiving, our baptismal rites, our confession of the faith – and converts them into acceptable worship to the glory of God. In worship, we are placed by the Spirit into the realm of grace, in which we discover the freedom to offer what we have and who we are, liberated from the pressure to 'get it right'! Who of us can claim to be 100 per cent committed, or offer perfect obedience? Our worship is not measured by how successful we are in 'crossing the line' to God, for God has already crossed the line to us. We simply cannot come to God in perfect self-offering as Christ has done, for he alone is our righteousness, our holiness, and our redemption. All we can ever do is to utter our 'Amen' to Christ's perfect 'Yes'. This is our worship, gathered up in Christ and sanctified by his grace.

The worshipping community

The theological motif of community is central to our understanding of the church, as we discussed in Chapter Two, and it is instructive to explore it more fully in relationship to the privilege of participating in the worship of Christ. The community dimension in worship reflects God's desire to fashion a *people* for himself. Though each Christian believer needs to nourish his or her own personal relationship with God through individual prayer and praise (something which we shall address in the final chapter of this book), the expression of communal worship follows from the truth that we have all been baptized by one

Spirit into one body (1 Cor. 12:13). The apostle Paul exhorts us to 'rejoice with those who rejoice; mourn with those who mourn' (Rom. 12:15), and another apostle, John, argues that our love for God implies our love for one another (see, especially, 1 Jn. 4:7–21). 'John thus turns his back on mystical experience as the high point in religion. Not for him retreat from the world of men into the privacy of a vision of God ... John's point is that loving one another is indispensable in a religion which longs to have a true knowledge of God.'[12]

To worship God together, therefore, is to enter into a shared experience of thanksgiving, prayer, praise, and service, through which the whole body of believers is edified, and simultaneously re-establishes or reinforces its identity in its participation in the life of the triune God. Expressed in terms of worship, this communal participation reminds us that the church is not a collection of individuals who happen to come together at certain times, but is 'that community within the world which in her worship anticipates the perfect community of the Kingdom, waiting for the marriage feast of the Lamb'.[13] In our worship we anticipate the ultimate eschatological community. So we do not participate in isolation, but in solidarity with each other, and in communion with the heavenly company of angels and perfected saints. We do not draw near to God on our own, but in the context of relationship, as Hebrews 10:22–24 makes clear: '*let us* draw near to God with a sincere heart ... *Let us* hold unswervingly to the hope we profess ... and *let us* consider how we may spur one another on towards love and good deeds' (italics mine). Our community life on earth, a life of mutual encouragement and of participation in Christ's mission in and for the world, derives from and is in fact an expression of our participation in the worship which characterizes the life of the triune God. In our worship and in our calling to serve God in the world we are a redeemed community, reflecting the loving communion into which we have been drawn by the Spirit.

In the midst of today's fragmented cultural climate in which many people have lost touch with each other, the context of congregational worship presents Christians with the opportunity to rediscover their roots not only in Christ but also in each other. In his discussion of the corporate disciplines of the Christian faith, Richard Foster refers to this as 'fellowship-in-worship'; he quotes the devotional writer Thomas Kelly, who wrote that when the people of God meet together a 'quickening Presence pervades us, breaking down some part of the special privacy and isolation of our individual lives and blending our spirits within a superindividual Life and Power. An objective, dynamic Presence enfolds us all, nourishes our souls, speaks glad, unutterable comfort with us, and quickens us in depths that had before been slumbering.'[14]

Kelly's reference to an 'objective' Presence is significant. In the Acts 4 incident referred to earlier the Christians recalled who God is as he has revealed himself in creation, through the Scriptures, and in their immediate circumstances.[15] In worship they respond to God's self-revelation. To remember who God is and what he has done avoids the danger of our coming to him so wrapped up in our own circumstances that our worship becomes an echo of ourselves rather than a response to the objective reality of God himself.

There has been an explosion of new songs within the life of the church over the past few decades, and many focus on the close-ness of a personal relationship with 'me and my God'. Whilst these songs have helped many Christians into a fresh awareness of God's love for them, transcendent truths about God have often been lost in the language of intimacy typical of their lyrics. Critics of charismatic worship may be too hasty in their rejection of contemporary choruses, and the repetitive singing characteris-tic of some congregations, but they do remind us of the need to anchor subjective experience of worship in the objective realities of a God who can help us precisely because he is greater than our problems or difficulties.

This perspective warns us not to squeeze the way worship is expressed into a particular mould or style. There are some Chris-tians who assert that their approach to worshipping God is more authentic or biblical than other modes of worship. Some insist on what they vaguely describe as 'the New Testament' model of worship. But this is to anchor our participation in the worship of Christ in the past without acknowledging the realities of the present and the uniqueness of each localized faith-community in its historical and contextual setting. In a powerful way, worship reflects the history and present-day story of local congregations.

A congregation is a specific, localized faith-community with its own history, and its own unique characteristics. These help to define the way the congregation expresses its worship in communion with the triune God of grace. Anchored in the objective truth of who God is, and liberated from the demands of those who would restrict worship to a single mode of expression, the local community of faith is encouraged in the power of the Spirit to experiment and explore contemporary and relevant styles of worship.

Walking along a country lane in England many years ago, I stopped underneath a large tree. It was in the middle of winter, and all the leaves had fallen, so I was able to see clearly the many different branches which spread out from the central trunk. As I looked up from the base of the tree, I sensed that God was speaking to me about his church. That day I had been discussing with some friends my concern over a claim made by one particular denominational group that they were the 'new breed' of Christians, through whom God would fulfil his eschatological purposes in the world. This was not a new claim, of course, but it was an urgent issue at the time. This Christian group was well-known for its vibrant style of worship, and often challenged the comparatively lifeless worship of the traditional denominations. They called Christians to leave the 'sterile' worship of their local churches in order to enter into the flow of their 'pure stream' of worship.

I was troubled by this claim, though as a young Christian I confess that I was attracted by the rousing and energetic, and at times deeply reverent, expressions of congregational worship that characterized their meetings. As I looked up at the tree, the Spirit of God helped me to see that just as there are many branches which emanate from the trunk, each bearing life because of its association with the trunk, so there are many

TREE — TRUNK IS
SOURCE OF LIFE
& WORSHIP

branches in God's church. I noticed that each branch was different, yet the same sap was flowing through each one, eventually to
turn bud into leaf. God does not compress his life into one
branch: eschewing monotonous uniformity, he delights to
express himself in glorious diversity in the worship of his church.

I continued to walk along the lane, reflecting deeply on what I
had experienced. I realized that what was important in worship
was not the outward expression but the inner source which gave
rise to worship. I came to understand that 'more important than
our experience of Christ is the Christ of our experience.'[16] I was
encouraged to explore this truth within the Anglican tradition
into which God had led me; whilst not rejecting the attractions of
more charismatic or Pentecostal styles of worship, I was motivated to learn how the richness of charismatic worship could be
developed within the established liturgical structures of the
Anglican church.

Grierson presents us with a contextual awareness of ministry
which is valuable in our understanding of the diversity of
worship expressions. Commenting on the individuality of each
community of faith, he challenges the assumption that local
churches are neat, tidy and generally civilized: 'A particular congregation is never neat, sometimes barely Christian and only
rarely civilized'![17] Accordingly, Grierson proposes six dimensions which 'name' a community of faith, which he defines as
'signs' of the hidden sources of meaning and significance which
constitute the people as a community of faith. These dimensions
are summarized as time, space, language, intimacy, consensus,
and circumstance.[18]

Time, the first dimension, has to do with a congregation's
awareness of its past, present and future: memory, vision, expectation, being stuck in the past – all relate to the 'time-sense' that
pervades the life of a community of faith. Grierson's second
'sign', *space*, has to do with how the people indwell their environment: 'The institutional order and organized arrangements
people give to their way of being is capable of telling their
hidden tale of their spiritual pilgrimage.'[19] *Language* functions
in circumscribing the people's reality: key words, phrases and

images all contribute to language as a powerful instrument of self-consciousness. The total experience of a people's shared life is implicit in the closeness, depth, and commitment involved in *intimacy*. *Consensus* defines what is commonly affirmed, reflecting the world-view of the congregation: this involves such things as its common belief system, and the values and truths which are shared and thus shape the congregation. Finally, every congregation is located in a specific context, which Grierson defines as its *circumstance*; geography, economic issues, ethnicity, social background, deprivation or abundance – all these create both opportunity and limitation for a faith-community.

Grierson's suggestion that congregations relate to these six 'signs' by valuing their past, claiming the present, and seeking their future causes us to appreciate the differing expressions of worship from one congregation to another. Every local church has its own 'remembered history' and 'heroes' of the past. C. S. Lewis once wrote: 'Humanity does not pass through phases as a train passes through stations: being alive, it has the privilege of always moving yet never leaving anything behind. Whatever we have been, in some sort we still are.'[20] Every community claims its own present through the important 'focusing concepts' of symbols, faith imagery, ritual, and gesture. Every gathered community addresses its own future by embracing an understanding of its destiny as a particular people in a particular place; this perceived future carries important images of hope and a vision which directs them as a people.

[margin annotation: always moving but never leaving anything behind]

Moltmann comments that 'every experience of life thrusts towards its expression in the people affected, whether it be expression through their Gestalt, their attitude to life, or through their thoughts, words and deeds, images, symbols and rituals.'[21] As we participate in the worship of Christ within the Trinitarian community, we acknowledge that there is no single way in which this worship finds expression within the earthly faith-community: our bodies and emotions, our minds and our creative energies, all are available to the Spirit who weaves the response of worship amongst the people of God, both spontaneously and through the employment of ritual and liturgy.

Drawing from the congregation's past memories, its present life-experiences, and its expectations for the future, the Spirit seeks to create an authentic tapestry of worship which reflects not only the rich diversity of life within God but also the unique life of each community of faith.

There will be common elements within the worshipping life of the Christian church as a whole, in which prayer, proclamation, singing, ritual and sacramental acts have a central place, but the creative Spirit of truth takes hold of that which is unique in each setting and translates it into a valid and relevant expression of that faith-community's own journey. Of course, where congregational leaders stifle the Spirit and, bound by traditionalism, resist needed change, worship becomes sterile and lifeless. The examples given in Chapter Three of Christians who have 're-packaged' church in order to make the gospel more accessible to the contemporary culture offer approaches to worship which are contextually vibrant and humanizing: the tragedy of much that passes for worship in many churches today is that people are not given the opportunity and freedom to discover who they are in relation to God and to one another. 'Since being human is to be made in God's image, spaces that do not allow people to express their humanity – even religious spaces – are ultimately contrary to the gospel.'[22]

These needed spaces cannot be assumed to occur whenever Christians gather together. Usually they have to be planned in a way that enables the mystery of God to be mediated to the participating congregation. The contemporary cultural climate embraces an acceptance of spirituality which challenges a modernist perception of Christianity, with its emphasis on cognitive, 'left-brain' responses to the presence of God. Traditional approaches to worship which adhere rigidly or mechanically to inappropriate structures can often inhibit the life of the Spirit. However, liturgy need not be so oppressive – in fact, liturgy can be a liberating vehicle for authentic worship, facilitating our response to God. 'Sometimes that response is carefully thought out, sometimes automatic, subconscious, unpremeditated.'[23] Because liturgy describes the normal patterns present in life itself –

not only in the accepted rites of passage, but also in small, even trivial, activities such as how we wash and dress – it is a natural means by which we can apprehend the reality and presence of God. The same may be argued for symbols and rites. The sacramental life of the church, expressed through material signs, often encapsulates theological truth in a way that verbal language cannot.

When I became the minister of a small congregation in West London in the 1980s, the life of the people was tied up in ritual, symbols, and liturgy which had, for many people, become more central than a living relationship with God himself. My response was not to dispense with these sacramental signs, but to proclaim the reality of the gospel life, to which these signs bear witness. For example, candles on the high altar were ceremoniously lit at the commencement of each service. When asked what they signi-fied, the typical response was that 'We've always had candles lit!' Nobody could satisfactorily articulate their significance. I con-tinued with the practice, teaching at the same time that the lit candles represented more adequately than words the reality of the risen Christ in our midst, the One who is present amongst us as 'the light of the world'. I introduced banners which declared biblical and theological truths in a colourful and immediate way. The Jewish model of life as a celebration was restored amongst us as we decorated the church, introduced special 'creativity days' to which members of the local community were invited, and explored new musical forms.

Clark Pinnock is not alone in arguing that the life of many churches needs to be enriched with more signs and symbols:

Iconoclasm has impoverished the life of the church and often reduced worship to a cognitive affair. This means that the Spirit is denied certain tools for enrichment. We are impoverished when we have no place for festivals, drama, processions, banners, dance, colour, movement, instruments, percussion and incense. There are many notes on the Spirit's keyboard which we often neglect to sound, with the result that God's presence can be hard to access. [24]

In his discussion of the relationship between liturgy and the renewing work of the Spirit in the Anglican church in recent years, John Leach helpfully offers twelve reasons 'why renewal needs the structuring which liturgy can provide':[25] the church needs a sense of rootedness and continuity with the past; the familiar territory of liturgical worship binds Christians together in a sense of belonging to a wider family; liturgical 'shape' moves the gathered congregation from a starting place towards an end, recapitulating the motif of journeying in life; the liturgical resources of calendar and lectionary, adopted by the historic churches, allow Scripture to be incorporated into worship within the context of special church 'seasons' like Advent, Lent, and Pentecost (too easily dismissed or even forgotten by some Christians); liturgy can help worshippers to stay doctrinally well-balanced; it proclaims truth and experience with a clarity often lacking in spontaneous expression; there is an economy in carefully thought out liturgical prayer which is welcome in the midst of the verbosity and jargon of some extemporaneous prayer; the aesthetic 'poetry' of liturgical texts is something that cannot be replicated in spontaneous worship; the logical flow implicit in the shape of the liturgy provides a sense of order and direction, within which spontaneity can find its place; liturgy allows children to participate more fully because children are liturgical by nature, craving routine from their earliest years; liturgy facilitates liberty by functioning 'not as a cage but as a scaffolding which can help support what we're building, and give it strength, shape and stability';[26] and, in the final analysis, liturgy is inevitable in life, in the sense that repetition and habit reflect the ordered world in which we all live. The vision of the valley of dry bones in Ezekiel 37:1–14, though exegetically inappropriate, is a helpful image for understanding the need for some form of structure within which the Spirit can breathe new life and hope.

Our discussion of worship has highlighted the themes of response, relationship, community, and liturgy. Each, in their own way, bring us back to the overriding motif of remembrance. In response, which is itself a gift of God to us as he draws us to himself, we remember the objective reality of God who has made himself known to us in history and who continues graciously to reveal himself to us. In relationship, we remember that this God holds us in his memory, and we are forever bound to him not through anything we do but because of his divine grace. As community, we remember one another as fellow-travellers in the journey of life, and we participate in one another's stories: in fact, each individual story is a strand in the story of the community to which we belong, which is itself part of the story of God and his people throughout the world. In liturgy and symbols, we remember 'that we are bodily creatures inhabiting a material world';[27] we need material signs to help us to comprehend the mystery of God.

Sacramental life in the community of faith

At the beginning of this chapter I suggested that worship can be properly understood only within the context of our communion with God. This is given sacramental significance in the rite of the Lord's Supper, and it is helpful to reflect on what took place between Jesus and his disciples immediately prior to his death as they gathered with him in the upper room in Jerusalem. When Jesus took the bread and wine of the Passover meal, giving thanks to his Father in heaven, he passed the elements round, inviting the disciples not only to remember his life and death in their midst, but also to receive the bread and wine into their own bodies.

Jesus was declaring by this act of pure grace that we are included in what was about to happen to him. Jesus' whole life was an offering to his Father, and his death was the climax of that self-offering on behalf of sinful humanity in obedience to his Father's will. All humanity participates in that self-offering, the ultimate expression of worship. When he died we died, and in his victory over death we too are victorious. This is the significance of Christ's baptism, into which we are called to participate in our own baptism. What happened to Jesus happened to all humanity: that is what we are called to remember in the Lord's Supper. Both sacraments declare the gospel of participation in the perfect worship of the Son, who has accomplished what we could not accomplish. When we receive the bread and wine at the sacrament of the Lord's Supper, we echo the cry of Jesus on the cross: 'It is finished!' Christ has done what I could never do.

But we do more than engage in a memorial service! The word *anamnēsis*, which translates into remembrance, is rich in meaning, signifying more than just mental acknowledgment; in particular, the Jewish understanding of the word conveys a sense of re-living the past as if it were real today. The Jewish celebration of the Passover, for example, conveys the idea of so entering into the event of the exodus as to make it one's own as a contemporary reality.

Remembrance, understood in this way, is active rather than passive: it accomplishes something profound and real in the life of a person. When war veterans return to the fields of battle as an act of remembrance, they always speak of the experience in terms of present reality; their impressions are invariably vivid, and many are affected emotionally. At a more domestic level, when I leaf through photograph albums with my family, I am often struck by the intensity of my recollection of times past and the power of those past memories even as I look at the images in the album. This is sacramental reality for me.

This perspective gives us an important insight into the significance of the Lord's Supper in the worshipping life of the church. Not only do we participate in shared and thankful remembrance of Christ's perfect self-offering on our behalf, but we also participate in Christ's continuing self-offering of himself on our behalf. We do not remember just the Christ of *history* – we remember the living Christ *today*, and the Christ who carries us into the *future*. So Barth declares that when the bread and wine are offered 'there takes place here and now exactly the same as took place there and then between Himself and His first disciples, immediately prior to his death and resurrection.'[28]

In a mysterious and compelling way, the sacrament powerfully draws past, present, and future together in the life of the faith-community. If *remembrance* brings the past alive, then the present is evident in the Lord's Supper as *proclamation, participation,* and *fellowship*. The future is clearly implied in the *anticipation* of the heavenly banquet. When Jesus gave thanks in the upper room shortly before his death, he literally 'eucharisted' ('gave thanks for') the bread and the wine; thus the theme of *thanksgiving* is of course a central motif in the celebration of the sacrament. These six words – remembrance, proclamation, participation, fellowship, anticipation, and thanksgiving – combine to offer a rich and profound interpretation of the Lord's Supper, though they do not, and cannot, contain its full mystery or theological significance.

Paul's explicit account of what he 'received from the Lord' in 1 Corinthians 11:23–26 alongside his teaching in 1 Corinthians 10:16–17 provide us with the biblical basis for the first five interpretations of the sacrament. Proclamation is explicit in Paul's words: 'For whenever you eat this bread and drink this cup, you proclaim the Lord's death until he comes.' The Eucharistic liturgy announces the historical truths of Jesus' death and resurrection, and has a similar impact to the *Haggadah* in Jewish narrative: those who hear the words are strengthened and affirmed in their faith in the God of history. 'The Eucharist, like the preaching of the gospel ... was thus a powerful factor in the early crystallizing of the passion story in a form recognizable in all four gospels.'[29]

It is a travesty of the gospel of grace when some ministers race through the Eucharistic words, and even more so when they hasten the administration of the elements of bread and wine: the people of God need time and space to absorb the truths of the gospel so that Christ's saving and healing power can become a present reality for them within the context of the sacrament. Rushing through the Lord's Supper displays a misunderstanding of the sacrament as a sacrament of participation in God's life. We are invited to engage with God and with each other in communion, and, as any person knows, it takes time to re-connect with each other.

The analogy of a family meal at home, or in a restaurant, is helpful: we do not rush through from one course to another, silent and unaware of each other: we prefer to take time to interact with one another, for personal, social, or other reasons. The meal is an *event in itself*, not a brief interruption in the busyness of life. Unfortunately, too many people have lost sight of the value of taking time out to enjoy meals together, which may have something to do with the busyness of contemporary society and the fragmentation of family life. Perhaps this is one of the reasons why we fail to give the Lord's Supper the significance it should have in our worship together.

It is worthwhile dwelling a little longer on the meaning of participation in the context of the Lord's Supper. In Chapter Two we suggested that the word *koinōnia* conveys the idea of being incorporated into a dynamic organism, and we developed this in the context of community life. In 1 Corinthians 10:16, however, Paul uses the word to express 'participation in the blood and body of Christ'. The Greek word *koinos* means 'common', and so by extension 'having something in common with'. In an unfathomable and mysterious way, we have something in common with Christ's body and blood.

Theologians have debated the meaning of this 'participation' throughout the centuries; the interpretation with which I am most comfortable is the one generally accepted, that those who receive the bread and wine actually receive into themselves the benefits that flow from all that Christ accomplished on the cross – forgiveness, peace with God, healing, and reconciliation. How this is made effective is a mystery: some argue that the faith of the believer is the critical factor; others maintain that the Eucharistic act conveys the grace of the gospel in itself, or *ex opere operato* ('by the work done'). Perhaps the liturgical proclamation of God's saving acts makes grace more efficacious: the creative power of the word is a robust theme in Hebrew thought. Others have suggested that whenever and wherever God's people are gathered together, united in their common identity, God's reality is more powerfully revealed.

Whatever position we hold, the issue essentially has to do with the nature of Christ's presence in the Eucharistic event. The Catholic doctrine of transubstantiation, in which the 'real presence' of Christ is interpreted in literal, physical terms, implies a sacrificial enactment of Calvary, which is biblically and hermeneutically unsustainable.[30] It is far more satisfactory to propose metaphorical significance to Jesus' reference to his own body and blood in Luke 22:19–20, similar to his claim to be 'the gate for the sheep' or 'the light of the world' – powerful representations of spiritual truth. In the Eucharistic liturgy the Spirit is invoked upon the elements of bread and wine that they might represent for participants the body and blood of Christ. Our interpretation of participation hinges upon a robust theology of the Spirit, who in some mysterious way makes Christ real amongst his people, and who simultaneously nourishes and blesses them.

We may take this further, however, in the light of our earlier discussion of the role of the Spirit in our response to God. As Torrance expresses it so poignantly: 'But what can we render to the Lord, for our lives are so unworthy, so broken and so sinful?'[31] And of course the answer is that we have nothing to offer him that is acceptable, and so Christ comes to us and he offers us himself: 'Take and eat; this is my body' (Mt. 26:26). Not only *has* Christ transformed us, making us righteous and perfect in himself, he *continues* to work in our lives through the power of the Spirit, who takes that which is of Christ and offers it to us again and again. So our remembrance, our *anamnēsis*, is given present and powerful reality for us as we participate in the communion of Father, Son, and Holy Spirit. We are nourished and renewed, and set on our feet again as we go out into the world. So our witness to Christ's presence in worship is not to be divorced from our witness to Christ's presence in his mission in and for the world.

Whilst we undoubtedly receive from Christ at a deeply personal level, we should remember that the sacrament also has effect within the wider body of believers. In the Lord's Supper, the Spirit takes hold of me and reminds me that I am not a 'lone ranger'

Christian: my identity is intrinsically tied up with who I am within the body of Christ. The fellowship of Christian community is clearly alluded to in Paul's words in 1 Corinthians 10:17: 'Because there is one loaf, we, who are many, are one body, for we all partake of the one loaf.' Vincent Donovan discovered the centrality of community as a way of life among the Masai of East Africa, so much so that they call the Lord's Supper 'the holy brotherhood'. Commenting on this, Donovan asks, 'Is the eucharist food for the individual soul, or the building up of an I-Thou relationship with Christ (or with anyone else), or the private domain of the priestly caste of an organization? Or is it not the sign and bond of unity and charity of a community?'[32] Paul was similarly concerned to correct individualism and factional strife amongst the Corinthian Christians, and he condemned their unworthy attitudes and behaviour at the Eucharistic table.

But of course the Lord's Supper does not end with the present reality of Christ amongst us. In 1 Corinthians 11:26 the words 'until he comes' are richly suggestive. The Passover *Haggadah* closes with a prayer to the Lord to 'restore the unnumbered congregation of thy people', an anticipation of the coming of the Messiah, who would gather all those who are dispersed and bring them finally and safely to Mount Zion. This eschatological perspective is the hope of the Christian church: 'Who hopes for what he already has? But if we hope for what we do not have, we wait for it patiently' (Rom. 8:24–25). In this life we do not receive all that awaits us in glory.

Peterson ties the two themes of fellowship and anticipation together, when he points out that 'local congregations or housegroups may be viewed as earthly manifestations of that heavenly assembly already gathered around God and Christ. The congregational meeting should thus be a way of expressing our common participation in that eschatological community, gathered, cleansed and consecrated to God by Messiah's work.'[33]

I am troubled by those who insist on claiming everything from God *now*, who emphasize the 'already' at the expense of the 'not-yet', and who live a triumphalism which is contradicted by the many biblical calls to suffering and costly discipleship. Not only does the Lord's Supper remind us of Christ's ongoing and gracious renewal of our broken lives through his self-offering in the bread and the wine; the sacrament witnesses to our frail and fragile life here on earth by pointing us to the glory that awaits us in heaven. Our temporal existence is contrasted with the eternity which awaits us. So there should be celebration and rejoicing, for we participate in a feast that anticipates the wedding supper of the Lamb. The community of the faithful who celebrate on earth will combine with all who belong to the Lord in an unending hymn of praise: 'Let us rejoice and be glad and give him glory! For the wedding of the Lamb has come, and his bride has made herself ready' (Rev. 19:7).

We have defined the Lord's Supper as the sacrament of participation in what Christ continues to do for us in our lives today; baptism is the sacrament of participation in what he has done by virtue of his all-sufficient death and resurrection: it is a covenantal sign, by which believers are called into lively participation in the life of the triune God. It is the sacrament of *initiation* into the family of God, whereas the Lord's Supper may be defined as the sacrament of *continuation*. The baptized are called into participation in Christ's death so that they might participate in his life. So baptism and the Lord's Supper are inseparable sacraments of participation.

Throughout history God has graciously taken the initiative in establishing and renewing a people for himself, and the idea of covenant reflects an important continuity between the Old Testament nation of Israel and the New Testament people of God. In his steadfast love God covenanted himself to his people, and signified his gracious promises through the rite of circumcision, by which individuals were initiated into the covenantal family life of God. In Colossians 2:11–12 Paul interprets the new covenant rite of baptism in a similar way: 'In him you were also circumcised, in the putting off of the sinful nature, not with a circumcision done by the hands of men but with the circumcision done by Christ, having been buried with him in baptism and raised with him through your faith in the power of God, who raised him from the dead.'

This is the language of grace! Baptism is first and foremost about God before it is about us. It is 'the divinely appointed rendezvous of grace for faith ... all is of God, who brings man to faith and to baptism, and in his sovereignty has been pleased to so order his giving.'[34] Community, covenant, and grace are three themes which are indispensable to a true theological understanding of baptism. They place the rite within the historic traditions of the universal church. They speak to us of the God in whose eternal story our own story of life unfolds: baptism reminds us that our lives are bound up in his and in the lives of all those who belong to him ... past, present, and future. Baptism is less a guarantee of commitment on our side as it is a guarantee that God remembers us all the way through our lives from the very moment of our birth, even before then. In a well-loved psalm David acknowledges before God: 'My frame was not hidden from you when I was made in the secret place. When I was woven together in the depths of the earth, your eyes saw my unformed body. All the days ordained for me were written in your book before one of them came to be' (Ps. 139:15–16).

This insight is helpful in the vexed issue of infant baptism. To welcome the children of believing parents into the community of faith through baptism is to acknowledge the grace of God who includes them on the basis of covenant love. He does not wait to see how they turn out at a later stage in their lives before including them. They may reject him, and many do, just as Esau failed to receive God's promises, even though he was circumcised. When baptized children choose at a subsequent stage in their lives not to remember the God who ever holds them in his heart, that does not invalidate infant baptism as a sacrament of covenantal love.

The first question in baptism, then, is neither *to whom?* nor *how?* but *what?* What is signified in baptism? To which we reply that baptism signifies what God has done for all humanity in Jesus Christ. Forgiven and cleansed, we are adopted into his family, and we are summoned to utter our 'Amen' to Christ's 'Yes', trusting that the Spirit of Christ will continue his faithful ministry in the lives of all who have been baptized, young and old alike. All are invited to participate not only in the baptism of Christ's own death and resurrection but also in the eternal feast of the triune God, foreshadowed in the Lord's Supper. So we are lifted up into the perfect and acceptable worship of Christ, in which we discover the fullness of our humanity as gift of the Spirit.

The grace of prayer

Although prayer is an expression of our individual life in Christ, Macquarrie cautions us against the dangers of egocentricity, suggesting that prayer 'takes place in the context of community, and, beyond that, in the context of Being'.[35] Whatever form our praying might take – whether inward in terms of adoration, confession, thanksgiving and supplication; or outward, in terms of intercession – the greatest joy comes when we realize that prayer is not so much what *we do* in presenting ourselves before God, but an entering into the prayer life of the triune God. This does not mean that prayer is a passive affair; there is active response on the human side. This response, however, is initiated and upheld by the Spirit who leads us in love, always at work in our lives to draw us into the perfect communion of God. That is his passion and his purpose for all humanity, that we might partake of the divine life in all its glory.

'Prayer,' Tom Smail once said, 'is all about entering into the stream of prayer which is forever taking place in the heavenlies.' In prayer, we participate in the 'conversation of heaven' as we dwell in the God who is ever interceding for us and for the world. 'To be true and serious, to be the prayer which is heard by God, it must first and last be the prayer of the One who as the true Son has the authority and power truly to address him as Father.'[36] Prayer therefore has to do with our listening before our speaking: it is an expression of our relationship with God, in whose life we are privileged to participate. We discover in prayer that God is for us and for all humanity: in his perfect love he knows our needs and the needs of the whole world before we ask. This is liberating, for we are thus free to come before God knowing, as Barth reminds us, that we are only creatures and not the Creator! Paul reminds us that 'the Spirit helps us in our weakness. We do not know what we ought to pray for, but the Spirit himself intercedes for us with groans that words cannot express. And he who searches our hearts knows the mind of the Spirit, because the Spirit intercedes for the saints in accordance with God's will' (Rom. 8:26–27).

In 1966 Michael Harper, seeking material for a book on the charismatic movement within the churches in the United States, travelled to the Episcopal Church of the Redeemer in Houston, Texas, and discovered there a remarkable work of the Spirit amongst the Christian community. (I quote this example because of its formative influence upon my own life shortly after my conversion to the Christian faith in 1972.) Harper was invited to address the church one evening, after which a number of the worshippers packed into a tiny prayer chapel in the basement of the church. The meeting impressed itself indelibly on his memory: in his own words, 'it was hauntingly memorable'.

> The people there obviously knew each other extremely well. There was no sense of rush about what was happening. One felt that two contradictory things were happening; at first sight it was as if they had worked it all out carefully before they had started, and yet, at the same moment, it was as if everything they said and did was new and fresh to them. There was an economy about it all. No time was being wasted. Some were prayed for as needs were expressed. Each person came forward and knelt at the altar rail. A tiny knot of people grouped themselves around the person. Hands were laid on them. Clear and appropriate words were spoken – the person nodding their head in approval. God was there. A gentle peace pervaded the chapel. No-one was in a hurry. There was no heavy hand of leadership, yet Graham was very obviously the leader. It was so clear that an unseen power was guiding the whole business.
>
> 'The Lord has given me a Scripture,' a woman told us, her tone of voice expressing partly excitement, partly mystery. 'The words are very strange,' she said.
>
> 'Never mind,' said Graham, 'let's hear them.'

'They're from Leviticus,' she said – 'thou shalt not uncover thy sister's nakedness.'

There was a pause, no-one knowing quite what to say. The strangeness of the words stunned everyone into silence.

'I reckon God is saying something here about our church,' said Graham slowly. 'God is saying that we are not to seek for or allow any publicity for the moment. This is a work of God which should not be uncovered.'

My heart gave a bit of a lurch. I could see a good story slipping from my grasp.

'We have a reporter here,' went on Graham. 'These words refer to you, Michael,' he said, turning and smiling at me.[37]

What is remarkable about the story of the Church of the Redeemer, a church which was shaped by the Holy Spirit into a compassionate, charismatic community of faith reaching out to society, is its openness to the mind of the Spirit expressed in a number of complementary and mutually reinforcing ways. The rector knew the inward call of God on his life, yet he was also aware of the need to submit himself to those amongst whom he was called to serve as leader. Direction came through the Spirit's ministry amongst the people of God, yet the mantle of leadership was not lifted from his shoulders. Charismatic gifting was evident in the prophetic word submitted by a member of the congregation: such manifestations of *charismata* were not uncommon in the everyday life of the church community. Within the tradition of the church, a joyful atmosphere of worship was evident, enhanced through liturgy and sacraments. At the same time, there was a high respect for the Scriptures, as Harper's account demonstrates.

When I was a young Christian, I was deeply affected by an incident that took place in the Anglican church to which I belonged. A visiting missionary speaker was present one evening to address us. Before he spoke, however, we participated in a time of worship and prayer, during which a remarkable thing happened. Someone received a mental picture of a flagpole in a clearing ... no more. Then another person added more detail to the picture, then another, and another, until a complete scenario was presented almost in technicolour! There was an expectant quietness for a while, as we waited for some interpretation of what had been communicated 'in the Spirit'. The silence was broken by the trembling voice of the missionary, who came forward and told us that what had unfolded before us in prayer described precisely his current ministry circumstances. The scenario which had been presented, and the subsequent interpretation, was a rich encouragement to him as he prepared for his return, and the man ministered powerfully to us out of all that the Lord had given to him through the gathered community.

The two incidents quoted here demonstrate the divine initiative in prayer operating through the gathered community. In both situations, those present were attentive to the Spirit, open to hear what he wanted to say and do in their midst. There was no hurry to get results, no striving in prayer, no demands placed on God, no 'naming and claiming'. The gathered community had learnt the meaning of participation in the prayer of God, and this was their acceptable and wholly refreshing worship.

To participate in the worship of Christ is to relinquish all efforts to perform before God. Yet the temptation to do so is always present when the high-priestly ministry of Jesus is disregarded. God is not a perfectionist, demanding that we perform with immaculate eloquence before him. He is a perfecter, receiving our flawed and fragile prayers and transforming them into something beautiful for him: 'For we do not have a high priest who is unable to sympathize with our weaknesses, but we have one who has been tempted in every way, just as we are – yet was without sin. Let us then approach the throne of grace with confidence, so that we may receive mercy and find grace to help us in our time of need' (Heb. 4:15–16).

If we do not understand this grace which resides in the heart of God, we will not interpret prayer as a privilege; rather, we will be dominated by an insistent pressure to 'bring God down' or 'press in for more of God'. This is the language not of true faith but of misplaced faith: it is faith in our own efforts, our ability to reach God, as if there were a great gulf between us and God. Prayer then becomes dependent on our formulae rather than God's faithfulness. This is evident in many different ways in the life and ministry of the church. Strategies are developed which have more to do with getting results than participating in a relationship. One church plans a 'prayer warfare' seminar; another group of Christians combine to 'pull down strongholds' through 'prayer walks'; others are engrossed in all-night prayer meetings in order to 'get the victory'. In some Christian gatherings, the decibel level of the praise is regarded as a measure of the presence of God!

Of course, when the people of God gather together, it is right that prayer and praise should characterize their assembly; we are rightly exhorted at times to 'shout to the Lord!' Paul encourages the Corinthians in their worship, teaching that when they come together 'everyone has a hymn, or a word of instruction, a revelation, a tongue or an interpretation' (1 Cor. 14:26). Nor must we diminish the importance of meeting together in prayer, whether for mutual encouragement, confession, or intercession. But when human endeavour usurps participation in the worship of Christ; when we move out of an understanding of God as a covenant-God, who delights to reveal himself in our midst, and replace him with a contract-God, whose actions on our behalf are dependent upon us in some way; when the focus of our worship has more to do with getting results than living in a relationship; then we have failed to live as worshippers in the grace of God.

Notes

1. John Calvin, *Institutes of the Christian Religion*, 4.17.2, tr. Henry Beveridge (Grand Rapids: Eerdmans, 1989), p. 558.
2. J-J von Allmen, *Worship: Its Theology and Practice* (London: Lutterworth Press, 1965), p. 184.
3. See James B. Torrance, *Worship, Community and the Triune God of Grace* (Downers Grove: IVP, 1996), pp. 66–7.
4. See Derek Kidner, *Psalms 73–150: A Commentary on Books III–V of the Psalms* (Leicester: IVP, 1975), pp. 343–6.

150   *Dancing in the Dark*

5. George Carey, *I Believe in Man* (London: Hodder & Stoughton, 1977), p. 32.
6. von Allmen, *Worship*, p. 210.
7. See, for example, C. Welton Gaddy, *The Gift of Worship* (Nashville: Broadman Press, 1992), p. 35.
8. John Leach, *Liturgy and Liberty* (Tunbridge Wells: MARC, 1989), p. 31.
9. ibid., p. 32
10. ibid., pp. 32–3.
11. Lawrence O. Richards and Clyde Hoeldtke, *A Theology of Church Leadership* (Grand Rapids: Zondervan, 1980), p. 240.
12. I. Howard Marshall, *The Epistles of John* – The New International Commentary on the New Testament (Grand Rapids: Eerdmans, 1978), p. 217.
13. Torrance, 'The Place of Jesus Christ in Worship' in Anderson (ed.), *Theological Foundations for Ministry*, p. 365.
14. Richard Foster, *Celebration of Discipline: The Path to Spiritual Growth* (London: Hodder & Stoughton, 1978), p. 143.
15. Richards and Hoeldtke, *A Theology of Church Leadership*, pp. 239–40.
16. Torrance, *Worship, Community and the Triune God of Grace*, p. 34.
17. Grierson, *Transforming a People of God*, p. 18.
18. ibid., pp. 53–93.
19. ibid., p. 66.
20. C. S. Lewis, *The Allegory of Love* (Oxford: Galaxy, 1968), p. 10.
21. Moltmann, *The Spirit of Life: A Universal Affirmation* (Minneapolis: Fortress, 1992), p. 19.
22. John Drane, *Faith in a Changing Culture: Creating Churches for the Next Century* (London: Marshall Pickering, 1994), p. 112.
23. Trevor Lloyd, 'Worship and the Bible' in Colin Buchanan, Trevor Lloyd, and Harold Miller (eds.), *Anglican Worship Today* (Bramcote: Grove Books, 1980), p. 14.
24. Pinnock, *Flame of Love*, p. 121.
25. John Leach, *Living Liturgy* (Eastbourne: Kingsway Publications, 1997), pp. 46–71.
26. ibid., p. 69.
27. ibid., p. 120.
28. Karl Barth, *Church Dogmatics*, IV/2 (Edinburgh: T & T Clark Ltd, 1958), p. 703.

29. F. F. Bruce, *1 and 2 Corinthians* – The New Century Bible Commentary (Grand Rapids: Eerdmans, 1971), p. 114.

30. For a statement of the classical evangelical position, see Millard J. Erickson, *Christian Theology* (Grand Rapids: Baker, 1983), pp. 1121–3.

31. Torrance, *Worship, Community and the Triune God of Grace*, p. 91.

32. Donovan, *Christianity Rediscovered*, p. 90.

33. David Peterson, *Engaging with God: A Biblical Theology of Worship* (Leicester: Apollos, 1992), p. 247.

34. George R. Beasley-Murray, *Baptism in the New Testament* (Grand Rapids: Eerdmans, 1973), p. 273.

35. John Macquarrie, *Principles of Christian Theology* (London: SCM Press, 1966), p. 440.

36. Barth, *Church Dogmatics,* IV/2, p. 341.

37. Michael Harper, *A New Way of Living* (London: Hodder & Stoughton, 1973), pp. 20–21.

Chapter Five

Participating in the Mission of Christ

Amazed and perplexed, they asked one another,
'What does this mean?'
Acts 2:12

In the last chapter we described worship as a way of life for the Christian community, in which our participation in the life of God naturally and necessarily impels us out into the world in other-centred service. Thus we are called into participation in the world, which is a contextual participation: 'Really to *know* one's context means to participate *in* it – not only physically and factually, which in any case is unavoidable, but consciously, deliberately, reflectively.'[1] Hall summons the Christian community into personal immersion 'in the problematic of its context', a participation which is, in fact, the *sine qua non* of communication. To worship the living God is to plunge into the particularities of people's lives in such a way that what takes place is not merely transmission of a message, but genuine communication and dialogue.

It is, therefore, a grave misunderstanding of the gospel to put a wedge between worship and mission: 'When we withdraw from the world and on behalf of the world worship the Father in the name of Christ, we are not making some pietist escape from the world and the needs and claims of the world ... So we call upon the world to participate with us in our participation in the death and resurrection of Christ, to participate with us in our participation in the New Humanity, and to look with us beyond death to the fulfilment of God's purposes for all creation in resurrection.'[2] The liturgies of the church insist upon an integral link between worship and service, as expressed in one of the Anglican post-communion prayers:

> Almighty God,
> We thank you for feeding us
> With the body and blood of your Son Jesus Christ.
> Through him we offer you our souls and bodies
> To be a living sacrifice.
> Send us out
> In the power of your Spirit
> To live and work
> To your praise and glory. Amen.[3]

As we go out into the world, strengthened and renewed by our participation in the worship of Christ, we summon the world to enter into the gift of life. This is the essence of mission. To be sent out in the power of the Spirit to live and work to the praise and glory of God is to participate in the life of the world, dancing in the dark and shining the light of the gospel of grace wherever we go. That is the privilege of the church in the power of the Spirit. It is a costly calling as well as a privileged one, for 'all Christians share in the prophetic ministry of Christ and are witnesses of the gospel.'[4] Moltmann reminds us that this prophetic mission in which we participate inevitably draws us into conflict with 'the powers of the past and the forces of the future, between oppression and liberation'.[5]

We should bear in mind that mission cannot be accomplished through programmes, but only through participation in the creative ministry of the Spirit, who choreographs the steps of all who are called into costly identification with the hurting world. Here we find no deistic God who stands apart from suffering, but a God who is intimately involved with his creation, calling us to share with him in his summons to life. 'Dancing in the dark' may therefore lead us into the same experience as those who uttered psalms of lament in the Old Testament. Whereas our emphasis in earlier chapters has been on participating in the dance of the

triune God with vibrant enthusiasm, here the dance takes on a
different form. Shouts of joy give way to sighs and groans, and
'where these sighs and groans are heard there is still hope for
redemption. Where everything in and around us is struck dumb,
hope dies too. Sighs and groans are hope's signs of life, in opposition to death.'[6]

In this chapter we will consider our participation in the continuing mission of Christ with particular reference to the activity
and operation of the Spirit. We observed in Chapter One that the
ministry of the church in the world is a continuation of the ministry of Christ in the power of the Spirit. We also noted that, by
virtue of his creativity and imagination, the Spirit invites the contemporary church to see its life as an adventure of faith, a participation in the active life of God in the world. This is a powerful
insight, for the church is then encouraged to discover what the
Spirit is doing, rather than formulating mission strategies and
programmes in its own strength. Harvey Cox reminds us that
our relationship to God derives from the work that we are privileged to do together: 'Rather than shutting out the world to delve
into each other's depths the way adolescent lovers do, God and
men find joy together in doing a common task.'[7]

THESIS   The thesis of this chapter is that to participate in the mission
of Christ is to enter into the reconciling ministry of the Spirit,
who is continuously at work in the world in both hidden and
improbable ways, with creative innovation and resourceful
ingenuity, and with concern for the particularity of context.
Whenever the Christian church ties the Spirit of mission down to
its own specific programmes, failing to recognize these essential
characteristics, it has lost sight of what it means to participate
effectively in the mission of Christ, which is at the same time participation in the world. We will examine these dimensions of the
Spirit's activity in the world in later sections of this chapter.
Firstly, however, we need to reaffirm the primacy of mission in
the ministry of Christ and his church.

From the sanctuary into the world

There is a wonderful and quite remarkable development recorded in one of Ezekiel's visions (Ezek. 47:1–12), in which a stream of water is seen to flow out of the sanctuary of the temple, getting wider and deeper as it reaches into the barren and dry places around the Dead Sea. No tributaries swell the stream: we are invited to respond to the vision as a symbolic picture of the blessings that come from God himself to his people. The sanctuary speaks to us of the place where human beings meet with God in worship: in that place we are reminded of all that God has done for us in Christ, and we respond with gladness and openness to the God in whose Trinitarian life we now participate as individual believers.

The Christian life, however, is not a private affair, though it is certainly very personal. Many people today assume that their Christian faith is something to keep to themselves, but the biblical emphasis is on the Christian community. Paul writes that 'we were all baptized by one Spirit into one body' (1 Cor. 12:13): God is interested in us as individuals, but his overriding purpose is to fashion us into a community which reflects his glory. That was his intention when he called Abram as his chosen instrument, not only to bring glory to him, but also to be a light to the nations of the world. Careful reading of the Old Testament testifies to God's unchanging plan to establish the Israelites as a community of faith which embodied his life as fully as possible.

In the pages of the New Testament, we recognize Paul as a man whose ministry found fulfilment in the founding and nurturing of communities of believers. We cannot understand Christianity unless we speak also of community in the same breath. Indeed, one of the distinctive ministries of the Holy Spirit in recent decades, especially through the charismatic movement, has been to draw individual Christians – within and across denominations – into a fresh awareness of their common identity and purpose in Christ. This communal identity finds expression in the richness of life in the river in Ezekiel's vision: wherever the river flows, there are 'swarms of living creatures' and 'large

numbers of fish … of many kinds'. Truly this is a river in whose
life we all participate; no mention here of our own little streams
in which to paddle!

It is a powerful thing indeed when the church declares the love
of Jesus by flowing as one in the stream of God's life. In his great
high-priestly prayer, Jesus prayed to his Father: 'May they be
brought to complete unity to let the world know that you sent me
and have loved them even as you have loved me' (Jn. 17:23). As
the church is 'given to the Spirit', drawn into the adventurous
and risky flow of his love and life, and carried along into the barrenness of the surrounding areas, new opportunities for ministry
will emerge. The transformation of the salt water in the Dead Sea
to fresh water symbolizes the transforming influence of the Spirit
who causes 'everything to live' – and we are invited to participate
in this glorious renewing ministry, characterized by healing and
fruitfulness.

There is an exciting unpredictability in this vision which
reflects the role of the Spirit in the ministry of the church, or,
more precisely, the role of the church in the ministry of the Spirit.
The vision defies logic, as does much of the Spirit's activity. The
trickle from the sanctuary turns unaided into a powerful river,
and continuously fruiting trees rise up out of nowhere. Likewise,
Spirit-filled Christian ministry will encounter the unexpected,
and lead us into surprising and supernatural experiences in our
engagement with God in the world.

The progression in the flow of the stream takes us from the
sanctuary into the desert. There is no future for a church which
espouses a 'private Christianity', hidden from public view in the
sanctuary: its life will dry up if it has no movement out into the
world. Our life in God is not a life to be hugged to ourselves, but
to give away. Embraced by the giving Spirit, we discover the joy
of giving ourselves. Such is the ministry of the Spirit, who leads
us through a personal progression from self-interest to service.
This is reflected in the following diagram:

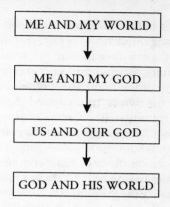

To be drawn out of our own selfish little worlds into the very life of the Trinity is a staggering reality, full of wonderful and eternal significance for individual Christians. To echo the community-life of the Trinity in our life as the body of Christ on earth, 'fellow-citizens with God's people and members of God's household' (Eph. 2:19), takes us into a greater depth of spiritual experience as we learn what it means to actually live in the unity of the Spirit as one people. But to see our common life as that which shines forth for the salvation of all people is to touch the very heart of God in his ministry to and for the world. Dancing in the dark – this is the core of Christian ministry. As we are drawn into the life of 'God-in-community', we discover the privilege and joy of incarnating that life in the world, participating in the continuing mission of Christ in the power of the Spirit. The progression out of 'me and my world' into 'God and his world' provides us, therefore, with a helpful paradigm for understanding the nature of that ministry.

The passion for mission in the heart of God

Human beings tend by nature to preserve that which exists or that which is working well, whereas the tendency of the Spirit is to orient us beyond that which exists to that which is yet to be revealed. The Spirit of God, who is the restorer of Israel – 'See, I am doing a new thing! Now it springs up; do you not perceive it?' (Is. 43:19) – is at work throughout the world, restoring and bringing life, at times in ways and in places that challenge the church's perception of ministry. The kingdom of God is not the church: to equate the two is 'to confound the Divine Rule with the people who live under it'.[8] Certainly the church has been given the authority of the kingdom, and is privileged to witness to the reality and power of the kingdom; and, straining forward, the church is the eschatological faith-community, expectantly awaiting the consummation of the kingdom; but the kingdom of God is a greater reality than the church, for it speaks of the sovereign activity and rule of God, who breathes life and hope into this broken world in the most unpredictable and powerful ways.

This should not surprise us, for the Spirit of God is the Spirit of mission. Reticent and humble in his desire to glorify Christ rather than seek his own glory, he is the ever-giving Spirit whose life in the church impels men and women in outward mission. This is his great passion. The history of the church is in fact the unfolding revelation of the kingdom of God, a continuation of the kingdom ministry of Jesus, who demonstrated in his own person the present reality of the kingdom: 'But if I drive out demons by the Spirit of God, then the kingdom of God has come upon you' (Mt. 12:28). The kingdom of God has come in the person of Jesus, anointed by the Spirit in fulfilment of Old Testament prophecy, as evidenced in Jesus' reading from Isaiah 61 in the synagogue in Nazareth at the commencement of his ministry.

But the kingdom motif also has an eschatological dimension: the Son of God presented his breaking into history as the fulfilment of something yet to be consummated. The kingdom has already come, expressed in the phrase 'realized eschatology',[9] but its complete fulfilment awaits us. It has both present and future reality (what some theologians have called 'inaugurated eschatology'). The kingdom of God radically challenges the agenda of the world (and, at times, the church!) whilst at the same time offering visible hope through the witness of the church in the world. So the church in the power of the Spirit is both

God's 'no' and God's 'yes' to the world. This perspective is necessarily missionary, embracing the mission of God who 'so loved the world that he gave his one and only Son' (Jn. 3:16). Moltmann's understanding of the church as a political reality is relevant here and finds support in the biblical tradition, with its revolutionary themes of promise, exodus, resurrection, and Spirit.

A true 'theology of liberation' is one that finds expression in many different forms, ranging from 'the economic abolition of the exploitation which results from the rule of particular classes, or the political vanquishing of oppression and dictatorship and the cultural elimination of racialism, down to faith's experience of liberation from the compulsion of sin and the eschatological hope of liberation from the power of death'.[10] The mission of the church is the kerygmatic proclamation, in word and deed, of a freedom which permeates many different dimensions of social disruption and disease; yet it is a freedom that 'can only be a single and a common freedom. It is the freedom for fellowship with God, man and nature.'[11]

Mission, however, is something that not only *creates* fellowship in all its richness: rightly understood, it *derives* from the faith-community's fellowship with the triune God. John Taylor argues that the church that will make a difference in society, the church that will 'send Christians into the fight', will be characterized by 'the quickening of compassion and the kindling of awareness by the Spirit of Jesus through the scriptures, worship and fellowship of the church'.[12] The role of the church is to be present in the world, because that is the arena of the Spirit's activity. The first few days of the New Testament church were marked by groups of believers 'who broke bread in their homes and ate together with glad and sincere hearts, praising God and enjoying the favour of the people'; the result was that 'the Lord added to their number daily those who were being saved' (Acts 2:46–47). The Spirit, who is the Spirit of fellowship, leading men and women into vital union with each other within the community-of-being of God himself, creates the very context within which mission takes place.

Elsewhere I have suggested that mission is what the church is called to *do* rather than what it actually *is*. This statement needs some qualification in the light of the preceding discussion. It relates to the distinction between 'mission' and 'missions' proposed by the eminent missiologist David Bosch: 'The first refers primarily to the *missio Dei* (God's mission), that is, God's self-revelation as the One who loves the world, God's involvement in and with the world, the nature and activity of God, which embraces both the church and the world, and in which the church is privileged to participate. *Missions* ... refer to the particular forms, related to specific times, places, or needs, of participation in the *missio Dei*.'[13] We might say, then, that mission is, ontologically, a defining characteristic of the church, for it expresses the inner impulse of the triune God to reveal himself through his church in the midst of the world. God delights to make himself known, and the church is both a sign of his kingdom, pointing to the reality of his rule of compassionate love, and a sacrament, a dynamic event of grace, in which he is present by his Spirit.

Functionally, however, the community of faith gives form and shape to that impulse under the inspiration of the Spirit through appropriate missionary strategies. Each faith-community is privileged to participate in the mission of Christ in the world, but each will be involved in that mission in its own unique way. No one local expression of mission is identical with another; it is the Spirit's prerogative to orchestrate the gifts and personalities of each congregation in creative ecumenism, weaving his own pattern of life and hope in a hurting and broken world.

Revisiting the incarnational imperative

In his development of incarnational theology, Karl Barth argues, on the basis of John 17:18 and John 20:21, that the church is formed under the imperative of the incarnation: '... the goal of the sending both of Jesus and of his disciples is the cosmos. The world is the third party to which they are sent, Jesus by the Father and the community by Jesus. Both his and their fully accredited embassy is to the world.'[14] But the world in which we live is one which is shaped by, and shapes, a diversity of belief systems. As Lesslie Newbigin points out, pluralism reigns where beliefs are concerned: we live today in a world characterized by religious pluralism, ethnic diversity and cultural relativism.[15] Participation in the mission of Christ requires the church to acknowledge these realities and to recognize that 'the eternal Spirit has been at work in all ages and all cultures making men aware and evoking their response, and always the one to whom he was pointing and bearing witness was the Logos, the Lamb slain before the foundation of the world.'[16]

Certainly the progress in global communication, international travel, and linguistics has contributed markedly to these social realities, particularly in the twentieth century. But history reveals that, though the intensity and scale of pluralism is more evident today in our 'shrinking world', it is not a new thing: diversity and tolerance were characteristic of the ancient Greek world and in the days of Jesus and the early church. Ziesler notes the cultural and religious traditions in which Paul stood, and observes that 'while pious Jews were holding the front door shut against foreign pressure, the back window was open enough to let mixing take place.'[17]

We recognize, therefore, important points of reference theologically and culturally when we relate the ministry of the church to the ministry of Christ. Theologically, as we discussed in Chapter One, the incarnation of God determines the orientation, meaning and purpose of the church. In Chapter Three we explored the diversity of views which people have about the world in which they live, and how they fit into it. The church is called into 'costly identification with people in their real situations as we see in the earthly ministry of Jesus'.[18] Though the church must beware the ever-present danger of capitulating to the culture, pluralism today is as great an opportunity as it was for the early church. Christian ministry is called not to deny culture, but to lead people beyond its often narrow, life-constricting confines, and into the liberty of the culture of the

162   *Dancing in the Dark*

kingdom of God, which was at the core of both Jesus' and Paul's teaching.

In fulfilling the commission to go and make disciples of all nations (Mt. 28:19), the church is equipped with the same power of the Holy Spirit as Jesus received at his baptism, the Spirit who knows no boundaries in the communication of the gospel from one cultural frame of reference to another. The Acts 2 narrative of the Pentecostal event 'provides a paradigm for redemptive relationships within a multicultural context ... in which the "breaking out" of the Spirit of Jesus was manifest in a multicultural, multigenerational and inclusive community of relationships.'[19] So Hinkle proposes the combination of the incarnational and Pentecostal paradigms in a model for pastoral ministry which shifts us out of cultural encapsulation into a rich and fruitful intercultural understanding in the power of the Spirit.

One of the central thrusts of Eugene Peterson's pastoral theology is that God's will and God's work must be incarnated 'in the actual *place* where the pastor lives amongst the *named* people with whom she or he lives'.[20] He quotes the story of the mythological giant Antaeus, whose strength derived from his proximity to the bare ground. In a wrestling match with the giant, Hercules lifted him high above the ground, so depriving him of his source of strength and ultimately life. Likewise, suggests Peterson, if Christian ministry is removed from its ground, it loses its strength to grapple with the complexities inherent in the work.

This is particularly evident in cross-cultural ministry. An Indian evangelist once said: 'Do not bring us the gospel as a potted plant. Bring us the seed of the gospel, and plant it in our soil.' Charles Kraft recounts his experience as a field missionary in northern Nigeria; he was frequently jolted by the perspectives of his Nigerian brethren, whose language and culture continually challenged his own way of seeing and doing things. Gradually he became aware that his growing attempt to 'integrate my anthropological understandings with my theological understandings was opening my mind to the probability that God wanted to lead the Nigerians in their attempts to be faithful to

Christ in a way different from the way he wanted to lead me and my people'.[21] So we can say that theology should be 'an ever-renewed re-interpretation to the new generations and peoples of the given Gospel, a re-presentation of the will and the way of the one Christ in a dialogue with new thought-forms and culture patterns'.[22]

Bruce Olson tells of a fascinating encounter with two warriors of the Motilone Indian tribe in Colombia, amongst whom he was working as a missionary.[23] The Motilones were a feared tribe, hostile to outsiders, but Olson befriended them and lived amongst them. By respecting their culture, and accepting their legends and understanding of life, he discovered that God was willing to work through the prophecy of a Motilone shaman in order to reveal Christ to these Indians. This remarkable event is characteristic of the unpredictable and surprising Spirit, who is ever at work in the cultures of the world to make Christ known. However, the possibility of a diminution of the Christian message is never far away.

In certain liberation-theology contexts, for example, the exodus tradition focusing on Moses has become more important than the story of Jesus. Robert Schreiter traces the rise of many independent churches in Africa and observes that 'their grasp on traditional Christianity seems to have been lost.'[24] A report in *TIME* magazine commented that in some regions of Africa a majority of men cannot receive communion because they have more than one wife. Reformers think the church should be tolerant of men who took several wives before they converted to Christianity and now feel committed to them. Others, however, vow that no amount of 'enculturation' – faith taking root in a new culture – will allow the church to bend on the issue.[25] An even more extreme example of enculturation permits the incorporation of tribal religions into African Christianity.

Where should the line be drawn? This is the constant challenge facing all who are committed to incarnational ministry in a pluralist and ethnically diverse world. Nor should we restrict cross-cultural ministry to overseas activity; ethnicity and multi-culturalism are domestic realities in many contemporary

societies, demanding sensitivity to world-views that are frequently ignored in the practice of Christian ministry. In the great
cities of the world, many different philosophies of life jostle with
one another in a rich mixture of human experience and
endeavour. It is precisely because authentic Christian ministry is
incarnational, directed towards individuals and people-groups
whose perceptions of reality and belief systems are very different
from our own, that we must give full attention to the variety of
ways in which the Spirit of Christ is active in mission in the contemporary world.

The inclusiveness of mission

Several years ago a young American man went to a meeting in
Pensacola, Florida, where some remarkable conversions have
taken place at the Brownsville Assemblies of God Church. At one
of the revival services there he was restored back to God. At his
baptism he spoke about his restoration, but what was particularly noticeable was his testimony about his relationship with his
own father, who was standing behind him in the baptismal pool.
With tears in his eyes, and in a faltering voice, he told of his
estrangement from his father, and then he turned round and said
in an emotional voice, 'I love you, Dad.' As his father embraced
him after his baptism, all who were there witnessed the grace of
the Spirit, who is ever at work, reconciling people back to God,
and to each other. It was a deeply moving moment.

In my early Christian life I worshipped in an Anglican church
in Yorkshire, England. I was privileged to be there at a time when
the Spirit of God was moving in a gentle and powerful way. It
was in the early days of charismatic renewal, and I witnessed
some remarkable works of God in people's lives. I shall always
remember one particular meeting when the presence of God was
almost tangible – suddenly two people moved towards each
other at the front of the church, slowly at first ... then they
rushed into each other's arms, and embraced one another. They
were husband and wife, separated, but now reunited as the Spirit

of God spoke deeply into their lives and brought them together. In another service at the church, a young girl cried out in the midst of our worship 'Lord, I believe!' and with rejoicing we praised God for his grace at work in her life.

These visible and dramatic examples of reconciliation can be repeated all over the world. They testify to the powerful work of the missionary Spirit, who works in many different ways to restore people back to God and to each other. However, the Spirit more often than not works in deep and hidden ways in creation to restore the world back to God. John Taylor encourages us to have a theology of mission which starts by being too inclusive rather than too narrow, suggesting that a passionate concern for the humanness of people may make a good beginning: 'As a first step we must begin to see our engagement in mission as a participation in the continuing work of creation and not simply in the redemption of that which was long ago created.'[26]

This interpretation of mission as a participation in the continuous creation of God in the world is not easily embraced by some Christians. The starting point in mission for most evangelicals, for example, tends to be exclusive rather than inclusive, and is expressed in the language of redemption-forgiveness-salvation rather than creation and wholeness. People are regarded as either 'saved' or 'lost', and the reconciling ministry of the Spirit is interpreted primarily in terms of transferring those who are 'outside' to a new life 'in Christ'. The examples at the beginning of this section are indicative of this understanding of the mission of Christ in the world.

Vital and significant as this understanding of mission is, I want to suggest that many Christians at the same time have failed to appreciate the amazing compass of the Spirit's mission throughout the world. Recently I came across the following incident related by a volunteer at Stanford Hospital in the United States. While he was working at the hospital he came across a little girl named Liz who was suffering from a rare and serious disease. Her only chance of recovery appeared to be a blood transfusion from her 5-year-old brother, who had miraculously survived the same disease and had developed the antibodies needed to combat the illness. The doctor explained the situation to her little brother, and asked the boy if he would be willing to give his blood to his sister. The volunteer who was present at the time saw the 5-year-old hesitate for only a moment before taking a deep breath and saying, 'Yes, I'll do it if it will save Liz.' As the transfusion progressed, he lay in bed next to his sister and smiled, seeing the colour return to her cheeks. Then his face grew pale, and his smile faded. He looked up at the doctor and asked with a trembling voice, 'Will I start to die right away?'

[margin note: BOY WILLING TO GIVE ALL HIS BLOOD.]

This story is a poignant example of one of the characteristic marks of the Holy Spirit at work in his creation. That little boy misunderstood the doctor, believing that he would have to give all his blood to his sister. What – or who – prompted him to give so sacrificially and willingly? May we not attribute his response to the loving ministry of the Spirit, who breathes life and compassion into the human heart, whether or not he is openly acknowledged? Do we have to insist on religious language in order to describe the gracious work of the Holy Spirit in our midst? Taylor exhorts us as Christians to 'come off our religious high-horse and get our feet on the lowly, earthy ground of God's primary activity as creator and sustainer of life.'[27]

Of course, we must avoid the trap of insisting that everything is mission, for then, as Neill has reminded us, 'nothing is mission'.[28] However, the church is perhaps in more danger of delineating mission too narrowly than too widely: we would do well to heed the words of Bosch, who describes mission as 'a multifaceted ministry, in respect of witness, service, justice, healing, reconciliation, liberation, peace, evangelism, fellowship, church planting, contextualization, and much more'.[29] The breadth of activity encompassed by this description challenges those who are inclined to reduce mission to having occasional guest services, inviting a visiting evangelist to 'conduct a mission' in the locality, or running introductory courses on Christianity at the church. None of these are to be dismissed, of course, but neither are they to be endorsed as primary indicators of the nature of mission.

To participate in the mission of Christ, therefore, is to come alongside those amongst whom the Spirit is already working and to work with him. We have noted frequently that mission is at the heart of the Trinitarian life of God and permeates his life in the world. This mission focus was evident during the first three centuries of the life of the church, although signs of the eclipse of the mission imperative were apparent in the second century as the church became more settled, and as ecclesiological concerns began to dominate. Following the conversion of Constantine in the fourth century AD, the church became institutionalized and the pre-eminence of mission gave way to 'mission projects', peripheral activities rather than a central conviction. This perspective still prevails in many parts of the Christian community.

What is needed in the church today is a recovery of the centrality of mission, such that all ministry is seen through the lens of mission. A colleague once observed that if we aim at ministry, mission will be marginalized; however, if we aim at mission, we will accomplish ministry. But the missionary perspective we need to embrace is one that is wide-ranging in its scope rather than narrow and reductionist. Taylor invites us to reflect on the enormous breadth and range of the mission of the Creator Spirit:

> It embraces the plant-geneticist breeding a new strain of wheat, the World Health Organization team combating bilharzia, the reconstruction company throwing a bridge across a river barrier, the political pressure group campaigning for the downfall of a corrupt city council, the amateur dramatics group in the new cultural centre, the team on the new oil-rig, the parents' committee fighting for de-segregated schools in the inner city. The missionaries of the Holy Spirit include the probation officer and the literacy worker, the research chemist and the worn-out school teacher in a remote village, the psychiatrist and the designer, the famine-relief worker and the computer operator, the pastor and the astronaut. Our theology of mission will be all wrong unless we start with a song of praise about this surging diversity of creative and redemptive initiative.[30]

Whilst Taylor's insights are helpful in pointing us away from a restricted interpretation of mission, they may be viewed by some as not being sufficiently anchored to the gospel story, at least not explicitly. What he is doing, of course, is swinging the pendulum towards inclusiveness; and there are risks in doing that. As a corrective, Bosch presents us with six Christological themes which need to remain central to Christian mission in order to avoid the communication of what he calls 'a truncated gospel': these are the incarnation, the cross, the resurrection, the ascension, Pentecost and the *parousia*. For Bosch, Christian mission must never lose sight of these central 'salvific events'. However, with Taylor, he warns us against the temptation to 'incarcerate the *missio Dei* in the narrow confines of our own predilections, thereby of necessity reverting to one-sidedness and reductionism'.[31] Mission, after all, is what *God* is doing. In order to participate in that mission, we need both the courage to look beyond our narrow evangelical and ecclesiological boundaries and also the wisdom to discern where the Spirit is at work, often in the unlikeliest places and in the most improbable ways.

When the Spirit was poured out upon the waiting disciples (Acts 2) they proclaimed the wonders of God in the tongues of every nation under heaven. Many people heard them: 'Amazed and perplexed, they asked one another "What does this mean?"' (Acts 2:12) Our reply is that it means that God has included all people in his act of grace in Jesus Christ – no one has been left out. Through Jesus' promise of the Spirit in Acts 1:8 and the reality of his coming on the day of Pentecost, God was teaching his church about the inclusiveness of his accepting love.

As Luke records the story of the church in Acts, we notice the remarkable incorporation of those who were thought by the Jews to be outside the saving grace of God. In Acts 8 Philip proclaimed the gospel of Jesus in the power of the Spirit, and many Samaritans, whom the Jews treated with hostility, put their faith in Christ. Peter was summoned to the house of the gentile Cornelius in Caesarea, where the Spirit fell upon all who were present in dramatic fashion (Acts 10–11). In fact, the Acts account of the workings of the Spirit reflect the unfolding history of salvation according to Acts 1:8, in which the disciples were privileged to participate.

The message of the Pentecostal outpouring of the Spirit for us today is that *God is for all people*: parents and children, husbands and wives, rich and poor, black and white, Jews, Muslims, Buddhists, gays and lesbians – all are included in God's forgiving, reconciling love. The Spirit is the reconciling Spirit who has been sent into the world to seek out the lost, the confused, the indifferent, and the rebellious. His mission is to bring them back to the Father, whatever their background, whatever their lifestyle, religion or cultic allegiance. The Holy Spirit at work in the world is none other than God amongst us, working in the midst of the mess of our lives, in the midst of our spiritual searching and religious confusion, in order to reconcile us to the Father.

This is the mission in which the church of God has been invited to participate. Caught up in the life of God, our hearts are to beat with his heart of reconciliation. The Greek word translated 'reconciliation' is *katallagē*, which literally means 'exchange'. In inclusive love, the Spirit of God reaches into the depths of the human predicament, offering to exchange his light for our darkness, his truth for our deception, his forgiveness for our condemnation, his peace for our torment. As he penetrates the alienation and confusion in human hearts, we must remember that the Spirit will not be bound by our neat theological formulae: he does things his way! That of course is the story of the Spirit in Acts – there is no monotonous uniformity there, but glorious diversity and unpredictability as the Spirit draws people into the triune life of God.

The Spirit continues what he began at Pentecost, recapitulating the gracious, inclusive love of Jesus through the ministry of the church. So passionate is his desire for reconciliation, so intense is his love for all humanity, that he will bypass the church if needs be in order to draw people back to the Father.

Many people today struggle with their sexual orientation, and their inner turmoil is aggravated by hostility and misunderstanding from different sections of the church. I have listened closely to the testimony of an American man who was trapped in a homosexual lifestyle for many years: his upbringing was severely dysfunctional, and he grew up craving the love of another man, for his father had not provided that love.

At one stage he planned a sex-change operation, but he was mercifully spared through what he calls divine intervention, though he did not immediately interpret what had happened in that way. At the time he was exploring a range of spiritual alternatives, and, as he wrestled with his sexuality, he sought comfort and peace in his hotel room. Quite unexpectedly he experienced the pure light and warmth of God enfolding him, and the Spirit brought to his mind words that he recalled from when he was a 5-year-old boy at church, as if angels were singing them:

> Jesus loves me this I know
> For the Bible tells me so.
> Little ones to him belong,
> They are weak but he is strong.

God is so much more gracious than his church! For years, this man had been told by the church that he had to get straight before God could accept him. That's what a 'contract-God' would say: 'You do this, then I'll do that!' But God is a God of covenant love, not a contract-God. The Spirit embraced the American in the midst of his wrestling, in the midst of his torment, saying to him, as it were, 'You *are* mine!' Reconciled to Christ through the gracious ministry of the Spirit, he discovered the healing power of God and is now happily married with a daughter.

We need eyes to see as God sees. We think the wind blows according to our doctrines, but 'the wind blows wherever it pleases' (Jn. 3:8). To participate in the mission of Christ is to be willing to have our eyes opened by the Spirit of God so that we may share in the joy of the Spirit's reconciling ministry. The homosexual man or woman craving for love, the Muslim seeking religious truth, the New Age devotee looking for inner peace, the political activist demanding justice for the oppressed, the drug addict searching for meaning in life … these are real people with deep longings, and if God is love he cannot pass them by.

So the Spirit reveals Christ in the most unexpected places and in the most improbable ways! 'We do not affirm the possibility of God's revealing himself outside Christianity begrudgingly – we welcome it! Not only does such a possibility suggest bridges in other cultures to enhance mission, but it also allows us to hear the word of God from others and deepens our own understanding of revelation.'[32] The Spirit is at work in all of life, because he is the Creator Spirit whose boundaries are limitless. He will go wherever he needs to go in order to point people to Christ and his saving love. If we do not understand that we will miss what the Spirit is doing in other cultures and other faiths. Pinnock suggests that 'without in any way being hesitant about making known the claims of Christ, we should listen and learn from the insights of others. Believing in the finality of Christ does not require us to be arrogant in our claims or closed to grace at work in other people.'[33]

A final story illustrates the power of the Spirit to penetrate other faiths, inviting us to respond to people with the same grace:

Gyalsang Tamang is a Sherpa, a member of the Tamang people, a Tibeto-Burmese people of around a million in number. His father was the overseer of a Buddhist temple and he led the worship songs at rituals held after people had died. Gyalsang helped his mother by looking after the sheep. One day when he was 10 years old, he lay down in the grass to doze for awhile. Two dark (what he calls) 'shadow-men' appeared before him as if in a dream, causing him to lose consciousness. His parents were very troubled. The men returned that evening, saying 'Don't worry. We want to use you. We want to show you the Buddhist way.' They told him to reassure his parents, and to sleep alone as they wanted to teach him each night.

And so this happened. With a Buddha image in front of him, he was taught the Buddhist way, and his parents were amazed as he reported to them all that he had learnt. He could even play instruments that he had never been taught! After some time the shadow-men revealed the Buddha image again, but it was different this time – there was a plate similar to a computer screen near the knees, and a voice explained the meaning of strange letters etched on the screen.

He wrote down these messages in a notebook in a language which to this day no one has been able to identify. Amongst the messages given to him was a list of 35 gods' names. The Dalai Lama was number 35. Then one day the message was given: 'After the Dalai Lama, bow down to Yesu' (which is Sherpa for Jesus, though Gyalsang did not know this). Month by month the name of Yesu rose higher in rank, and with his name came teaching about this unknown God. Gradually the whole biblical story of creation and redemption was unfolded through the messages on the Buddha screen. One day his father brought in a Tibetan tract about Jesus left behind by some tourists: it confirmed what had been revealed to Gyalsang.

Then three missionaries arrived, Jon, Dan and Jay. They met Gyalsang's brother, Mingmar, and in the course of their visit shared with him about Jesus. Mingmar was amazed that what they told him was exactly the same as his brother had shared with the family over three years. The missionaries then met Gyalsang, and by this time Yesu had jumped to second in the list of gods' names. As they explained the Christian faith, Gyalsang got excited and checked everything in his notebook: it was exactly the same, except that in one place he had mixed up Pilate's name with Caesar's!

That night the shadow-men came as usual and escorted him to the Buddha image. He heard a voice: 'Today my kingdom is finished in you and you no longer need to serve me. One comes after me who is greater than I. Do what the missionaries tell you and follow Yesu.' In the Buddhist tradition Buddha forbade others to worship him, and spoke of one who would come after him and who is worthy of worship. That was Gyalsang's last vision. Morning came and he felt a heavy burden lifted from him. The missionaries explained more about Jesus, and as they spoke Gyalsang tore the charms and beads from his neck and told Yesu that he wanted to follow him. Others did the same, burning their Buddhist things.

Mingmar and his wife went on to Bible school in Pokhara, and both of Gyalsang's parents confessed faith in Christ. Gyalsang can

no longer read what he wrote in his notebook as he cannot understand the language any more; now he has the Bible. His father com-
poses hymns in the Sherpa language and leads the singing when the
villagers gather for worship. Many of the villagers became Christians as a result of this remarkable move of the Spirit in the life of one
young man.

Gyalsang and his father spend much of their time visiting the surrounding villages explaining what it means to be a Christian. Many
people are wondering and asking about their unfamiliar faith.
Gyalsang also leads the services where local believers have built a
church. That building is in plain view of the village, and there are no
photos or statuary, emphasizing the fact that God is a Spirit, not a
graven idol. [34]

This well-attested narrative of the Spirit at work in the Buddhist
tradition reminds us that God is at work in other faiths precisely
because he is the reconciling God of grace, and 'religions play a
part in the history of grace, as the Spirit moves the world towards
the kingdom.'[35] This does not mean that the church must be
unquestioning in its response to other faiths, for undoubtedly
there are deficiencies and error in the non-Christian religions of
the world. Other religions do not present us with an understanding of God as triune being, nor do they speak of God's work of
grace for all humanity in Jesus Christ. What this story does
mean, however, is that we are to be open to the Spirit working
outside our frequently narrow, confined paradigms of mission,
so that we can participate fully and creatively in Christ's continuing mission in the world today.

Engaging with the postmodern agenda

A further area which has provoked great caution in the ministry
enterprise of the church is the phenomenon of postmodernism.
We have argued at some length in this book that all ministry is
contextual, that no ministry takes place in a vacuum; there is a
unique context which the gospel addresses each time it is

proclaimed, whether in word or deed. But there is substantial disagreement over the extent to which the Christian church should 'take on board' some of the fundamental tenets of what has been described as the 'postmodern context'. Actually, convinced postmodernists would squirm at the very idea that the philosophy behind their world-view can be characterized by fundamental tenets: after all, the very idea of postmodernism challenges the existence of absolutes in favour of a relativistic interpretation of both truth and values.

Throughout this chapter I have been arguing that God's calling to us as his church is to be a community of grace, vulnerable and accessible to a confused and searching world. For too long we have presented ourselves as a remote institution, lacking life and relevance. Our privilege and responsibility is to convey a life of grace and freedom, accepting fellow-travellers in our midst without imposing on them a narrow, dry evangelicalism that stifles and restricts. That will demand of us boldness and wisdom as we undertake *theologia viatorum* as the people of God. My plea is that we do not see postmodernism as a threat, renouncing it as an enemy of evangelical and biblical faith; rather, let us receive it, at least in part, with enthusiasm, and embrace it as an ally to assist us in our calling to be church in the world.

There is, as we have already suggested, considerable debate concerning the nature of postmodernism as a philosophical and cultural phenomenon; indeed, we may want to ask whether it can be defined as a world-view at all. Postmodernism has been with us as a philosophy of life for long enough for some to inquire about its successor! I am not among those who see postmodernism as 'a pause, a wrinkle in time',[36] nor do I interpret it as a *fin de siècle* (end-of-century) phenomenon.[37] As a cultural and social phenomenon, I believe it has considerably more resilience than its critics would suggest – and this resilience has a lot to do with its beneficial and positive features, some of which we explore below.

Both epistemologically and ethically, we live in disturbing and changing times, and the Christian mandate is to deliver an unchanging message in what has come to be regarded as a 'post-Christian' culture. The major issue today is seen by many as an ecclesiological one as much as an epistemological one. In other words, if the postmodern insistence upon relativism demands of the church a vigorous declaration of the truth claims of the gospel, it is also incumbent upon the church to 'get its own house in order' in order to communicate effectively to a world that is tired of an institution that seems to lack both lustre and relevance. As Christians, we also need to take note of those who have something to say to us about the times in which we live. The American philosopher, Diogenes Allen, has remarked that 'the embargo on the possibility of God has lifted.'[38] We might well be living in a post-Christian age, but it is a spiritual one nonetheless.

Christianity is once again an acceptable option, but now only one out of a smorgasbord of spiritual and religious alternatives; a wide range of spiritualities are now on the menu, offering gods of our own making, gods that suit us. The modernist worldview – characterized by rationalism, scientific progress and the fundamental tenets of secular optimistic humanism – put self very firmly on the throne of life, rejecting intervention from any supernatural source. The postmodern agenda retains the modernist focus on self; indeed, the current distrust of modernism – consider the alienation, violence and greed of modern society – affirms the centrality of self in its rejection of absolutes. The postmodern creed declares that I am my own master, with my own gods (if I want them), and I am free to live my life my way.

All this, of course, is enough for many Christians to throw up their hands in horror and disavow postmodernism in its entirety. How can we ally ourselves with a life-philosophy that rejects any notion of absolute truth and advocates not just an epistemological shift but an epistemological *vacuum* into which we are invited to construct our own versions of reality? And to make matters worse, the logical companion of such a phenomenon is ethical pluralism. But such a hasty repudiation is, I suggest, both inappropriate and ill-considered, and inevitably leads us to 'throw the baby out with the bathwater'. Although I hear the critics of postmodernism with sympathetic ears,

especially those from within a Christian world-view perspective,
I would like to swing the pendulum the other way and argue that,
far from being totally negative, chaotic and irrational, as some
commentators have suggested, postmodernism may be presented
in a more positive, hopeful light.[39]

Recent critics of the evangelical church have commented on
what they perceive as the church's capitulation to modernism.
This has been articulated in a number of interrelated ways: as an
embrace of *theologia gloriae* at the expense of *theologia crucis*;
as a willingness to seek results through pragmatic programmes
rather than Pentecostal reality; or as a focus on rational
discourse and intellectual debate at the expense of a holistic
experience of God. Although these issues are of enormous
importance, we need to lay them on one side as we address the
crucial ecclesiological question: are there better ways of *being
church* so that we participate more effectively in Christ's mission
in today's world?

The truth is that we live in a world which is far removed from
the modernist version of reality, with its rational, clinical and
superficial presentation of life. 'The world is too complex, too
contradictory, too enigmatic, pock-marked with guilt, flawed
with folly and pride, scarred by ignorance and arrogance.'[40]
Postmodernism rightly highlights ambiguity, mystery, paradox,
and confusion in its understanding of reality, so presenting us
with emphases that need to be acknowledged if we are to participate compassionately in the turmoil of the world around us. The
missio Dei speaks of a God who plunges urgently and relentlessly
into the chaos and pain of a world that is in desperate need of
healing and redemptive love. To participate in the mission of
Christ requires us to give sympathetic consideration to the
postmodern agenda, and to listen to the voice of the Spirit who
invites us into his dance of love in the darkness of the human
predicament.

The current way of 'being church' corresponds with an
Enlightenment way of thinking that has much to do with structure, order, and predictability within a framework of propositional truth. However, we need to hold in creative tension the

idea of divinely ordained order and structure in the universe and the presence of randomness and unpredictability in creation, as suggested by recent advances in chaos theory and quantum mechanics in the physical sciences.[41] An insistence on order at the expense of spontaneity can lead to a 'reductionist' view of a God who is boxed into a narrow modernistic paradigm which denies ambiguity, mystery, paradox and unpredictability. Such a view can all too easily carry into the life – or lack of life – of the church. Now this is perhaps not news to those who have been reared within the confines of the institutional church, but it needs a response if faithfulness to the Word is to be accompanied by relevance to the contemporary world. It is not propositional truth which is in question here, but the clothes we put on this truth. What is needed is an imaginative, creative and fundamentally *Pentecostal* approach in clothing the truth of the gospel such that it is received and actually *heard* by many who would otherwise be passed by. Indeed, if the Spirit is who he is, challenging us to creativity and glorious diversity in our expression of unchanging truth, then postmodernism, in its challenge to tired structure, sits very comfortably with the richness of charismatic and Pentecostal life.

We need to be those who, like the men of Issachar of long ago, understand the times in which we live and know what should be done (1 Chr. 12:32). This, of course, is the stuff of theology, and connects directly with the ongoing discipline of 'doing theology', a concept which we examined in Chapter Three. Consistent with this discipline, I suggest that we need a more positive assessment of postmodernism as we gear up for ministry in a new millennium. Imagine that we are all on a playing field, kicking a ball around within a clearly defined and limited space. We know the rules, and we are, more or less, familiar with the way we each play the game. Then along comes somebody who extends the boundaries so much that we are initially confused about how we are to cope with the new possibilities engendered by the change. Confusion leads to frustration, and antagonism is felt by some, even anger, as the goal posts are widened. Why, even the shape of the ball seems to be changing! This really is a new ball-game.

Some of us are threatened by what is happening, and a cry is heard: 'Come on everybody, let's stay within the old boundaries, and stick by the rules we all know.' Others, however, are excited by the new opportunities created by these changes; after all, the purpose is still the same – to get the ball between the goalposts. The game retains all the same thrills and challenges, but its context is different.

This parable has a lot to do with Christian ministry in a changing world. Toffler's 'future shock' rings in our ears as we consider the enormous changes that have taken place both culturally and technologically in recent years. I am reminded of Helmut Thielicke's oft-quoted words that 'the Gospel must be constantly forwarded to a new address, because the recipient is repeatedly changing place of residence.' It *is* a new world out there, and we need to both understand it and respond appropriately to the challenges presented by the postmodern world in which – whether we like it or not – we now live.

Postmodernism is, as Hans Frei once described hermeneutics, 'a word that is forever chasing a meaning'.[42] An American academic theologian once referred to postmodernism as 'intellectual velcro dragged across culture'[43] – an adhesive label picking up anything random that floats across the surface of our culture. Whatever else one may think about such a label, at least it has the merit of alerting us to an important signifying motif in postmodernism: its rejection of transcendent absolutes of any kind. The French social theorist, Jean-Francois Lyotard, argues that the essence of postmodernism is the 'incredulity towards metanarratives':[44] that is, there are no overarching explanations of the human condition, such as those claimed by either Christianity or any other political or social 'order'. So free rein is given to relativism and subjectivity, and all are not only free, but *encouraged*, to believe whatever they wish, for there are no absolutes in life. Objective truth, according to the postmodernist, is a myth, a viewpoint that conveys obvious ethical implications.

But we must look beyond these initial interpretations, for postmodernism opens up the door to new and optimistic expressions of freedom, imagination and creativity, epitomized in the challenge to Le Corbusier's architectural straight lines. Right-brain creativity, with all its ambiguities, flamboyance, irreverence, and stylized pastiche, offers hope and encouragement (albeit at times only transitory) to a generation tired of structure, order, and left-brain sterility. It is, I suggest, too easy for those who mourn the loss of stable values and the abandonment of unequivocal truth-statements, particularly in the realm of theology, to dismiss this more positive evaluation of postmodernism.

Whilst I do not wish to ally myself exclusively either with those who wholeheartedly espouse the postmodern ethos or with critics like Allan Bloom and David Wells,[45] I do want to present a Christian case for postmodernism which recognizes its contribution to an understanding of the human condition today. Looking back, we need to hear postmodernism's critique of modernism, and its protests against narrowness, intolerance, rationalism, the pursuit of materialism, and so-called scientific progress. Looking forward, we need to embrace postmodernism's emphasis on experience, awareness of others, tolerance, and the value of the individual. We need to acknowledge postmodernism's concern for marginalized groups even as we reject its repudiation of metanarratives.

Of course, there is a need to give the pendulum a push back in the other direction, especially in recognition of postmodernism's epistemological and ethical vacuum, where style has replaced substance and self-reference is the central creed. After all, postmodernism's fatal flaw may be its lack of commitment to anything at all – except itself! Bloom insists that 'one has to have the experience of really believing before one can have the thrill of liberation',[46] and it is precisely this need for conviction and commitment that keeps alive the relevance of Christianity, both doctrinally and ethically.

One way of exploring this further is to present the argument in diagrammatic form, similar to layouts proposed in articles and books that seek to present a distinction between the modernist and postmodernist paradigms. This one draws from material developed by John Drane. Drane acknowledges that 'there is a good deal of debate about the precise difference between Hebrew (biblical) thinking and Greek (secular) thinking.'[47] His labels are therefore typological, not exact; the paradigms are suggestive and are meant to be neither complete nor culturally rigorous.

Conservative Evangelical / Contemps Culture

LEFT-BRAIN, SCIENTIFIC, 'GREEK' WORLD-VIEW	RIGHT-BRAIN, POETIC, 'HEBREW' WORLD-VIEW
PRECISE	IMPRECISE
REASON / INTELLECT	EMOTIONS / INTUITION
PERMANENT	PROVISIONAL
PHYSICAL	SPIRITUAL
ABSOLUTE	AMBIGUOUS
SCIENCE / TECHNOLOGY	VALUES
PROPOSITIONAL	APPROXIMATE
WESTERN CULTURE	ETHNIC WORLD-VIEWS
RATIONAL	INTUITIVE
MEN	WOMEN
LITERAL	SYMBOLIC
CHURCH	SPIRITUAL QUEST
WORSHIP	PERSONAL NEEDS

Each reader will zone in on areas of contrast and tension which have to do with his or her own areas of preference and interest. Some will find themselves drawn like a magnet to the explicit gender implications! Perhaps others will focus more immediately on cultural or philosophical distinctions. Whatever our response, we can use this 'paradigm-contrast' model as a way into expressing the tension that exists between our church culture (more specifically here the conservative evangelical tradition) and contemporary culture. It is instructive (though not necessarily appropriate in all cases!) to label the left-hand side of the diagram 'CONSERVATIVE EVANGELICALISM' and the right-hand side 'CONTEMPORARY CULTURE'. We will then find ourselves discovering a number of areas which challenge traditional or conventional ways of 'doing ministry', ways which have created major credibility gaps in the church's witness to the world.

A number of words in Drane's diagram have to do with the nature of reality as perceived by modernists and post-modernists. Modernists tend to rely upon a 'left-brain', analytical understanding of life; words which relate to this perspective are 'precise', 'absolute', 'propositional', 'literal', and 'rational'. Postmodernists, however, put a premium on creativity and imagination in their interpretation of reality, and the corresponding words which reflect their world-view, as suggested by Drane, are 'imprecise', 'ambiguous', 'approximate', 'symbolic', 'intuitive'. The emotional side of human personality also takes on greater importance, in contrast to the left-brain emphasis on the reason/intellect. It is evident that there is a substantial distinction here between the objective and the subjective in the interpretation of what is real and true. For example, sociological assessments of contemporary culture suggest that narcissism is possibly the central clinical problem of the present period, replacing guilt. The problem today is that many people have no guilt at all, whilst leading hedonistic, permissive lifestyles which fail to provide deep, lasting satisfaction.

But it is too easy – as some Christians are wont to do – to cluster words like imprecise, ambiguous, approximate, and intuitive, and dismiss them as inappropriate descriptors of either theology or ministry. Rather, they say, let us hold fast to that which is precise, absolute and propositional. The danger here, of course, is that Christian truth then becomes something which is dry, dusty, and inaccessible to the postmodern mind. It fails to engage with the 'right-brain' mentality of many people today. Of course, a wholesale espousal of what Millard Erickson has called 'hard postmodernism' (which deconstructs truth such that no meaning is discernible save the meaning that the hearer or reader wishes to find) leads us into even more danger.[48] Let me represent the options as follows:

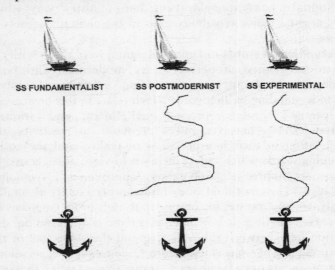

Three sailboats are bobbing around on a stretch of water. The first boat is attached firmly and rigidly to an anchor at the bottom, such that it has no opportunity for manoeuvre. The second boat is beginning to pick up a freshening wind, and moving into the distance – it has been cut off from the anchor to which it was originally tied. The third boat is moving around, but close observation shows that its freedom of movement is restricted within a diameter made possible by the slack in the rope attached to the anchor: there is freedom to explore, but it is not unlimited freedom.

We may liken the first boat to the fundamentalist variety of conservative evangelicalism, in which its adherents are so rigidly tied to dogmatic, propositional expressions of the Christian faith that there is no room for exploration of alternatives. This 'theological boat' could be labelled the 'SS FUNDAMENTALIST'! The focus is on 'the Word' as God's self-expression, perhaps even to the point of 'bibliolatry' – the Holy Spirit is left out in the cold, particularly in hermeneutics. The church, to adopt the distinctions put forward by Zizioulas (see Chapter Two), is founded on the authority of Christ, but fails to experience the creativity of the Spirit. Ecclesiology has more to do with structures and permanence than imaginative and provisional engagement with the Word and the world. The people on board this first boat function as a miscellaneous collection of individual sailors rather than a team community.

The response to such rigidity, of course, is not to cast away all restraint and abandon the anchor altogether (as with the second boat, the 'SS POSTMODERNIST'). There is need for all that the first boat represents: the primacy of Scripture, church authority, individual conversion. To dispense with these foundational imperatives is to lose sight of the essentials of our Christian faith. To drift off to sea will inevitably leave the boat at the mercies of the elements, ultimately to suffer shipwreck. But Erickson recognizes that there is a 'soft' version of postmodernism, which rightly challenges the church, acting as a 'wake-up call' in the disturbing and exciting times in which we live. This is where the third of our three boats comes in, which I have named the 'SS EXPERIMENTAL'. If the church is to be faithful to the gospel (attached *firmly but not rigidly* to the anchor of Christ), and if it is to be relevant to the world which is crying out for meaning and reality, then there needs to be that flexibility to manoeuvre within the area permitted by the slackness of the rope.

Many of us, quite understandably, will want to debate how long that rope should be! The point is that there needs to be a greater willingness to experiment with what it means to 'be church' in the community, an eagerness to resonate with and adapt to the surrounding culture. This does not mean that all we need is a band and a warehouse to start a church; bread, wine, and 'the book' are indispensable 'givens' and cannot be laid aside. But the Spirit of the church invites us into new modes of expressing the life of Christ. Jürgen Moltmann eloquently declares: 'The essential impediment to the charismatic experience of our potentialities for living is to be found in our passive sins, not our active ones. For the hindrance is not our despairing attempt to be ourselves, but our despairing attempt not to be ourselves, so that out of fear of life and fear of death we fall short of what our lives could be.'[49] So the Spirit invites us into new possibilities for living, not just at the individual level, but also in our corporate life together.

The ambiguity of the 'right-brain' paradigm also offers a more creative hermeneutical approach to the study of the Scriptures, encouraging us to be willing to live with diversity as we receive what the Spirit of God has to say to us through the given text. What is true-for-me can be held in creative tension with what is true-for-you *so long as both are consistent with the ultimate Truth that resides in the person and work of Christ*. Here postmodernism and the creativity of the Spirit engage with each other, offering the possibility of new theological insights as we interact with the cultures of our day. Indeed, postmodernism may be a catalyst for a fresh understanding, even experience, of Pentecost!

Other possibilities emerge as we engage with the terminology of the paradigm contrasts. Many evangelical churches are wary of symbols, fearing a drift into pre-Reformation superstition, but symbols are powerful reminders of deep and lasting truths. More especially, particularly in the sacraments, they evoke mystery and wonder, enhancing worship. The rapid growth of Celtic spirituality is, I suggest, more than just a fad; in its Christian expression, it resonates powerfully with a longing for a way of living that is sacramental in itself, reflecting outwardly the fullness of God's grace. The evangelical church has much to learn here in espousing a spirituality that is characterized more by mystery than by methodology.

Patterns of worship need to reflect today's cultural expectations and limitations, rather than adhering slavishly to a 'New Testament model', whatever that may be! This principle has its application in many other areas of Christian ministry. Our evangelistic efforts demand a radically different approach in today's postmodern age, in which propositional truth-statements are treated with suspicion, if not hostility. Getting people's attention requires communication skills radically different from those employed in earlier times. Of course, there are doctrinal and ethical norms which we would all agree are neither time-specific nor culturally bound, such as the work of Christ on the cross, his resurrection, the benevolent fatherhood of God, the reality of judgment, the efficacy of forgiving love, the ethic of love towards our neighbours, God's hatred of sin, and so we could go on.

The matter becomes more urgent if we ask *What is sin?* What do we say to a person who enjoys smoking a cigar after an evening meal? Where do we draw the line regarding sexual behaviour within the marriage relationship? Is it wrong to have a beautiful Hindu carving adorning the living room? Should Christians be tolerant of films in which crude language, violence, or sexual activity are present? The Bible is not at all clear about such issues, and so we are dependent upon the creative ministry of the Holy Spirit to guide us into truth in these matters – truth that cannot be enshrined in propositional statements or a specific scriptural text, but truth that accords with the underlying thrust of the Word and life of God. Perhaps a guideline is to ask: *Does this behaviour or belief allow me greater or lesser freedom in my relationship with God?* Our churches need to be places in which we encourage people to explore their freedom in Christ, rather than imposing rules on them. That's risky, but perhaps that is the very nature of grace.

Our inquiry into postmodernism suggests that there are significant ministry opportunities awaiting Christians who are willing to enter into the world-views of those whose lives may be very different from their own. The bankruptcy of naturalistic world-views is becoming increasingly evident, thus creating a vacuum within which Christian theism may again find a central role amongst competing world-views. Effective Christian ministry demands a robustness that has often been lacking in the final century of the second millennium. Francis Schaeffer argued that in the twentieth century the church embraced 'a defective view of Christianity' in its capitulation to humanistic values.[50] Likewise, Harry Blamires bemoans the loss of intellectual morale in the contemporary church: 'we Christians in the modern world accept, for the purpose of mental activity, a frame of reference constructed by the secular mind and a set of criteria reflecting secular evaluations.'[51] For both Schaeffer and Blamires, this mental bankruptcy has caused the Christian church to surrender to secularism, compromising its beliefs in the process.[52]

However, it is not just heightened intellectual prowess, commendable though that may be, that is needed in Christian ministry. The opening years of the new millennium will be increasingly characterized by a fascination with experience, especially *spiritual* experience, and this offers real hope for those engaged in Christian ministry. Only when we understand the perceptions and assumptions that people have about 'The Ultimate Question of Life, the Universe and Everything', as Douglas Adams put it in one of his nihilistic science-fiction novels,[53] can we effectively relate the Christian gospel to those who, in their search for meaning and purpose in life, are embracing revived pagan ideas. Clark and Geisler accurately observe that Christians today stand once more on Mars Hill:

> In the first century, Saint Paul debated with two groups of Greek philosophers at a place in Athens called Mars Hill. Paul's antagonists were the Epicureans and the Stoics. Like Paul, Christians today are locked in debate with both Epicureans and Stoics. When the American Atheists met in Denver recently, Madalyn Murray O'Hair declared that there is no God. Shirley MacLaine soon came to town to pronounce that she and all her listeners are gods. Shortly thereafter, in a Denver crusade, Billy Graham preached that Jesus alone is God. These well-known champions of three world-views have rekindled that ancient Mars Hill debate.[54]

The particularity of context

In Chapter Three we considered the concept of world-view through the lenses of philosophy, theology, history, and culture. These four dimensions offer the possibility of a rich understanding of the content and shape of individual and corporate (cultural) world-views. This is significant because the integration of world-view and ministry provides the church with a useful framework within which to explore its participation in the mission of Christ in the world. If we represent the relationship between world-view and ministry in a matrix format, showing, for example, how different aspects of pastoral activity intersect with the key metaphysical issues of truth, existence, values and destiny – interpreted, for example, in terms of Sire's seven world-view questions, summarized in Chapter Three – important concerns are raised which may suggest the need for a paradigm shift in order authentically to relate the gospel to other people. And if not a paradigm shift, at least a willingness to enter into alternative perceptions of reality, to see things differently.

In order to develop such a matrix, or taxonomy, for analysing ministry opportunities, we need to be clear about how to represent the ministry axis. Theologically, as we discussed in Chapter One, the ministry of the church has been described as incarnational, kerygmatic, and diaconal.[55] However, if, as Dulles suggests, all ministry is diaconal; and if the *kērygma* of the church is 'a representation of God's presence in the world as the eternal one',[56] then these theological descriptors, foundational as they undoubtedly are for our understanding of ministry, are not discrete enough as a paradigm for exploring different ministry activities.

An alternative approach is to adopt the biblical pattern summarized in Ephesians 4:11, in which the ministry of the church is encapsulated in what David Sheppard calls 'the five callings':[57] apostles, prophets, evangelists, pastors, and teachers. In whatever way these five spheres of ministry may operate within a local church context, they have usually been regarded as foundational ministries within the wider church.[58] The value of this paradigm lies not just in its biblical pedigree; if the ministry of Christ is programmatic for the ministry of the church, then the fact that Christ perfectly fulfilled each of the five 'callings' of Ephesians 4:11 points to their adequacy as identifiable elements of Christian pastoral ministry.[59]

So the ministry of Christ is the prototype and inspiration for the ministry of the church: as supreme apostle, prophet, evangelist,

pastor and teacher, Jesus is 'paradigm minister'. And the promise
to the disciples of 'another counsellor, to be with you forever'
(Jn. 14:16) is a promise of another of the same kind (as implied by
the Greek *allos*); so the Holy Spirit's ministry recapitulates the
ministry of Christ on earth. In Harper's words, 'the Holy Spirit's
role is not to depart from the pattern of Christ, but rather to work
out that pattern corporately in the life of the church.'[60]

ἄλλος

Another way of looking at the ministry of the church is
through the lens of ecclesiology, and Dulles' work on models of
the church is useful here, as we suggested in Chapter Two. The
five models that Dulles presented – the church as institution,
mystical communion, sacrament, herald and servant – and his
subsequent sixth model, the church as a community of disciples,
are representative types that reflect different perceptions of ministry. It is not appropriate here to examine in depth each of
Dulles' models, neither is it necessary to evaluate them as appropriate ecclesiologies. However, we may note the author's own
view that the institutional model is not a primary one, but secondary in the sense that 'institutions are subordinate to persons,
structures are subordinate to life.'[61] Accordingly, if we discard
for our purposes the institutional model, we may retain Dulles'
remaining original four plus his discipleship model as paradigmatic for Christian ministry.

Dulles' ecclesiologies highlight important ministry imperatives
identified earlier, such as *kērygma* and *diakonia*, and give added
significance to a characteristic of ministry implicit in the notion of
pastor in the biblical paradigm, namely *koinōnia*. Recent emphasis on the 'community model' for pastoral care refocuses care as
a ministry of the people, rather than a ministry conducted by
individuals (often regarded as professionals). So 'the church and
other caring communities are a community of ministers who are
together not primarily to be together, but because as human beings
their members need one another in order to do the work of ministry.'[62] The interpersonal model of the church as *koinōnia* makes
room for the spontaneous initiatives of the Spirit amongst the
people of God and responds to the felt needs of many for warm,
loving, accepting community.

Other paradigms of ministry may present themselves besides those proposed above. The biblical and ecclesiological paradigms put forward are suggestive rather than exhaustive, and they offer opportunities for fruitful insights for the mission of the church when interpreted within a matrix format alongside a world-view axis. Following the Ephesians 4:11 biblical paradigm for ministry, the matrix looks like this:

MINISTRY AXIS

WORLD-VIEW AXIS ↓	Apostle	Prophet	Evan-gelist	Pastor	Teacher
What is prime reality?					
What is the nature of external reality?					
What is a human being?					
What happens to a person at death?					
Why is it possible to know anything at all?					
How do we know what is right and wrong?					
What is the meaning of human history?					

This type of grid needs to be handled in a flexible and fluid way; as we have seen, world-view and ministry components are not as discretely unique as their labels imply. But the taxonomy is helpful as a conceptual tool in focusing the practice of ministry as a contextual activity:[63] it demands that those in ministry seek to understand those amongst whom they are working, whether they are different cultural groups (as in cross-cultural ministry), a specific segment of the local community (such as the youth sub-culture), a characteristic sociological/demographic group (for example, 'baby boomers'), or specific individuals within the community. The responsibility of the church is to discern how and where the Spirit is at work in the particularity of each context, and to participate with him in the outworking of Christ's mission.

Within the grid, certain segments will assume more importance than others as the task of contextual ministry unfolds. For example, the prevalence of ethical relativism in contemporary western society – an axiological issue, represented by the question 'How do we know what is right and wrong?' – is clearly a significant one for the evangelist seeking to present the gospel of Christ's Lordship over the whole of life. Aboriginals have a radically different understanding of time and history from that of white Australians, which presents a challenge to the pastor or teacher seeking to relate a Christian view of history (linear and teleological) to a group of Aboriginal Christians.

The example quoted earlier in this chapter of Bruce Olson's experience among the Motilone Indians of Colombia suggests the need to revise one's understanding of how prophecy operates within God's purposes: a western biblical concept of 'the prophet of the Lord' gave way under the inspiration of the Holy Spirit to an understanding of prophecy within the world-view of the Motilone tribe. The 'Word of the Lord' came from 'a tall man with yellow hair' (Olson) who was himself the fulfilment of shamanistic prophecy. God spoke to the Motilones in the context of *their* legends and history, specifically their understanding of God and how he related to human beings at death. Olson's openness to the Spirit gave him entry into the Motilone world-view and led to the conversion of the whole tribe.[64]

Within contemporary Australian society, Philip Hughes notes that young people do not see God in cosmic terms, as 'the One who sustains the system. Rather, God is seen in more personal terms, as a powerful, beneficent friend and resource. They see God as involved in the events of daily life rather than sustaining the world processes in which we live.'[65] This observation is significant for those involved in ministry among young people today, especially those with pastoral and evangelistic concerns. What sort of God do young people believe in today? Along our world-view axis, this corresponds with the question 'What is the nature of external reality?' Probing for answers to this question will open up doors for ministry, directing youth to an understanding of a God who is concerned as much for the whole world as he is for the needs of each individual.

Speaking at a seminar on postmodernism and the gospel at a centre for urban mission in inner-city Melbourne, John Smith highlighted the need to grasp the language of today's youth subculture, a language which easily offends many Christians: 'If we get into the "native village" of postmodernism, we will find that much of the language and images are totally inaccessible to us. That will put us in a situation where we have to cry out to God and love the people to whom we're sent – and not be so darn touchy and self-protective.'[66] For Smith, mission is all about 'God inviting us into something that he's already working with'. So, under the guidance of the Spirit, the church needs to experiment creatively and imaginatively with alternative mission approaches in order to learn how to communicate with contemporary youth.

In the examples above, the challenge is to listen to other people in order to see things from their perspective. As we have observed in this chapter the Spirit of God is at work in a rich variety of ways to reveal Christ in the world. The church is privileged to participate in this contextual mission 'consciously, deliberately, reflectively'.[67] To respond to the Spirit's creative (even improbable or outrageous!) initiatives is to participate in the adventure of God as he seeks to reconcile those whom he loves to himself. Just as unity-in-diversity is a characteristic feature of each individual faith-community, so it describes the partnership of local congregations in their witness to the love of God in the world. The idiosyncrasies of each local setting within which Christians gather, combined with their unique personalities and talents and the creative ministry of the Spirit, suggest a flexible, and at times provisional and spontaneous, expression of 'church' in the world.

This interpretation of the mission of Christ in the world offers a further, more personal, dividend, which has to do with a growth in self-awareness: those involved in ministry are encouraged to question their assumptions about how they, and others, perceive reality. 'The cost of not doing so is to be captive to a mind-set, your own or another's, that does not afford the liberty to learn, grow, and exchange error for truth.'[68] This invitation into what we described in Chapter Three as the discipline of 'doing theology' is not an option. Not only are Christians encouraged through *theologia viatorum* to go where they have never gone before, they have the privilege, the responsibility, and the authority to lead others in the faith-community into similarly new and open pastures, where the gospel has power to come alive for those who would otherwise be passed by.

Notes

1. Hall, *Thinking the Faith*, p. 81.
2. Torrance, 'The Place of Jesus Christ in Worship' in Anderson (ed.), *Theological Foundations for Ministry*, p. 358.
3. *The Alternative Service Book 1980* (London: Hodder & Stoughton, 1980).
4. Moltmann, *The Church in the Power of the Spirit*, p. 85.
5. ibid., p. 83.
6. Moltmann, *The Source of Life*, p. 132.
7. Harvey E. Cox, *The Secular City* (London: SCM Press, 1965), p. 264.
8. A. M. Hunter, *Introducing New Testament Theology* (London: SCM Press, 1957), p. 25.
9. See C. H. Dodd, *The Parables of the Kingdom* (London: Nisbet & Co, 1935).

10. Moltmann, *The Church in the Power of the Spirit*, p. 17.
11. ibid.
12. Taylor, *The Go-Between God*, p. 147.
13. David J. Bosch, *Transforming Mission: Paradigm Shifts in Theology of Mission* (Maryknoll, NY: Orbis, 1991), p. 10.
14. Barth, *Church Dogmatics*, IV/3, p. 764.
15. See Lesslie Newbigin, *The Gospel in a Pluralist Society* (Grand Rapids: Eerdmans, 1989), pp. 14–26.
16. Taylor, *The Go-Between God*, p. 191.
17. A. Ziesler, *Pauline Christianity* (Oxford: Oxford University Press, 1983), p. 8.
18. Newbigin, *The Gospel in a Pluralist Society*, p. 154.
19. John E. Hinkle Jr, 'Culture and Care' in Carroll A. Wise (ed.), *The Meaning of Pastoral Care*, revised by John Hinkle Jr. (Bloomington IN: Meyer-Stone Books, 1989), p. 145.
20. Eugene H. Peterson, *Five Smooth Stones for Pastoral Work* (Atlanta: John Knox Press, 1980), p. 14.
21. Kraft, *Christianity in Culture*, p. 8.
22. Bengt Sundkler, *The Christian Ministry in Africa* (London: SCM Press Ltd, 1960), p. 211.
23. Bruce E. Olson, *Bruchko* (Altamonte Springs, Florida: Creation House, 1973).
24. Robert J. Schreiter, *Constructing Local Theologies* (London: SCM Press Ltd, 1985), p. 102.
25. 'Africa: Fertile Soil for Catholicism', in *TIME*, 25 April 1994, pp. 54–5.
26. Taylor, *The Go-Between God*, p. 36.
27. ibid., p. 39.
28. Stephen Neill, *Creative Tension* (London: Edinburgh House Press, 1959), p. 81.
29. Bosch, *Transforming Mission*, p. 512.
30. Taylor, *The Go-Between God*, p. 38.
31. Bosch, *Transforming Mission*, p. 512.
32. Pinnock, *Flame of Love*, p. 208.
33. ibid., p. 205.
34. For a full transcription of this remarkable story, see Gyalsang Tamang, 'The Name Above All' on {http://users.aol.com/tailenders/npnmaa.htm}.
35. Pinnock, *Flame of Love*, p. 203.

36. See Howard A. Snyder, *EarthCurrents: The Struggle for the World's Soul* (Nashville: Abingdon Press, 1995), p. 230.

37. See John Docker, *Postmodernism and Modern Culture* (Cambridge: Cambridge University Press, 1994), pp. 108–14.

38. Diogenes Allen, *Christian Belief in a Postmodern World: The Full Wealth of Conviction* (Louisville: Westminster/John Knox Press, 1989), esp. pp. 1–19.

39. A number of the arguments developed below first appeared in my article, 'Swinging the Pendulum – Theology for a Changing World: Re-assessing the Challenge of Postmodernism', *PCBC Journal*, 1:1 (Oct. 1997), pp. 4–6.

40. James H. Olthuis, 'Dancing Together in the Wild Spaces of Love: Postmodernism, Psychotherapy, and the Spirit of God', *Journal of Psychology and Christianity*, 18:2 (1999), pp. 140–52.

41. See, for example, Paul Davies, *The Mind of God: Science and the Search for Ultimate Meaning* (London: Penguin Books, 1993); Ted Peters (ed.), *Cosmos as Creation: Theology and Science in Consonance* (Nashville: Abingdon, 1989).

42. Hans Frei, *Types of Christian Theology* (New Haven: Yale University Press, 1992), p. 16.

43. Tyron Inbody, 'Postmodernism: Intellectual Velcro Dragged Across Culture?', *Theology Today*, 51:4 (Jan. 1995), pp. 524–38.

44. Jean-Francois Lyotard, *The Postmodern Condition: A Report on Knowledge* (Minneapolis: University of Minneapolis Press, 1984).

45. See, for example, Allan Bloom, *The Closing of the American Mind* (New York: Simon & Schuster, 1987); and David F. Wells, *God in the Wasteland* (Grand Rapids: Eerdmans, 1994).

46. Bloom, *The Closing of the American Mind*, p. 43.

47. Drane, *Faith in a Changing Culture*, p. 35.

48. See Millard J. Erickson, *Postmodernizing the Faith: Evangelical Responses to the Challenge of Postmodernism* (Grand Rapids: Baker, 1998), pp. 17–20.

49. Moltmann, *The Spirit of Life*, p. 188.

50. Francis A. Schaeffer, *A Christian Manifesto* (Westchester: Crossway, 1981), p. 18.

51. Blamires, *The Christian Mind*, p. 4.

52. Two helpful books which flesh this out in the context of modern Protestant America are Os Guinness and John Seel (eds.), *No God but God* (Chicago: Moody, 1992); and Michael Scott Horton (ed.),

Power Religion: The Selling Out of the Evangelical Church? (Chicago: Moody, 1992).

53. Douglas Adams, *Life, the Universe and Everything* (New York: Pocket Books, 1983).

54. David K. Clark and Norman L. Geisler, *Apologetics in the New Age* (Grand Rapids: Baker Book House, 1990), p. 7.

55. See Ray S. Anderson (ed.), *Theological Foundations for Ministry*, pp. 493–751.

56. ibid., p. 496.

57. David Sheppard, *Built as a City* (London: Hodder & Stoughton, 1974), p. 298.

58. See, for example, Markus Barth, *Ephesians* – The Anchor Bible (New York: Doubleday, 1974); Andrew T. Lincoln, *Ephesians* (Dallas: Word, 1990); C. Leslie Mitton, *Ephesians* – New Century Bible (Grand Rapids: Eerdmans, 1973). A helpful discussion of the five ministry-gifts can be found in John R. W. Stott, *God's New Society* (Leicester: IVP, 1979), pp. 159–66.

59. See, for a development of this insight, Michael Harper, *Let My People Grow* (London: Hodder & Stoughton, 1977), pp. 61–71.

60. ibid., p. 66.

61. Dulles, *Models of the Church*, p. 198.

62. J. Patton, *Pastoral Care in Context: An Introduction to Pastoral Care* (Louisville: WJKP, 1993), p. 42.

63. For an example of how the taxonomy can be applied in a specific mission context, see Graham Buxton, 'A Qualitative Study of School Chaplaincy Ministry' (M.Min. thesis, Melbourne College of Divinity, 1997).

64. Olson, *Bruchko*, pp. 140–41.

65. Hughes, *A Maze or a System?*, p. 15.

66. Smith, 'More than Babbling Tongues', p. 47.

67. Hall, *Thinking the Faith*, p. 81.

68. Hoffeker, *Building a Christian World-View* (vol. 1), p. xi.

Chapter Six

Participating in the Compassion of Christ

'Jesus, remember me when you come into
your kingdom.'
Luke 23:42

In the summer of 1991 I was driving across British Columbia
with my wife and three children, on our way from Calgary to
Vancouver. A week earlier we had packed all our belongings into
a large container ready for shipment from London to Adelaide,
where I was to take up my new appointment at Tabor College.
We flew to Calgary and picked up a car so that we could enjoy
the spectacular scenery of the Rocky Mountains and Banff
National Park. Our enjoyment of the trip, however, was tinged
with more than a little misgiving, for my wife and I were struggling with the enormity of our decision to start a new life in
Australia as migrants.

As we were travelling through the rolling plains, our anxiety
grew. We had left so much behind – family, friends, a rewarding
ministry in London, our beloved homeland. From our perspective, the future was uncertain: would everything work out?
Financially, we were taking a step of faith and there were times
when we found it hard to trust that God really would look after
us. Though we knew God's presence with us, paradoxically we
also felt vulnerable and alone. Repeatedly we cried out to God
for reassurance that we were doing the right thing.

As we made our way along the highway approaching
Kamloops, we were feeling particularly unsettled and some edgi-
ness crept into our conversation. Suddenly my wife noticed a

placard announcing the availability of free coffee, which seemed a good idea at the time. We pulled up by the roadside, and our two daughters scampered off to the toilets, to return a few minutes later, each clutching a tiny cardboard box in their hands with the words 'Take Me' written on the lid. In each box there was a folded piece of paper on which a child had written some verses of Scripture: 'Be anxious for nothing, but in everything by prayer and supplication with thanksgiving, let your requests be made known to God, and the peace of God ... will guard your hearts and minds through Christ Jesus' (Phil. 4:6–7); 'Seek first the kingdom of God and his righteousness, and all these things shall be added to you' (Mt. 6:33); and 'My God shall supply all your needs' (Phil. 4:19).

We stood there for a moment, overwhelmed by the gracious compassion of our Father, who knew all about our inner struggles and fears. In his utter faithfulness, he had orchestrated events by his Spirit in such a way as to reach deep into our lives at a time when we needed it most. Little did the children who had created those boxes realize how faithfully they had participated in the compassionate ministry of Christ – or perhaps they did (Ps. 8:2; Mt. 18:3)? Knowing nothing about our situation they had entered into the ministry of the One who understands everything.

To participate in the compassion of Christ implies a freedom to respond to the impulse of the Spirit, whose activity in the world reflects the truth that God holds all whom he has created in his memory. Remembrance and compassion are two sides of the one coin. In Old Testament times, the Israelites may be forgiven for thinking that Yahweh had forgotten them during their enslavement in Egypt, but the Lord could not be false to his nature: 'God heard their groaning and he *remembered* his covenant with Abraham, with Isaac and with Jacob. So God looked on the Israelites and was *concerned* about them' (Ex. 2:24–25). To remember is to be concerned, and to be concerned is to act.

In an imaginative and visionary interpretation of the text of the Old Testament as a resource for contemporary preaching, Walter Brueggemann offers the motif of 'exile' as a rich and supple metaphor not only for preaching but also for the more general practice of ministry. The Israelites of old cried out to God in lamentation and complaint, reminding him of their sense of forsakenness; but they also responded to Yahweh with thanksgiving and doxology as they recalled his mighty deeds. Nor was the communication one-way: in his faithfulness and unchangeableness, God offered both assurance and promise to his people. His lovingkindness, goodness, and promise of peace are 'more than enough to override the flood, to overcome the absence and shame, and to overmatch the terror of exile'.[1]

Implicit in Brueggemann's understanding of the relationship between disconsolate human beings and their God is the notion of remembrance: the people dare to recall their God as one who will still act for them, and the God to whom they cry still remembers his people. What makes his analysis particularly powerful for the contemporary church, however, is the correspondence between the church of today and the exilic community in Babylon, and his suggestion that we can learn much from the way in which that community related to their God.

Like the Israelites driven out of their own land, the contemporary Christian church is in desperate need of *good news* in a social and cultural climate from which they are becoming increasingly alienated. So it is instructive to be reminded that, rather than driving the Jews to even greater despair, the experience of exile 'evoked the most brilliant literature and the most daring theological articulation in the Old Testament'.[2] Exile gave birth to rich and creative expressions of faith and enlivened the community in its real and actual existence in exile. The context – characterized by deep feelings of forsakenness, rootlessness, despair, and shame – was the crucible within which the Israelites were able to rediscover their identity.

A paradigm of remembrance for pastoral ministry

The Japanese word for 'crisis' is represented by two characters: the first means 'danger', and the second conveys the idea of 'opportunity' and 'promise'. Christians have always been a 'people of crisis', living dangerously in a hostile world, residents in an alien land, yet motivated by the promise of the future, which is the hope of the gospel. But the community of faith cannot exist for very long without referring back to its roots, for the ground of its being is the historical reality of the One who is 'the same, yesterday, today and forever' (Heb. 13:8).

However, remembrance as a motif for understanding the nature and practice of pastoral ministry does not have its origins in the church's memory of God. The starting point for any theology of remembrance is the covenant faithfulness of God himself, who is ever mindful of his people: 'Can a mother forget the baby at her breast and have no compassion on the child she has borne? Though she may forget, I will not forget you!' (Is. 49:15)

God's loving concern brings remembrance alive in a way that inspires action: at the heart of God's memory is his will to act on behalf of those he loves. For God, remembrance implies action. It is inconceivable for God to remember without doing something to redeem the situation. The narrative of his acts throughout the biblical story, and supremely in the event of the incarnation and atonement, is a history of active engagement based on covenant love. Ultimately, God does what he does because he is who he is, not the other way round. He holds all whom he has created in his memory, and works *for* them because he is love.

Participation in the compassionate ministry of Christ has its starting point in the realization that God holds all people in his memory: we are not forgotten. In his covenant love, God takes the initiative to bless, irrespective of the failures and weaknesses of those to whom he binds himself. Theologically, the idea of covenant carries no *quid pro quo*, and thus differs from the notion of a 'contract'. As the Israelites prepared to enter Canaan, they were encouraged by the truth that 'the Lord your God is a merciful God; he will not abandon or destroy you or forget the covenant with your forefathers, which he confirmed to them by oath' (Deut. 4:31). This does not mean that God does not mete out punishment; the history of God's dealings with his people is a repeating cycle of obedience-rebellion-punishment-deliverance.

But God's very nature means that he cannot erase his people
from his memory.

This theological truth establishes the context within which all
pastoral ministry takes place. Because God remembers us, we
are to be like-minded: to live as God's people is to open our
hearts in the same vulnerable, caring and giving way. John
Patton, a pastoral theologian, interprets pastoral care 'as a
ministry of the Christian community that takes place through
remembering God's action for us, remembering who we are as
God's own people, and hearing and remembering those to
whom we minister'.[3]

In the last chapter, we interpreted the faith-community as a
community which is called to look beyond its own boundaries
to the world, to be light in the darkness. It is therefore
summoned both to remember those who need to hear and
respond to the grace of God, and to participate in the proclamation of the good news in word and deed. This reflects the
biblical mandate that we are saved and healed in order to live as
moral, responsible beings in God's world. Exhorted to live
together in unity, Christians must beware the temptation of
'separating themselves from brothers and sisters with whom
God has made it clear his saving love is to be shared, both in
receiving and giving'.[4]

We must insist, then, that pastoral ministry has its source in
God's gracious memory of all people. Without that, we are all
doomed; even the despairing Job waits in the hope of God's
remembrance of him: 'If only you would set me a time and then
remember me! ... You will call and I will answer you; you will
long for the creature your hands have made.' (Job 14:13,15). The
prophet Hosea records God's tender words to Israel: 'How can I
give you up, Ephraim? How can I hand you over, Israel?' (Hos.
11:8). God's memory of his covenantal love for his people always
leads to action. God's remembrance of rebellious Israel transformed his anger into compassion. He did not sit neutrally on the
sidelines, leaving his people to whatever fate might await them;
he acted in deliberate response to their plight and rescued them
from exile.

Similarly, God's people are not called to live passively in his love: their identity is bound up in active response that flows upward to God, inward towards each other, and outward to the world. Activity characterizes the Christian life. This is not to be confused with *activism*, a concern which we will address in the final chapter of this book. Passivity and activism are two perennial dangers within the church. The first is rooted in a failure to understand that God has called us into a life of service for the sake of the world, recapitulating the servanthood of Christ; the second derives from our failure to realize that we are fallible and limited human beings who need to learn how to rest in God before trying to reclaim the world for him!

In Chapter Four, our discussion of worship reminded us that we are not isolated individuals, but integral parts of the rich tapestry of God's love and grace woven through creation. This sense of belonging, which is fundamental to all that is involved in being a human being, is given more explicit recognition in the sacramental life of the church, as family identity is expressed through baptism and the Eucharist. As God's Word is proclaimed in the power of the Spirit, God himself reminds us that we are children of grace, and the fullness of his self-revelation in Jesus Christ directs us to a way of life that is both healing and light in the darkness of this world. In all of these pastoral acts the Spirit seeks to bring to our remembrance all that is needful for our wholeness, that we might experience life, 'and have it to the full' (Jn. 10:10).

More than this, the Spirit is active amongst the people of God as they gather together, weaving his own unique liturgy. The community of faith needs to be continually attentive and open to his direction, so that the will of the Father is accomplished as his children meet with him and with each other. Writing to the Corinthian Christians, Paul reminds them that, when they come together, 'everyone has a hymn, or a word of instruction, a revelation, a tongue or an interpretation. All of these must be done for the strengthening of the church' (1 Cor. 14:26). Those who are responsible for leading the gathered congregation are accountable to the Spirit, and need to be open to his creative and, at times, unpredictable, ministry amongst people.

However, there are times when the help people need cannot be secured through these broad dimensions of pastoral care. More specialized help may be necessary, often in the form of one-to-one ministry, so that those who are disturbed or distressed in any way can cope with the pressures they face in life. This is the province of the more specific discipline of pastoral counselling, to which we now give some detailed attention.

It is important to realize that the principles outlined in this chapter are of value to all who are engaged in caring for others, whether or not the caring context is formalized in the language of 'pastoral counselling'. Larry Crabb identifies three levels of counselling which can be integrated into the life of the Christian community.[5] At the most basic level, all Christians should be involved in the first level, that of encouragement, which 'depends upon an awareness of painful emotions in a member of the [Christian] family and a sincere effort to understand them, growing out of an attitude of compassion and concern for the person who hurts'.[6] The ministry of encouragement is one which all people can exercise (1 Thes. 5:11; Heb. 3:13, 10:25). The second of Crabb's levels, that of exhortation, has more to do with the adjustment of behaviour than the management of problem feelings, and training in interactional skills may be helpful in facilitating this type of change. The third level – enlightenment – demands more specialized training: 'If we are to profoundly change how a person functions, we must help him change what he believes.'[7]

In recent years, Larry Crabb has become more aware of the concept of community as the context within which change, even at the most profound level, can take place:

> Rather than thinking in terms of therapists, counsellors, pastoral counsellors and lay counsellors, I propose thinking of a healing community as providing two kinds of relationships: *spiritual friendship*, which exists among spiritually minded peers who share their lives together, and *spiritual direction*, which takes place when time is specially set aside for one person to present his or her life to a respected (not always familiar) person who agrees to listen, pray, think, and speak, preferably without pay.[8]

This shift away from a structured, analytical approach to helping people through their struggles and difficulties to one which is essentially communitarian is significant. With its roots in Trinitarian theology, as we discussed in Chapter Two, the communitarian model proposed by Crabb invites us to participate as fellow-travellers with Christ *and with each other* in the power of the Spirit. As a community of faith, we are not alone, for Christ comes alongside us to transform us in our journey, and we all learn and grow together.

Christian pastoral ministry is not about being involved with needy people inside or outside the church, armed with all our experience, training and techniques, as if we have nothing to learn. It has to do with engaging sympathetically and compassionately with others, so that in the process *Christ* ministers; and his ministry may be as much to the person who offers help as to the one who seeks it. The goal of Christian counselling is to lead people out of merely coping and into an enjoyment of life in Christ characterized by freedom, growth and relational acceptance: in that process we ourselves may discover afresh the healing grace of Christ.

However, there is an ever-present danger for pastoral counselling to so emphasize healing and wholeness *within* the faith-community that those who are *outside* the boundaries of the visible church are forgotten. The truth is that the two dimensions of care are inextricably linked. We are healed and saved not just for ourselves, but to enable us to live as moral, responsible beings in God's world. As the church engages in Christian ministry in the new millennium, there has rightly been a call for unity, for denominations to link arms in a demonstration of the reality of our oneness in Christ. This is surely to be commended, but only so long as unity is not perceived as the final goal for the Christian community.

In his high-priestly prayer to his Father in John 17, Jesus explicitly states that there is a goal beyond unity, a goal to which unity actually contributes, which has to do with the salvation of the world: 'As you sent me into the world, I have sent them into the world' (Jn. 17:18); 'May they also be in us so that the world may believe that you have sent me' (Jn. 17:21); 'May they be brought to complete unity to let the world know that you sent me and have loved them even as you have loved me' (Jn. 17:23). Three times Jesus points beyond unity to reveal the compassionate heart of the Father, who longs that all may come to know his saving love in their lives.

Our concern with pastoral counselling therefore takes us beyond healing within the church and directs us to a wider understanding of God's healing grace within the world. Speaking through the prophet Isaiah, the Lord reminds the Israelites that true righteousness is measured by a deep concern for the welfare of others: '... if you spend yourselves on behalf of the hungry and satisfy the needs of the oppressed, then your light will rise in the darkness, and your night will become like the noonday' (Is. 58:10). Throughout the Scriptures, God's people are exhorted to display justice and righteousness by helping to mend the broken lives around them.

Patton quotes the insights of Parker Palmer in an address to the Association for Clinical Pastoral Education in 1987: 'Remembered means to re-member. It means to put the body back together. The opposite of remember is not to forget, but to dis-member. And when we forget where we came from ... we have in fact dis-membered something.'[9] To remember someone in this way is to be a part of their healing.

To respond to a person's cry, 'Remember me!', whether in a home or in a hospital, is to live in solidarity with that person in their struggle and pain; to tell someone that you will not forget them offers hope and reassurance in the midst of loneliness and despair. In pastoral counselling, not only do we remember who we are as God's people, we also 're-member' one another; so we participate in God's ministry of reconciliation and restoration. To remind one another *whose* we are, as distinct from *who* we are, can be a powerful healing word in people's lives.

But we also have the privilege of 're-membering' those outside the life of the church whose lives have disintegrated: we are the bearers of good news, and through us the Spirit of God is able to rebuild broken lives. As the community of faith, we are privileged to participate in the ministry of Jesus, who declared in the synagogue in Nazareth: 'The Spirit of the Lord is on me, because he has anointed me to preach good news to the poor. He has sent me to proclaim freedom for the prisoners and recovery of sight for the blind, to release the oppressed, to proclaim the year of the Lord's favour' (Lk. 4:18–19). So we are healed to heal, we are blessed by God in order to bless others. This is a moral imperative in pastoral counselling, one that needs to be emphasized in today's cultural climate, where personal blessing is seen as the primary goal of life.

Therapy as a dance of blessing

In an article exploring 'a postmodern, postsecular model for psychotherapy', James Olthuis resonates with the theme of this book in proposing the metaphor of 'dance' in his interpretation of the nature of Christian therapy:

> The people we work with are strugglers, stragglers, wounded, just like all of us – their wounds bearing/baring (carrying and exposing) the evidence of their stories' truth and power – who need to be received, seen, heard, held, and accompanied in all their suffering. In brief, they need blessing: an attitude of deep respect, affirmation, and openness to the other which evokes a prayerful hope that God's love may surprise and surround, empower and convict, encourage, redeem, and heal. This transforms therapy into a dance of blessing which recognizes that we are all in this together, brothers and sisters in the skin, gifted and vulnerable, reaching out and drawing back, expectant and wary.[10]

For Olthuis, psychotherapy needs to be understood as care rather than cure, as art rather than science, as adventure rather than treatment, and as spiritual process rather than psychology-plus-prayer. This does not mean that techniques and methods should be dismissed: they are valuable so long as they are used flexibly and are not allowed to take over.

We notice this in the ministry of Jesus as he compassionately engaged with hurting and needy people. He was absolutely clear about the moral framework within which he related to all around him, 'and yet his dealings with people were consistently characterized by grace and an absence of coercion.'[11] When techniques are dominant, the possibility of coercion, or at least control, is never far away; people may be viewed as 'cases' for whom solutions need to be found. This was not how Jesus related to people. He saw them as individuals in need of freedom; he respected the dignity of each person he encountered, and did not restrict himself to any particular technique or style of counselling.

For example, Jesus was direct with the rich ruler who came to him, asking what he must do to inherit eternal life (Lk. 18:18–25); he did not chase after him, as some of us might have done, but allowed him to face the consequences of his own decision. He was similarly direct in his dealings with the woman caught in adultery (Jn. 8:3–11), and when a notorious woman ventured into the home of Simon the Pharisee and anointed Jesus' feet with perfume, he discerned Simon's silent disapproval and told him a story which exposed his critical judgment of the woman (Lk. 7:36–50). In none of these incidents did Jesus seek to control or 'get results'. His attitude to the rich ruler, to the woman caught in adultery, and to Simon was one of accepting love, in which he offered them the freedom to choose their own response.

In acknowledging the person-centred ministry of Jesus, we must not minimize the contribution of secular insights in the church's participation in the compassionate ministry of Christ. Whilst many people have been concerned that the Christian community has been too ready to embrace the insights of secular psychology in its desire to help hurting people back into wholeness, it is important to remember that both counselling and psychology are concerned with 'constructive change and the central nature of the helping relationship'.[12] We must beware the trap of putting Christianity and psychology into separate boxes, as if they had nothing to do with each other.

Many well-known writers in the field of Christian counselling, such as Collins, Narramore, Crabb, Hurding, McMinn, and Siang-Yang Tan have been trained in psychology and acknowledge its relevance in helping us to understand the inner turmoils, anxieties and insecurities that beset the human race.[13] But the danger of capitulating to the seductive pragmatism of secular therapies remains: as Olthuis declares, the goal of all therapy 'is not decisive conclusions or valid interpretation, but transformed connections, changed lives, the surge of mercy, a drawing nearer to each other, and to God. Not: "Have I mastered the technique?" But: "Has the person been seen, heard, and blessed?"'[14]

Counselling as an activity of the Christian community should not be perceived as a monochrome activity; within the pastoral ministry of the church, many alternative approaches rub shoulders with each other, reflecting the different world-views which exist under the umbrella of Christian theism. Prior to emphasizing the Christian perspective, Gary Collins amusingly invites us to consider how different counsellors today might have assisted the despondent Martin Luther, who was plagued by depression throughout his life. Depending upon their background and counselling predisposition, Luther might have been prescribed antidepressant medication or a course on stress-management techniques! Freudian psychoanalysts would have delved into his past, whilst the family therapist would have concentrated on Luther's social network. Others might have told Luther to 'pray and trust God', or invited him to a charismatic healing service.[15]

The point of Collins' anecdote is that counsellors should be flexible and open in their approach to helping troubled people: there is great merit in what he calls 'responsible eclecticism' in drawing from the wide range of available counselling methodologies. However, he rightly reminds us that the Christian community needs to exercise wisdom and discernment in the face of the nonbiblical, even anti-Christian, assumptions which undergird many of the psychological techniques and approaches in current vogue: Christian truth and values may too easily be sacrificed in favour of pragmatic methods. Someone once wryly observed that in the current cultural climate the church must be on its guard not to embrace a ministry philosophy which exalts 'what works is true' at the expense of 'what is true works'! For the community of faith, remembering each other and remembering God go hand in hand.

The uniqueness of Christian pastoral counselling has methodological as well as epistemological implications. As argued earlier, a professional secular counsellor is often expected to *do* something, to 'deliver the goods', as it were – perhaps because he or she is paid to do so. A Christian counsellor, however, tends to focus more on the person than on the problem, since the ultimate concern is a person's wholeness rather than the solution of a problem. This observation is clearly a generalization and should be interpreted neither as an endorsement of amateurish conduct nor as an aversion to techniques. Boisen comments on the unique contribution of the minister of religion to the task of helping those in distress; such a person

> recognises the fundamental need of love, and dark despair of guilt and estrangement from those we love, and the meaning of forgiveness through faith in the Love that rules the universe and in whose eyes no one is condemned who is in the process of becoming better. In such insights lies the important contribution of the competent minister of religion rather than in any particular techniques.[16]

Christian counsellors, therefore, seek to direct counsellees, at least ultimately if not immediately, into a 'healthy dependence upon and fellowship with God as a prerequisite of true security'.[17] That was Jesus' own motivation in his ministry amongst people: to draw them into abundant life, summed up in himself: 'I have come that they may have life, and have it to the full' (Jn. 10:10). To participate in the dance of life is to experience *shalom* wholeness at the deepest level, and it is that invitation which we are summoned to offer to all who need healing in their lives. But those who are privileged to journey as care-givers are also called to participate in the healing process as a spontaneous journey of faith and adventure, recapitulating the motif of dance: 'It is a sojourning together, a lingering in stages and phases, a sometimes struggle, sometimes dance, always adventure, on the way to renewed and deepened connections and reconnections with self and others.'[18]

Secular therapists, however, operate within a humanistic paradigm: their belief in the self-sufficiency of human beings is fundamental to the counsel they offer. For example, in Rogerian counselling, in which optimistic humanism is the foundational life philosophy, the wisdom of the Bible is replaced by a 'person-centred' free-floating openness in the cause of 'unconditional positive regard, empathy and genuineness'.[19] Carl Rogers' emphasis on tolerance and the individual's right to choose, and his insistence on experience as the highest authority in human behaviour, are highly regarded in contemporary postmodern society, challenging the truth-statements and authority of the Christian community.

Difference and diversity in pastoral ministry

However, in the spirit of my earlier comments in Chapter Five about the positive dimensions of postmodernism, we must acknowledge the contribution of postmodernism to the exercise of Christian compassion. Perhaps the most important characteristic on which to focus in this regard is the celebration of difference, understood in a social rather than philosophical sense.[20] Postmodernists argue that human beings 'tend to construct perspectives, world-views and metanarratives that erase difference and marginalize whatever does not fit'.[21] However, 'difference and diversity occur within a larger context of creational cohesion and unity',[22] and this is of enormous importance in the therapeutic ministry of the church.

Just as Christ, in his ministry on earth, treated each person as unique and important, so we are to participate in his ongoing concern for the individual. As Christians, we are not called to press people into some clone-like pattern of life and behaviour, a common fear among those who do not really understand God.

Rather, we are to 'descend into detail, past the misleading tags, past the metaphysical types, past the empty similarities to grasp firmly the essential character of not only the various cultures but the various sorts of individuals within each culture, if we wish to encounter humanity face to face.'[23] It is altogether too tempting to treat people as homogeneous rather than as a diverse and colourful multitude of unique individuals, each with their own history, hopes and fears. To participate in the compassion of Christ is to 'listen to the singular *who*' and seek to multiply differences.[24]

The diversity of pastoral ministry activity, therefore, mirrors the diversity of human nature itself as much as it reflects the events and circumstances which individuals face as they journey through life. This variability has been recognized for centuries as important in soul care. The Cappadocian Father Gregory of Nazianzus wrote these pertinent words in the fourth century:

> The principle is this: just as the same food and medicine is not appropriate to every bodily ailment, so neither is the same treatment and discipline proper for the guidance of souls ... Some persons are better motivated by words, others by example. Some who are sluggish and dull need to be stirred up to the good, while others are already inordinately fervent and so rushed about that they need to be calmed. Praise will benefit some, while correction will benefit others, provided that each is administered in a seasonable way. Out of season your counsel may do more harm than good.[25]

So as human beings we react in very different ways to the exigencies of life. The Old Testament scholar Gerhard von Rad, commenting on Genesis 1 – 11, suggests that the great problems of humanity are subjected in this narrative to the light of revelation: creation and nature, sin and suffering, man and wife, fraternal quarrels, international confusion.[26] This leads Oglesby to trace five particular areas of relevance to pastoral care and counselling, rooted in the Genesis material: initiative and freedom, fear and faith, conformity and rebellion, death and rebirth, and risk and redemption. These themes remind us forcefully of the complexity of problems that are grist to the mill of the pastoral counsellor.

Clinebell similarly observes that pastor and people struggle together with basic theological issues at a deeply personal level: 'Sin and salvation, alienation and reconciliation, guilt and forgiveness, judgment and grace, spiritual death and rebirth, despair and hope, are interwoven in the fabric of the healing-growthing interaction between pastor and parishioner.'[27] Of course, there are many other factors that impinge upon the way an individual may or may not be coping with the sort of issues raised here. In particular, we should recognize that every person lives within a unique environment of interpersonal relationships involving family, work colleagues, neighbours, and the wider community. We are, as we observed in Chapter Two, 'being-with' creatures more than many of us may realize.

Furthermore, the journey that each person has travelled in life contains a history which the counsellor needs to understand if he or she is to interpret Scripture effectively into that person's present situation. We need to have what Oates calls a 'feelingful entrée' into a person's own context, or frame of reference for life, if we are to counsel them appropriately – our earlier discussion of contextualization and world-view in Chapter Three emphasized this as a feature of all Christian ministry.

We must also note diversity in the goals of pastoral counselling ministry. In their discussion of the way narrative works in the Bible, Fee and Stuart helpfully distinguish between three levels in the Old Testament, which together comprise a hierarchy of narratives.[28] Individual narratives represent the first level, embracing, for example, stories about the great heroes of faith in Israelite history; these stories fit into the second narrative level, which has to do with God's special relationship to Israel with its repeating cycle of obedience, rebellion, punishment, and deliverance. This middle level is in turn a part of the ultimate narrative of salvation history, or *Heilsgeschichte* – the whole universal plan of God worked out in creation and redemption. A similar tripartite pattern is observable with regard to the goals of pastoral counselling.

In the same way that a narrative text may be confined to the story of a particular individual, or a sequence of events in the life of a biblical character, a person may seek help within his or her own limited world, perhaps afraid to step out beyond a secure comfort zone. An example of this would be someone who has experienced bereavement, and who is unwilling to find solace beyond his or her own grief. At this stage, all a counsellor may be able to do is to offer a listening ear, alert to opportunities to lead the grief-locked person into the wider world of other human beings. In the same way that biblical narrative may shift out of the first level of individual stories to the second level of the story of Israel, a counsellor's goal may be to lead a troubled individual beyond his or her limited world of pain and confusion into an awareness of their place within the wider concerns of humanity.

This remembrance of who we are as 'human beings in community' is a powerful and necessary stimulus to wholeness, as hurting people are invited into participation in a context wider than their own. When Jezebel pursued Elijah after the contest on Mount Carmel, Elijah's understandable fear turned into self-pity as he complained to the Lord (1 Kgs. 19:1–18). God's response to his protest was to instruct him to return and anoint kings in Damascus and Israel and a successor to himself. At times we need internal spaces in order to cope with our pain; but a time must also come for us to 'gird up our loins' and join the rest of humanity in our common shared life in the world.

This implies an important social-ethical dimension, or moral imperative, in pastoral care. Remembrance within the Christian community must embrace the stranger in our midst, and not just those who are privileged to be members of the faith-community: 'Being with another in ministry is more important than the satisfaction of simply being with.'[29] There is a discernible trend in pastoral care in which subjective experience replaces objective purpose, the personal supplants the social-ethical, a sense of individual mysticism usurps the moral dimension and self replaces other. If the pursuit of happiness is substituted for a life of other-centred holiness within the counselling arena, the church may end up as a community of like-minded people, living ghetto-lives divorced from the real world of pain and suffering.

This perspective on the ultimate goal of pastoral care echoes the concern of those who criticize the unqualified espousal of 'power encounters' with demonic forces in the ministry of the church. The motive of those who rightly insist upon the need in our hurting world for the 'demonstration of the Spirit's power' (1 Cor. 2:4) is surely to be commended; however, some 'signs and wonders' advocates have overlooked the context of Paul's words. His emphasis is on the cross of Christ, and the language he adopts is the language of incarnational, kenotic love, of God's power in human weakness, not, as Smail cogently argues, the language of *theologia gloriae*:

> When we take our bearings from the cross, we can see that the only power with which Jesus works is the power of that utterly self-giving love that was itself weak and helpless on Calvary. He overcame all the violent force and energy of evil that fell upon Him there, not by exercising greater force and violence, but by renouncing them altogether ... a church in which healing, renewal and effective evangelism can happen is a church that is open to receive Christ's Calvary love, to demonstrate it in specific ways in the relationships of its members to one another, and to extend it to those outside its own fellowship with whom it comes into contact. Such a church will get near to the people by its acceptance of them and will intercede for people in a way that takes its inspiration from the kind of intercession that Jesus made when He identified himself on the cross with the sinners and sufferers of the world and offered himself to God on their behalf.[30]

Notice here the deliberate emphasis on caring for those who are outside the boundaries of the community of faith. What most impresses the majority of people is a quality of love which finds its fullest expression in the humility and obedience of Christ, who 'being in very nature God, did not consider equality with God something to be grasped, but made himself nothing, taking the very nature of a servant ...' (Phil. 2:6–7). <u>Sacrificial, other-centred love is the crucible within which the power of the Spirit is most at home</u>: within the flowing tide of *agapē* love God's edifying, healing and restoring power reaches out to touch and transform even the hardest heart. <u>A charismatic theology which holds cross and Spirit in the closest possible association is a theology which offers the greatest hope for all people, both inside and outside the church</u>.

Oden's discussion of soul care corresponds to this critical concern for all whom God has created. He views the pastor as a person who is more likely than other helping professionals in society 'to compassionately behold the parishioner's whole existence – physical, moral and spiritual – in the context of salvation history or universal history seen in relation to eternity'.[31] Remembering those who are not yet part of the community of faith identifies pastoral care and counselling as a ministry which 'seeks to nurture small communities and persons within those communities who will contribute to the redemption of the whole society. Anything less than the whole seems to misunderstand the hope of Christian mission for the world.'[32] Such ambitious, yet wholly appropriate, goals for pastoral counselling correspond with Fee's and Stuart's third and ultimate level of biblical narrative, *Heilsgeschichte* – what Bar-Efrat describes as 'the vast canvas of history'.

In the same way that individual narrative stories fit as cameos into this larger canvas of biblical history, so each individual person struggling with issues in life can be encouraged to view his or her life as significant in God's wider purposes in the community and ultimately in the world. For example, the stories of Joseph, Gideon and Esther, among many other Old Testament heroes, offer hope and purpose to an individual wrestling with opposition, self-doubt or adversity. God is in control of our lives and may yet use them in ways which are beyond our present understanding (see Gen. 45:7–8; Judg. 6:14; Esth. 4:14).

I recall during a time of prayer in a church meeting receiving a picture in my mind's eye of a pastoral scene in jigsaw format. The details in the foreground were typical of rural life: farm buildings, animals, farmhands working in the fields, tractors and other equipment standing nearby. Above, a vast expanse of blue sky extended over the whole scene. But one piece of the jigsaw was missing in that sky. I sensed the Lord speaking into my spirit that there were some present who felt like that piece of blue sky, unimportant and insignificant – how much better and more exciting to be part of the foreground! However, as the prophecy made clear, every piece is important. In fact, the pieces that are most noticeable by their absence are those in the blue sky: the busyness of the foreground would have disguised a missing piece in that part of the jigsaw. I went on to affirm each person in the gathering, especially those who felt themselves to be insignificant, encouraging them to believe that they had a special place in the purposes of God: he remembers each one of us within the 'vast canvas' of life, and incorporates our own personal stories into his own great metanarrative. As we care for one another within the community of faith, we do well to offer this perspective to all who may feel uncertain about their place within God's 'big picture'.

The hierarchy of goals suggested above – which we may define as *personal*, *communal* and *universal* – is a further consideration in sensitive application of the Bible in pastoral counselling situations. The wise counsellor will select biblical material appropriate to the goals within a given context, whether they are expressed implicitly or explicitly. Some situations may lend themselves to overt presentation of the gospel, in which case the issue of the relationship between counselling and evangelism arises. For Adams, Christian counselling is *biblical* counselling, in which people need to be confronted with the need to grow up into the fullness of the stature of Christ: 'counselling involves helping people to put off old patterns which grow out of rebellion towards God, and helping them to put on new practices which grow out of obedience to God.'[33] His goal is Christlikeness for everyone, and for him this necessarily involves presenting the gospel of Christ – in an explicit evangelistic sense – at some stage in the counselling process. Rejection of the gospel is a valid enough reason to terminate the interview.

This perspective, however, is in danger of putting biblical counselling into the straightjacket of evangelism, and does not give sufficient weight to those whose frame of reference for counselling is undoubtedly biblical but not as overtly direct and confrontational. Adams's gospel emphasis is commendable, but gospel-centred counselling need not be as 'nouthetic' as he seems to suggest is necessary.[34] Aldrich, for example, proposes a style of evangelism based upon an incarnational/relational model, in which the Christian, freed from the pressure to proclaim biblical truths, 'plays the music' of the gospel by lovingly accepting other people: 'What you know is not as important as what you are.'[35]

Pruyser, whilst not dismissing the kerygmatic emphasis in pastoral ministry, takes a similar view, observing that 'seeing how far anyone is from the Kingdom requires some perspicacity and attentive listening to the client's groping for self-evaluation.'[36] His concern is the development of appropriate pastoral strategies for intervention, and he argues that proclamation of the Word of God 'presupposes a respectful recognition of another person whose integrity is to be met'.[37] Compare this with Adams's statement that a genuinely concerned pastor 'will not mince words or spar around with people. Rather, he will be specific about personal problems and straightforwardly attempt to correct them.'[38]

We must therefore recognize diversity in the way evangelism is interpreted within the ministry of pastoral counselling. Whilst the avowed goal of all pastoral care finds its centre in Colossians 1:28–29, where Paul seeks to present everyone complete or mature in Christ (which is the correct translation of the Greek word *teleios*), there are conflicting views as to how such a goal is to be achieved. Some may focus more overtly on evangelism than others as a precondition for effective change; others give greater emphasis to a person's life journey and to 'the complex interweaving of feelings, experiences, thinking and action'[39] which characterizes an individual's personal story. It is not surprising, therefore, that the way in which the Bible is used may differ significantly from one counsellor to another.[40] This leads us to a consideration of counselling styles.

Counselling styles and the role of story

It is helpful to distinguish between three broad approaches to counselling: directive, permissive and interactional. In directive therapies 'the counsellor is viewed as an expert who diagnoses and analyses a problem, sometimes labels and categorizes behaviour, decides on solutions for the counsellee's problem and in various ways communicates these solutions to the counsellee.'[41] Adams's 'nouthetic' style of counselling slots into this category. In permissive counselling 'the counsellor is the facilitator who stimulates people to solve their own problems and who creates a permissive environment where this problem can be solved and personal growth can occur.'[42] Permissive counselling has been strongly advocated by many Christians because it avoids the trap of 'playing God' in the lives of others. It also demonstrates the crucial importance of disciplined listening and responding to an individual's feelings.

Interactional counselling, at times referred to as 'relationship counselling', lies somewhere in the middle, and in its Christian development owes much to the example and teaching of the Swiss medical practitioner Paul Tournier, whose emphasis is on two human beings working together at burden bearing and problem solving. His approach is essentially participative, in which 'soul-healing' takes place in the presence of God. For Tournier, the counsellor is 'as guilty, as powerless, as inferior and as desperate' as the one seeking help, 'a companion in repentance and in waiting for grace'.[43]

Tournier's many writings display great gentleness and openness, combined with an eclectic and flexible approach which encourages frank dialogue between those involved in the counselling process. His style is essentially pastoral and conversational, compared with the prophetic-confrontational nature of directive counselling and the priestly-confessional character of the permissive approach.[44]

There is a considerable degree of overlap between these three styles, and counsellors may typically move from one to another within a particular encounter. Sometimes confrontation is needed, at times deep and reflective listening, and sometimes there is much mutuality and sharing. We need not regard these styles as alternatives, but as complementary approaches in the task of helping troubled people in their journey towards wholeness. No one style has a monopoly on hearing the voice of God: all offer the possibility of prophetic insight.

However, listening to God must never squeeze out the importance of listening to the person who comes for help. Bonhoeffer acutely observes that 'he who can no longer listen to his brother will soon be no longer listening to God either; he will be doing nothing but prattle in the presence of God too.'[45] In similar vein, Oates is concerned that no one be pressed into any 'prearranged or patent interpretation': 'The spontaneous intelligence of a person in the press of a felt difficulty quite often lays hold of a more realistic interpretation than does the mind of the minister who does not feel the pressure so keenly.'[46] Pastoral authority must not dominate to the point where the one offering counsel imposes his or her pathology on another.

The ultimate controlling guide in Christian counselling is God's word. Capps quotes Faber's and van der Schoot's discussion of the value of pastor-initiated Bible reading, in which they suggest that 'the moment the Bible is read a certain change will take place. Even though the pastor reads, he and the parishioner are in a very similar position because both of them are addressed by the same word of the Lord.'[47] Whilst imposition of a particular interpretation may still occur (and even the choice of passage may be open to the criticism of being diagnostic, prescriptive and possibly judgmental), it is evident that there is great benefit in allowing people to hear God speak directly into their own lives through his word. This is particularly true in the case of stories, to which we alluded in Chapter Two in the context of their ability to teach and instruct vicariously.

Pruyser relates the history of the pastoral contact between a minister and a young woman in her mid-twenties who was consumed by the guilt of her adultery which had led to divorce. The pastor, sensing her inability to receive God's forgiving grace, felt that he needed to confront her as a 'man of God' in order to move her through confession to restoration. So he retold her the story of the woman caught in adultery (Jn. 8:3–11) and applied the story to her life. The young woman's response was to identify with the adulterous woman, and she broke into tears at the assurance of forgiveness given by the minister.[48] Here the biblical story functioned in a *prescriptive* way. Such is the dynamic of narrative where confrontation is needed within the counselling context. Biblical stories announcing the living Word of God have power to penetrate even the most resistant shells, and they often enable counsellors to prescribe the needed medicine in a very directive way.

In conversational counselling, however, biblical stories tend to function *descriptively*: 'living biblical insights, stories and metaphors are right brain ways of communicating profound truths about life.'[49] In other words, they represent creative, intuitive, imaginative means by which biblical truths can enter human experience in a positive life-transforming way. This is particularly important within a postmodern paradigm of reality, where the medium of narrative conveys the possibility of transformation often unattainable through direct propositional truth-statements. Left-brain approaches, on the other hand, focus on techniques, and are characterized by analytical, intentional, problem-solving methodologies which are at the core of many secular counselling therapies.

When a biblical story is introduced, and even discussed, in a non-threatening, conversational way, points of contact are created between that story and the personal story of the one seeking help. As we allow the narrative text of Scripture the opportunity to penetrate our personal spaces, it becomes 'living and active', offering succour and encouragement, comfort and guidance. In the same way that Christ told stories, drawing his hearers in to teach them and offer direction in their lives, so we participate in his continuing ministry in the lives of those around us as we allow his Spirit to reveal his love and grace in the complexities and confusion of contemporary life. Instead of searching for a means of entry into the lives of others as we counsel them, even to the point of extracting what may seem to be the most appropriate technique from our own array of counselling methodologies, we engage with others within the vibrant context of Scripture as story, which has its own power: 'Sharper than any double-edged sword, it penetrates even to dividing soul and spirit, joints and marrow' (Heb. 4:12).

Before examining this further, we should note that the counsellor's own story may be of value in the therapeutic process: those who have been exposed to the realities of pastoral ministry and the many circumstances which envelop people's lives are the ones most likely to discern what is needful and appropriate in subsequent situations. In addition, the experiences of others, not just the counsellor, may add to the inventory of stories which have relevance to a given pastoral issue. So Oden proposes personal and social experience as one of the branches of a quadrilateral of theological method for pastoral theology, the other three being Scripture, tradition and reason.[50] This quadrilateral, as Oden points out, is based on the well-known fourfold source for understanding God's self-disclosure in history. The experiential nature of personal and biblical stories as descriptive rather than prescriptive tools is fundamental to the conversational, relationship-centred counselling of Tournier, for example, who encourages counsellors to 'think biblically' rather than using biblical texts as 'magic formulae'.

In non-directive confessional counselling, centre stage is given to the story of the person seeking counsel; the role of the pastoral counsellor is to bring God's mercy to bear on that story. It may or may not be appropriate to introduce biblical material explicitly in such a context. The key, rather, is empathetic listening: acute sensitivity to the personal story of someone in distress, leading to the spoken word of forgiveness, is often more valuable than using the Bible as 'the sword of the Spirit' (Eph. 6:17), whether in story form or not. However, the introduction of biblical narrative may offer needed moral guidance and direction because of its capacity to teach in an implicit rather than explicit way.

Sir Philip Sidney, the English Renaissance poet and essayist, claimed that the final end of poetry, in which he embraced fictional narrative, 'is to lead and draw us to as high a perfection as our degenerate souls, made worse by their clayey longings, can be capable of'.[51] The power of literary artistry is affirmed by Peterson, who claims that 'the Greeks were the best storytellers that the world has ever known. We keep telling their stories to each other to locate ourselves in the human condition. The stories of Odysseus, of Oedipus and Electra, of Narcissus and Sysiphus are diagnostic as we try to get our bearings and keep our balance.'[52] We need to rediscover the art of telling stories to one another, if we are to avoid relying upon those educators who like to present us with moral dilemmas in our search for truth, inviting us to draw our own conclusions through moral reasoning. These strategies offer us the freedom to write our own stories, inputting our own values; this, of course, reflects the spirit of contemporary society, an age of relativism rather than absolutes.

Stories have an inductive role, which is important in the context of pastoral counselling where, for example, troubled people need guidance and help to resolve their problems. We suggested in Chapter Two that stories work because they have power to draw us into the reality, the experience, the events being described. Stories, of course, can be well told, or they can be poorly told: so craftsmanship in the construction of the story is important. To accomplish their purpose, stories must arrest us; they must have movement that carries us. Hein argues that nearly all good novels move from quest to illumination, from problem to solution or meaning.[53] They offer a satisfying conclusion, in contrast to the open-ended uncertainties prevalent in much moral education today. The value of form, and its power to convey meaning within the context of pastoral care, will become evident in our brief investigation of the Ruth narrative at the end of this chapter.

Stories also work because, to quote the Horatian dictum, they are pleasurable as well as profitable. This is the major thrust of Leland Ryken's studies in the value of literature.[54] His complaint, echoed by many today, is that our generation is illiterate – not in the sense that we *cannot* read, but that we *do not* read, in spite of our universal education system and advanced means of communication. In fact, technological progress has contributed to modern illiteracy, with videos, television, and computers occupying the greater part of individual leisure activity (or inactivity!).

In referring to the pleasurable aspect of stories, I am not necessarily referring to form, although the aesthetic structure, balance, and style of a story understandably gives pleasure just as good poetry leaves one with a sense of satisfaction in the way words, images, and rhythm convey meaning. But there is pleasure also simply in the reading, just as gazing at a majestic mountain peak fills one with wonder and joy. God has given all good things for our enjoyment, including good literature, which has intrinsic power to please. To read Keats or Wordsworth, Dickens or Shakespeare is a pleasurable experience. The utilitarian perspective is that aesthetic beauty may act as a catalyst for the meaning of the words to penetrate the mind, touch the heart, and move the will.

So we are encouraged to pursue energetically the possibility that lives can be changed as divine truths reach into the hearts and minds of hurting, confused and inquiring people through the medium of the biblical text in all its literary richness. Exposure to the liberating power of language with all its performative efficacy may accomplish far more than specific Bible verses trotted out mechanically by the pastoral counsellor. Thus 'language is by no means merely an expression, nor a stimulant, but a real medium of information',[55] information which is actually transformative by becoming present reality in the lives of those who receive it into the depths of their being. C. S. Lewis observes that to be told that it is a very cold night hardly compares to the evocative words of John Keats, who opens his poem 'The Eve of St Agnes', with these famous words:

> St Agnes' Eve – Ah, bitter chill it was!
> The owl, for all his feathers was a-cold;
> The hare limped trembling through the frozen grass,
> And silent was the flock in woolly fold:
> Numb were the beadsman's fingers...

The Bible is rich in this sort of language and structural form, appealing to human sensibilities in a way that factual statements cannot.

Acknowledging the Bible as great literature as well as great theology means that we are free to respond to scriptural truth not only through our God-given faculties of reason, will, and emotions, and not only as the Holy Spirit reveals the once-hidden things of God to us, but also through our *imagination*. In no way is this meant to detract from the truthfulness of the Bible as the Word of God; nor do I wish to minimize the reality and impact of Spirit-inspired scriptural texts, charismatic insight or words of prophecy, which may speak powerfully into the human condition, bringing consolation, direction or conviction. Rather, we are encouraged to recognize that 'through the dim and broken history of the Bible there passes a strange procession of events and images which alone can shadow forth, and in part satisfy, man's groping recognition of many kinds of hidden yet vital life; that the roots which the images send deep into our minds draw from the depths something that satisfies, we do not know how, the deepest needs of the psyche.'[56] This leads us into the realm of biblical interpretation, for we are now encouraged not to dismiss the literary qualities of the text in our anxiety to 'get to the truth'.

The hermeneutical task is a process in which the reader is ideally drawn into the biblical text, a task which reflects a cycle of wonder, leading to curiosity, leading to more wonder. Here there is no last word, for it is not a question of the interpreter 'getting to the bottom' of the text, but, in the final analysis, being willing to so engage with the text that it becomes, for him or her, the living word of God in a deeply personal way, shaping, healing, and transforming life. Biblical authority must therefore be defined as more than canonical authority: it has, it *is*, authority to change our lives. It allows the Bible's literary qualities to come to the fore, such that the literary and the theological intertwine in symbiotic union.

My point is simple: a hermeneutic which reduces all of Scripture to an elementary, uniform series of statements or block of teaching does violence to its creativity as the work of both God and human beings. This creativity has been explored by Capps, who expounds the theme of diversity in the relationship between biblical literature and pastoral counselling.[57] Three different counselling situations are posited, corresponding with Oates's earlier-mentioned functions of comfort, instruction, and diagnosis. The first is concerned with the limits of our endurance, and the consequent need for comfort: in this context, he proposes a non-directive approach utilizing the psalms as a means of providing help in clarifying feelings in the midst of the experience of transition. The quest for permanence and stability is Capps's second counselling context; here he suggests the use of proverbs which are more directive in seeking to generate change in a person's moral behaviour. Thirdly, the insecurity of radical change is addressed, in which he highlights the value of parables as being particularly appropriate in conditions that demand action and change: typically, a permissive environment is more suited to this context.

More specifically Capps suggests that the three biblical forms of psalms, proverbs, and parables can be applied, respectively, to such areas as grief counselling, premarital counselling and marriage counselling. Whilst his overall framework gives an appearance of tidiness, and interlocks the elements of diversity perhaps too neatly in order to advance his goal of realizing unity in diversity, Capps undoubtedly succeeds in illustrating the need for wisdom and flexibility in the relationship between the Bible and counselling. Different literary forms function in different ways in pastoral counselling ministry. Those who are involved with others in a caring context are therefore privileged to witness the variety of ways in which Scripture is able to access the many different dimensions of personal pain, opening up windows for them to participate in all that Christ is doing by his Spirit to bring healing and hope.

As a specific example of this general thesis, we now turn to the genre of biblical narrative, which predominates in the Old Testament, accounting for over forty per cent of the text, and which typifies much of the gospels and Acts. Whilst pastoral counselling may frequently be undertaken without reference to narrative material, I emphasize its value here because it is all too often neglected as a medium through which God's truth may be accessed by the troubled soul.

The Ruth narrative in pastoral ministry

Earlier in this chapter we noted Fee's and Stuart's hierarchy of narratives in the Old Testament, consisting of three levels, ranging from individual stories to the ultimate narration of God's salvation plan in history (*Heilsgeschichte*). Awareness of this hierarchy is valuable in appreciating the way narrative works: no individual story is isolated from the fuller picture of God's self-revelation in history. Each story points beyond the individual characters involved towards the One who is working out his purposes through the relationships and events portrayed.

For example, the Joseph cycle is not only a story of a young man who experiences both favouritism and rejection, slavery, imprisonment, the rise to secular power and ultimately reconciliation with his family. It is also a story of God's intention to bring life to the nations through his people Israel: it is redemptive, salvific, and ultimately eschatological. Joseph declares to his brothers: 'But God sent me ahead of you to prepare for you a remnant on earth and to save your lives by a great deliverance. So then, it was not you who sent me, but God' (Gen. 45:7–8; see also 50:20).

This hierarchical approach in our understanding of the narrative material in the Bible helps us to keep our eyes on God's overall goals, rather than confining ourselves to specific details. The details are important because they speak to us about our human condition, our struggles and weaknesses, our experiences of both pleasure and pain, our hopes and our fears: they represent to us the reality of our own lives, and so speak to us vicariously. But we also need to see the God who is at work in all human life, often 'behind the scenes'. This is a particular feature of the Ruth narrative. As a person is drawn into the events and characters involved in the biblical narrative, he or she is also drawn beyond them, even out of them, to acknowledge the sovereignty of a God who is greater than the events, and whose purposes cannot be thwarted, a God who is able to work in the present (and the future) as he has in the past. For someone who is, to use Stuhlmacher's phrase, 'open to transcendence',[58] narrative as a genre is powerful in offering the reward of a more personal encounter with God, who is ever waiting to speak through the experiences of others to those willing to enter into them.

Writing about the literature of the Old Testament, Clines suggests that texts are like monuments: 'they signal the purpose of what is dead but "survives" and can be awakened ... Any literature worth the name jumps the time-gap of its own accord. For this reason, the church is entitled to regard its scripture as "living oracles".'[59] The book of Ruth may be regarded as one such 'living oracle', though its first impression is one of simplicity and charm: an attractive, indeed compelling, story of loyalty among ordinary folk. However, if we probe beneath the superficial exterior and examine the book as a literary work of art containing significant theological insights, we discover that it is a narrative which has been carefully constructed in the best traditions of Hebrew literature.

Throughout the book there is a dominant motif of emptiness-fullness. The emptiness theme is established as an orderly development in chapter 1, where reference to the barrenness of the earth is followed by Naomi's sense of emptiness at the loss of her husband and two sons, and her awareness of her own 'barrenness'. Her situation appears hopeless ... yet the harvest context, central to chapter 2, permits the working out of the restoration theme. From a literary viewpoint, we note the foreshadowing of fullness to come in Ruth 2:12,14 as the ideas of reward and satisfaction are suggested. In chapter 3 the theme is one of completion, of ingathering: '... the arms of Boaz gathering in to himself the maiden Ruth, the arms of the young men drawing into the barns the grain'.[60] Full restoration is achieved in the final scene of the story as Ruth gives birth to a son, significantly laid in Naomi's lap: for Naomi, Obed is her fullness, so much so that the women of Bethlehem declare that 'Naomi has a son.' Ultimately it is God who rewards those who are faithful to him: in Ruth's first meeting with Boaz, he declares, 'May you be richly rewarded by the Lord, the God of Israel, under whose wings you have come to take refuge' (Ruth 2:12).

The thematic development in Ruth is complemented by its structural artistry, in which the typical Hebraic features of symmetry and parallelism predominate. This is particularly noticeable in chapters 2 and 3; in both scenes, among the harvesters and on the threshing floor, a meeting takes place between Boaz and Ruth, with Boaz inquiring about the girl's identity and blessing her for her kindness (firstly to Naomi, then to himself); Ruth then returns to Naomi with barley from Boaz, and the next course of action is discussed. Thematically, Ruth's reception of barley from Boaz and presentation of it to Naomi prefigure the birth of Obed, thus carrying the narrative forward to the sense of fulfilment which dominates the end of the story. The heightened sense of expectation afforded by these literary devices reinforces the emptiness-fullness motif which gives the story its underlying unity.

Other literary refinements add to the narrative's artistic shape. The book is in the form of a short story, or *novella*, and Campbell identifies a number of key attributes associated with this form-category: brevity, a plurality of episodes, a distinctive and well-wrought structure, an element of fiction, and a purpose for which the story was written.[61] In addition, word play is common throughout the narrative, and through a masterly use of sentences the author helps the reader to make the transition from one act of the story to the next as the story unfolds. This is particularly evident in the final verse of chapter 1 as Naomi's despair contrasts with the hope offered by the harvest; the author 'by this exhibition of perfect poise convinces us beyond any doubt that all is well'.[62] There is also a careful managing of pace, which keeps the story moving without damaging the important scenes of encounter between the central figures.

Turning to the major theological themes, we detect three people, Naomi, Boaz and Ruth, living lives that reflect the *ḥesed* character of God himself in his dealings with them: *ḥesed* is difficult to render in English: it refers to such qualities as faithfulness, lovingkindness, loyalty, constancy and sheer goodness, especially in the context of the love that binds two parties together in covenant relationship. It arises from within, rather than from external legal obligation.[63] In Ruth this *ḥesed*-living takes place in the context of 'an inexplicable famine ... and an inexplicable series of calamities'.[64] Amidst these trials and sorrows God is seen to be at work, for he is the One who remembers his people. Ruth declares that Naomi's God will be her God; his name is invoked as first Ruth and then Boaz commit themselves by oath (Ruth 1:17; 3:13), so acknowledging him as their God; and the Lord's name is praised by the women of Bethlehem following the birth of Obed. In spite of her deep grief and pain, Naomi has not forgotten the Lord; the Israelite belief in Yahweh's all-causality is absolutely implicit in her acceptance of all that has happened to her. In her misfortune she acknowledges the hand of God, whose blessings are seen in the midst of adversity.

As the story unfolds, we recognize that God's remembrance of his people, affirmed by the leading characters, is complemented by their remembrance of him and their remembrance of one another. Ruth's loyalty towards her mother-in-law finds a gracious echo in Boaz's response to her. Ruth is a story about people – ordinary people, not 'superstars' – and we notice in their behaviour, towards God and one another, a deeper meaning to the words loyalty and kindness than perhaps we had ever known before. Of course, Boaz's generosity as kinsman-redeemer towards Ruth foreshadows the extravagance of the great Redeemer, who was to descend from him. It cannot be purely coincidental that the redemption motif characterizing Boaz's action is most supremely expressed in the life of one who is descended from him, and part of whose genealogy is listed in Ruth 4:18–22. God's actions in Ruth are set within the context of salvation history, of *Heilsgeschichte*: the story is more than a tale of everyday life; in a powerful way it relates to the redemptive history of God's people through the ages.

Childs has observed that the theological witness of Ruth is inseparable from its form: the literary and theological are dependent on one another.[65] The story does not explicitly declare God's providence in the face of the calamitous events recorded in Ruth, suggesting that more often than not God works in a hidden way in people's lives, working his purposes out 'behind the scenes'. We see in the superb literary artistry of the book a means by which *God's activity is revealed in its hiddenness*. It is precisely here that the narrative which we have been examining has its power in pastoral counselling. We may not be immediately conscious of its poetic elegance, nor of the craft of the storyteller in weaving the major themes of redemption and restoration into an appealing record of life in a particular period of Israelite history. We do not have to be fully aware of such expertise, in the same way that enjoyment of a movie or novel does not require of us today a familiarity with film-production techniques or writing skills. It is sufficient that the final product does what it is intended to do.

However, recognition of the literary quality of Ruth will undoubtedly add to our appreciation of the book's value, and we will see more in the text for ourselves than would be possible with a cursory reading. For example, the pastoral counsellor's approach to a person groping for security and significance will be influenced by the insights suggested in the paragraphs above. As the troubled person is encouraged to read the story of Ruth, identifying perhaps with the alienation of Ruth or the despair of Naomi, the craft of the storyteller generates hope and encouragement in a far more powerful way than the mere reciting of theological platitudes or the quotation of specific Bible verses could achieve.

Earlier, we recognized a hierarchy of counselling goals within the pastoral ministry of the church, defined as personal, communal, and universal. At the personal level, someone may lament with Naomi, claiming with her that 'the Lord has afflicted me; the Almighty has brought misfortune upon me' (Ruth 2:21). It is not uncommon for individuals to feel as if they have been 'cursed' by God in some indefinable way, believing their plight to be a punishment for some sin or past failing. Is there no hope for them? On the contrary, the power of the narrative draws them into the story as they identify with Naomi's feelings, and the possibility of blessing becomes real for them as well.

Beyond the personal goal of restoration for Ruth and Naomi as Boaz enters their lives, we recognize the 'hidden hand of God' at the larger communal and universal levels. The story is one of community involvement as the people of Bethlehem – the harvesters, the townspeople, the elders at the gate, the women – contribute to the resolution of the crisis. Though God is the main participant, Ruth is also a story of human activity and commitment. So we participate in each other's stories, sharing in the sorrows, the decisions and the joys which unfold. Wounded people can be encouraged to involve themselves in the ordinary affairs of life and living, rather than withdrawing into self-pity. In sharing their hurting and confused lives with others, opportunities arise not only for personal healing, but also for the blessing of those who participate in their sorrows. So Boaz is rewarded with a wife, and the women of Bethlehem delight in the birth of their child: community life is immeasurably enriched.

The universal level reminds us that our own personal stories fit, like pieces of a jigsaw, into the larger story of God's creative and redeeming work in the world. Sittler observes that 'ultimate desolations are made both more bearable and significant when the story is the Ultimate Story.'[66] Paradoxically, the ordinariness of life is more than ordinary. Beyond this, the Ruth genealogy points us to the One who alone has the power to redeem our lives, who gives 'the oil of gladness instead of mourning, and a garment of praise instead of a spirit of despair' (Is. 61:3). Though we may feel alone in this world, the truth is that in God no one is left out. The pastoral counsellor who understands the importance of helping people to discover their identity as individuals who are valuable in God's sight and who *belong* in God's big picture of life will readily point to the genealogical appendix, which takes the reader of Ruth beyond the story of *ḥesed*-love into the universal story of redemption.

Earlier we considered a variety of contexts within which the pastoral counsellor may operate. Here we may present a few themes in Ruth which identify with the complexities and realities of human experience. The search for personal significance has already been suggested, whereby the counsellor has opportunity to explore with the person coming for help the implicit truth found in the story that we matter to God. The emptiness-fullness motif in Ruth, related to loss and barrenness and the experience of grief, is another potent theme in the church's pastoral ministry. A sense of lostness and hopelessness frequently invades the lives of the bereaved, and the Ruth narrative addresses those who seek help in this area of personal sorrow. Peterson reminds us that 'Naomi got into the story by complaining':[67] her response to what had happened to her contributed to the outworking of the solution.

In fact, both Naomi and Ruth are portrayed as active participants in the story. They avoid the temptation to sink into a morass of self-pity. Naomi had one card left – a small piece of land in Israel and a distant relative, and it is quite possible to characterize her as a desperate woman playing her last card! As God's purposes unfold, in the hidden way so typical of his dealings with us, we recognize the twin themes of human and divine activity. God calls us into a co-operative venture with him, so that we contribute to *his* solution. How much more powerfully is this truth conveyed to the postmodern mind by the Ruth narrative than by Paul's words in Philippians 2:12–13: '… continue to work out your salvation with fear and trembling, for it is God who works in you to will and to act according to his good purpose.'

The story is also an outstanding witness to God's acceptance of our imperfect humanity. Neither Naomi nor her complaints are rejected by God, even though she blames him for her situation. We may even question the purity of both Naomi's and Ruth's motives in the events involving Boaz, which unfold in chapters 2 and 3. Sasson exposes the provocation and resourcefulness of both women, and teasingly inquires regarding the threshing floor encounter: 'Is Ruth merely to remove the covers at his feet? Or is Naomi asking her to risk a bolder move?'[68] We are left to wonder. Counsellors are encouraged to be patient as struggling people pour out their complaints, but the story reminds us that there are times when 'the pastor collaborates in story making by encouraging persons to step out and speak their own lines'[69] even to the point of asking for what they want.

Ruth is a story of conflict resolution, with all the features of a good plot, satisfying Aristotle's requirements for a beginning, a middle, and an end. The concept of conflict resolution is important in understanding the dynamics of storytelling in pastoral counselling. Though the story may start with tears, there is the promise of joy at the end. Ruth is a story which reminds us of the truth that, in God's providential plan, 'in all things God works for the good of those who love him, who have been called according to his purpose' (Rom. 8:28). The pastoral implications of this biblical truth are rich beyond measure, and we have touched on only a few of them. We are reminded that God holds all people in his memory, unable because of his own nature to dismiss or forget them. To embrace a Moabite woman and place her in the very centre of his salvation purposes speaks to us of a God whose grace is beyond human understanding, who deals with us not according to our background or condition, but on the basis of his own *hesed*-love.

So the story points us in the direction of reaching out to those who are outside our own man-made boundaries, for ultimately there are no boundaries with God, certainly none that restrict the flow of compassion from the community of faith. God's love is inclusive, not exclusive; to be 'in Christ' is to have the same heart for all people that God has. God remembers us; and we remember him most truly when we remember not only those who are our brothers and sisters within the faith-community, but also those who are strangers and foreigners in our midst: 'For I was hungry and you gave me something to eat, I was thirsty and you gave me something to drink, I was a stranger and you invited me in, I needed clothes and you clothed me, I was sick and you looked after me, I was in prison and you came and visited me' (Mt. 25:35–36).

To care in this way is to live in the power of the Spirit. In so doing, we participate in the compassion of Christ, who lovingly and urgently invites all people into his dance of life. Writing about the value in soul care of the sort of exploration and discovery through conversational engagement which we have been describing in this chapter, Benner suggests that we need to surrender to and embrace the motif of dialogue in our compassionate response to sinful and struggling humanity: 'Much like moving into a flowing stream of water, one must enter dialogue ready to let go and be carried along on a journey. We create *opportunities* for dialogue, and we participate in it.'[70] This was the approach of Christ in his liberating concern for all people; he respected their freedom to choose their response to his presence in their lives. He *listened* to them, and by his Spirit invites us to be attentive too. 'It is the good listener, who listens in the quiet places to God and then mediates his compassion and God-given wisdom, who brings solace.'[71]

Notes

1. Walter Brueggemann, *Cadences of Home: Preaching among Exiles* (Louisville: Westminster John Knox Press, 1997), p. 19.
2. ibid., p. 3.
3. Patton, *Pastoral Care in Context*, p. 15.
4. Eugene Peterson, *Five Smooth Stones for Pastoral Work*, p. 24.
5. See Lawrence J. Crabb, *Effective Biblical Counselling* (London: Marshall Pickering, 1977), pp. 156–84.
6. ibid., pp. 159–60.
7. ibid., p. 175.
8. Larry Crabb, *The Safest Place on Earth: Where People Connect and are Forever Changed* (Nashville: Word Publishing, 1999), pp. 9–10.
9. Patton, *Pastoral Care in Context*, p. 28.
10. Olthuis, 'Dancing Together', *Journal of Psychology and Christianity*, 18:2, p. 147.
11. David G. Benner, *Care of Souls: Revisioning Christian Nurture and Counsel* (Grand Rapids: Baker Books, 1998), p. 146.
12. Hurding, *The Bible and Counselling* (London: Hodder & Stoughton, 1992), p. 67.

13. For an alternative perspective strongly promoting the sufficiency of Scripture, see Ed Hindson and Howard Eyrich (eds.), *Totally Sufficient* (Eugene: Harvest House, 1997).

14. Olthuis, 'Dancing Together', *Journal of Psychology and Christianity*, 18:2, p. 147.

15. See Gary R. Collins, *The Biblical Basis of Christian Counselling for People Helpers* (Colorado Springs: NavPress, 1993), pp. 11–24.

16. Anton T. Boisen, *The Exploration of the Inner World* (New York: Harper & Bros, 1936), p. 285.

17. Wayne E. Oates, *The Bible and Pastoral Care* (Grand Rapids: Baker, 1991), p. 71.

18. Olthuis, 'Dancing Together', *Journal of Psychology and Christianity*, 18:2, p. 148.

19. See Carl R. Rogers, *On Becoming a Person: A Therapist's View of Psychotherapy* (London: Constable, 1961).

20. For a discussion of the philosophical distinction between 'difference' and '*différence*' in postmodernist thought, see Stanley J. Grenz, *A Primer on Postmodernism* (Grand Rapids: Eerdmans, 1996), pp. 142–7.

21. J. Richard Middleton and Brian J. Walsh, *Truth Is Stranger Than It Used to Be: Biblical Faith in a Postmodern Age* (Downers Grove: IVP, 1995), p. 170.

22. ibid., p. 154.

23. Clifford C. Geertz, *The Interpretation of Cultures* (New York: Basic Books, 1973), p. 53.

24. Olthuis, 'Dancing Together', *Journal of Psychology and Christianity*, 18:2, p. 145.

25. Quoted in Oden, *Pastoral Theology*, p. 197.

26. Quoted in Oglesby, *Biblical Themes for Pastoral Care*, p. 38; for a fuller discussion, see Gerhard von Rad, *Old Testament Theology* (London: SCM Press, 1975), vol. 1, esp. 136–65.

27. Clinebell, *Basic Types of Pastoral Care and Counselling*, p. 50.

28. Gordon D. Fee and Douglas Stuart, *How to Read the Bible for All Its Worth* (Grand Rapids: Zondervan, 1982), pp. 74–5; for a similar and fuller development, see Shimon Bar-Efrat, *Narrative Art in the Bible* (Sheffield: Almond Press, 1989), pp. 93–140.

29. Patton, *Pastoral Care in Context*, p. 23.

30. Tom Smail, 'The Cross and the Spirit: Toward a Theology of Renewal' in Tom Smail, Andrew Walker and Nigel Wright, *The*

Love of Power or the Power of Love (Minneapolis: Bethany House Publishers, 1994), pp. 27–8.

31. Oden, *Pastoral Theology*, p. 188.
32. ibid., p. 195.
33. Jay E. Adams, *Competent to Counsel* (Grand Rapids: Baker, 1970), p. 71.
34. The Greek word '*noutheteo*' means to admonish or warn, which Adams interprets in terms of 'confrontation'. In the light of the many criticisms levelled at 'nouthetic counselling' (some complain that the compassionate and gracious side of God seems at times to be lacking in Adam's counselling approach) it is important to note that, for Adams, 'nouthesis' is motivated by love and deep concern.
35. Joe Aldrich, *Lifestyle Evangelism* (Sisters, Oregon: Multnomah, 1993), p. 80.
36. Paul W. Pruyser, *The Minister as Diagnostician* (Philadelphia: Westminster, 1976), p. 61.
37. ibid., p. 61.
38. Adams, *Competent to Counsel*, p. 63.
39. Roger F. Hurding, *Roots and Shoots: A Guide to Counselling and Psychotherapy* (London: Hodder & Stoughton, 1985), pp. 275–306.
40. For further discussion on this, see Capps, *Biblical Approaches to Pastoral Counselling*, pp. 17–46; Hurding, *Roots and Shoots*, pp. 275–306.
41. Gary Collins, *How to Be a People Helper* (Nashville: Vision House, 1976), p. 165.
42. ibid., p. 60.
43. Paul Tournier, *Guilt and Grace* (London: Hodder & Stoughton, 1958), p. 112.
44. Collins, *How to Be a People Helper*, p. 174.
45. Dietrich Bonhoeffer, *Life Together* (New York: Harper & Bros, 1954), pp. 97–8.
46. Oates, *The Bible in Pastoral Care*, p. 74.
47. Quoted in Capps, *Biblical Approaches to Pastoral Counselling*, p. 28.
48. Pruyser, *The Minister as Diagnostician*, pp. 115–18.
49. Clinebell, *Basic Types of Pastoral Care and Counselling*, p. 51.
50. Oden, *Pastoral Theology*, pp. 11–12.
51. Sidney, in Jones (ed.), *English Critical Essays*, p. 11.

52. Peterson, *Working the Angles*, p. 19.
53. Rolland N. Hein, 'A Biblical View of the Novel' in Leland Ryken (ed.), *The Christian Imagination: Essays on Literature and the Arts* (Grand Rapids: Baker, 1981), pp. 255–62.
54. See, for example, Leland Ryken, *How to Read the Bible as Literature* (Michigan: Academie, 1984); *Words of Delight: A Literary Introduction to the Bible* (Grand Rapids: Baker, 1992).
55. C. S. Lewis, 'The Language of Religion' in *Christian Reflections* (London: Geoffrey Bles, 1967), p. 170.
56. T. R. Henn, *The Bible as Literature* (London: Lutterworth, 1970), p. 20.
57. Capps, *Biblical Approaches to Pastoral Counselling*.
58. Referred to by Arden C. Autry, 'Dimensions of Hermeneutics in Pentecostal Focus', *Journal of Pentecostal Theology*, 3 (Oct. 1993), pp. 29–50.
59. David J. Clines, 'Story and Poem: The Old Testament as Literature and Scripture', *Interpretation*, 34:2 (April 1980), pp. 115–27.
60. D. F. Rauber, 'The Book of Ruth' in K. R. R. Gros Louis et al (eds.), *Literary Interpretations of Biblical Narratives* (Nashville: Abingdon, 1974), pp. 163–76.
61. Edward F. Campbell, *Ruth* – The Anchor Bible (New York: Doubleday, 1975).
62. Rauber, 'The Book of Ruth' in Gros Louis et al (eds.), *Literary Interpretations of Biblical Narratives*, p. 167.
63. See Bernhard W. Anderson, *The Living World of the Old Testament* (London: Longman, 1978) pp. 286–8.
64. Campbell, *Ruth*, p. 30.
65. Brevard S. Childs, 'Ruth' in *Introduction to the Old Testament as Scripture* (London: SCM Press Ltd, 1979), p. 567.
66. Joseph Sittler, *The Ecology of Faith* (Philadelphia: Muhlenburg Press, 1963), p. 39.
67. Peterson, *Five Smooth Stones for Pastoral Work*, p. 82.
68. Jack M. Sasson, 'Ruth' in R. Alter and F. Kermode (eds.), *The Literary Guide to the Bible* (London: Collins, 1987), pp. 320–8.
69. Peterson, *Five Smooth Stones for Pastoral Work*, p. 85.
70. Benner, *Care of Souls*, p. 151.
71. Hurding, *The Bible and Counselling*, p. 106.

Part Three

Pastoral Temptations

Chapter Seven

Participation and Pragmatism

'And so you will plunder the Egyptians.'
Exodus 3:22

Earlier in this book I mentioned my background in business management, and referred to my early struggles as I attempted to reconcile the commercial realities of marketing with my understanding of the Christian faith. In common with many people, I regard myself as a traveller on a journey, a pilgrim with much to learn, but that was not my attitude when I embarked on my journey of faith. At first, I believed that there was a yawning gap between Christianity and the way the world goes about its business of life and living, and in some respects this is so. However there is an unfortunate tendency in some Christians – and I was one of them – to dismiss everything that the world has to offer in terms of wisdom and experience, to the point that an unreal dualism begins to shape the way life is perceived: the world lives according to secular principles, and God's people live according to spiritual, or sacred, principles. And so the divide between sacred and secular took root in my mind, contributing to an unhealthy and, at times, narrow superspirituality, which allowed little room for theological exploration and discovery.

My introduction to life in the community of faith was certainly exhilarating, challenging the mediocrity of life without God: I discovered that God could actually change people's lives, healing and restoring in glorious ways. I experienced the powerful and loving ministry of the Holy Spirit amongst hurting, lonely, ordinary people in an inner-city Anglican parish in the

north of England. I encountered the gracious *charismata* of God
at work not only in the church, but also outside the boundaries
of the community of faith of which I was a part. There was no
thought of introducing techniques, programmes or methodologies into the ministry of the church. Imperceptibly an intensity
crept into my experience of Christian life, a zeal which was not
altogether healthy. I was not sufficiently confident or mature to
admit my condition to those around me, but two years of study
at theological college exposed my shallowness, and gradually I
deepened my understanding, and began to grow in many areas of
my spiritual life.

In particular, I became aware of the concept of stewardship
in ministry. The insights I had gained and the lessons that I
had learned in the business world did not appear to be as
inappropriate as I had at first imagined in my zeal to embrace the
Spirit's way of doing things. I discovered also that the gap
between what I had taught in a university business school and
what I was doing in Christian ministry was not so yawning after
all! There were points of contact between the church and the
world. Jesus relates a parable in which a dishonest manager,
accused by his master of irresponsibly wasting what he had been
given to look after, acted in a shrewd, though fraudulent, manner
to preserve his own interests (see Lk. 16:1–13). In his comment
on the parable, Jesus commends the steward not for his fraud nor
for his self-centred goals, but specifically for his wisdom and
perspicacity: 'For the people of this world are more shrewd in
dealing with their own kind than are the people of the light'
(Lk. 6:8).

The point of the parable is that those who have been given
responsibility in the kingdom of God should be alert to all the
resources that may be available to them in the fulfilment of what
they are given to do. Whilst Jesus goes on to connect the parable
to friendships and the stewardship of money, it is helpful to
consider his teaching in the context of opportunities to draw
from the wisdom of the world in the affairs of the kingdom of
God. May not the world have much to teach the 'children of
light' with regard to intelligence and astuteness? The chasm

between Athens and Jerusalem was beginning to close in my mind as I reflected on the contribution that management could make to effective – and efficient! – local church ministry. When God called Moses to lead the Hebrews out of slavery in Egypt, he added that he would 'make the Egyptians favourably disposed towards this people so that when you leave you will not go empty handed' (Ex. 3:21). So the Hebrews were enabled by God's grace to plunder, or spoil, the Egyptians of silver and gold and clothing, articles that they would find useful for their journey to the promised land. Likewise, the Christian community may find valuable resources available to them to facilitate their ministry in the world, resources which are not exclusive to those who do not participate explicitly in the life of the church.

All people are created in God's image, and all receive gifts of his grace in their humanity. One aspect of the doctrine of 'common grace' is that everyone is a recipient of God's gracious blessings, whether or not they confess Christ as Lord. Paul reminds the unbelieving crowd in Lystra that God 'has shown kindness by giving you rain from heaven and crops in their seasons; he provides you with plenty of food and fills your hearts with joy' (Acts 14:17). Whether God's gifts are expressed in terms of his gracious provision and sustenance as Creator, or in terms of unique human attributes, such as intelligence, manual dexterity, or musical giftedness, they are given without distinction. Paul Enns reminds us that 'when people participate in the material blessings of God ... it ought to make them reflect on the goodness of God.'[1] It is the use to which we put the resources given to us by God that is significant.

Our participation in the ministry of Christ is predicated on the prior understanding that all who have been created in the image of God are privileged to participate in the blessings that flow from God's universal Fatherhood. I argued in Chapter Five that the Spirit of God is the reconciling Spirit who is at work in all of life, seeking to draw all humanity into a conscious awareness of the Father's forgiveness and loving embrace. If that is so, then it is inconsistent to claim that those who do not confess the name of Christ are somehow denied the generous tokens of the riches of his grace. All that is lovely and beautiful and true comes from God's hand, and his glory is revealed by and within the whole created world (Rom. 1:20).

So in a mysterious and profound way the world is in some measure already participating in the activity and purposes of God. Baxter Kruger recounts the story of Eric Liddell, the Scottish runner, whose athletic career was immortalized in the film *Chariots of Fire*:

> Who can forget that scene under the mountain in Edinburgh when Liddell spoke to his sister? He said, 'God made me fast, and when I run I feel *His pleasure*.' Running, winning, being an Olympic champion were for Liddell but the mere expression of participation in the delight of the Father in His Son. Running was but the outer form of the event of the Spirit, the expression of the concert of the Father's pleasure. How wonderfully free he was to move on from running to other, seemingly less noble, forms of participation. But for Liddell, it was all of a piece. It was participation in the pleasure of the Father in His Son, whether in racing for Olympic gold, shovelling mud or suffering persecution on the mission field.[2]

Liddell attributed the glory in his running not to himself, but to God. Great composers have been inspired by God to create musical masterpieces, and wherever music gives joy to the human soul, there we may fittingly claim that the Spirit is at work. When I lived in England, I was awakened occasionally by the glory of the 'dawn chorus', as multitudes of birds joined in song at the break of a new day. At such times I was reminded of Calvin's comment that all living creatures are 'animated by angelic action'.

Indeed, in his *Institutes* Calvin specifically legitimizes the ministry of the 'ungodly', arguing that '... if the Lord has been pleased to assist us by the work and ministry of the ungodly in physics, dialectics, mathematics, and other similar sciences, let us avail ourselves of it, lest, by neglecting the gifts of God, spontaneously offered to us, we be justly punished for our sloth.'[3] These are challenging and incisive words, and invite all who are involved in Christian ministry to reflect on their willingness to discern opportunities to participate in God's giftings to all humanity. However, Calvin is clearly a long way from saying that everything in which the world is engaged reflects the character of its Creator. In today's imperfect and pragmatic age, we need great wisdom and discernment in differentiating between that which finds its genesis in the will of God, and that which originates in the desires of the human heart. The two must not be seen as mutually exclusive, of course, but neither must they be perceived as indistinguishable.

The temptation to rely on Egypt

Church leaders are often under great pressure within their denominations to develop strategies for growth. In the second half of the twentieth century, the Church Growth movement, with which Donald McGavran and Peter Wagner are particularly associated,[4] unwittingly contributed to this pressure, though, paradoxically, it also offered hope to those who were struggling to get their local church out of ruts and into renewal. The literature, tapes, seminars and conferences spawned by this movement seemed to promise new life: take the pulse, read the signs, develop five-year plans, distribute questionnaires, design new organizational patterns, set targets ... the techniques and methodologies proposed were endless.

In its early days as a pioneer of church growth, the Institute of Church Growth (ICG) under the leadership of Donald McGavran promoted a missiology which emphasized kerygmatic proclamation above incarnational presence. McGavran's 'theology of harvest' – in preference to a mere 'search theology', which he criticized for its failure to focus on results – was unequivocally growth-oriented, and his emphasis on the quantitative dimensions of growth led to charges of triumphalism, which he cheerfully accepted. 'McGavran's concern for the priority of evangelism in mission arose from his own experience and involvement in the Christian mass movements in India.'[5] His theology arose out of a unique context, and may be fairly criticized for failing sufficiently to allow for the incarnational dimension as a *primary* mission focus. Furthermore, his pragmatic recommendations – including growth methodologies, training programmes and gift-discovery techniques – have at times obscured his overriding conviction that mission has to do with participation in the will of God. With this conviction we must surely concur. It is with regard to the implementation of that mission that the debate has been most heated.

Many of those churches which were enamoured of ICG teaching discovered that for all their efforts nothing really changed. Pragmatism offered so much, yet delivered so little. The bookshelves of pastors were full of 'how to' texts, designed to get the local church out of maintenance mode into growth and mission. 'Spiritually loaded' numbers, especially seven and twelve, appeared in the titles (*7 Steps to ...* or *12 Keys to ...*) as if to guarantee divine authenticity or inspiration. Authors encouraged pastors to be success-oriented and growth-conscious, and a pragmatic 'what-works' mentality began its subtle invasion of the pastoral ministry of the church.

Certainly, there are good things to be discerned out of all that has been championed, and we will consider these later in this chapter, but my primary concern has to do with what is left unsaid rather than with what is proclaimed. There is a well-known parable which likens the Christian life to a ride on a tandem bicycle:

TANDEM BIKE

As a kid, I loved bikes. From the beginning I enjoyed the races. But how does a small boy win the right to ride in the biggest race of all? At first I saw God as a judge who would determine whether I was good enough to enter the race and if my efforts merited a prize. I was quite sure I would recognise God if I saw Him, but I didn't know Him at all. Later, I recognised He was the coach who had taught others how to ride. He explained that life was like a bike ride. He made me see that life was a tandem bike, and I noticed that God was in the back seat helping me pedal. Man, this was great! I could control the bike, but He gave me the power to really move! One day we got to travelling so fast that I lost control and we crashed into a tree. That was when He suggested that we change places. The race has never been the same since. With God providing the power and the steering, the race of life is very exciting! When I had the controls, I knew the course I would take. The race was sort of boring and predictable. I always took what seemed to be the shortest distance to the finish line. But, when God took the handle bars, He knew exciting long cuts, up over the mountains and down into deep valleys. I would never have ventured in these paths, let alone at breakneck speeds! Sometimes it was all I could do to hang on. Even though God provided all the power needed, He still said that I should pedal. I became worried and anxious and asked, 'Where are you taking me?' He laughed and didn't answer. I had no choice but to trust because you can't get off a moving bike. Very soon, I forgot my boring life apart from the tandem bike. Even when I was scared there was a thrill about this ride and I was calmed when He reached back to touch my hand. God took us racing through our homeland where people I had never met before gave us gifts for our way. What great joy to have them share a cool drink when we paused to rest. Then we were off again. He said, 'Give the gifts away because they weigh too much and will slow us down.' So I did, and as we travelled through foreign lands we taught and fed hungry children. For some reason, each time we gave away a heavy parcel, we received back more than we gave, but the burden on our bike still grew lighter and lighter. I did not trust Him at first because I was sure that if He controlled the bike, He would wreck it. But, you know, I found that He not only provided power and direction for the journey, He also provided special ability to race, because He built the bike. He knew exactly how much to lean into a curve and how to jump over high rocks. At times, He made the bike just fly. And I am learning to just trust and pedal through the strangest places. I am beginning to enjoy the view, the cool breeze on my face, and my delightful constant companion. It's like I love my companion more than I do the bike or the race. And on those days when I think that I cannot keep riding any more, He just smiles and says ... 'Just trust me and pedal!'[6]

The seduction of pragmatic methodology as the panacea for church sickness lies in its invitation to Christian leaders to get wrapped up in the bike or the race rather than their 'delightful constant companion'. The parable speaks to us of perseverance and trust in the context of a long-distance race. When the going gets tough, we are all tempted in different ways to turn to sources other than the Lord for help. The short-cut is favoured at the expense of the long-haul; instant answers and exciting possibilities are understandably attractive to those dispirited by church decline and weary of ministry. There are times when pastors doubt the Lord's ability to accomplish his will in their churches, in the nation, even in the world. At times, the Israelites were tempted to seek outside help from the Egyptians, as Isaac did when there was famine in the land (Gen. 26:1–3). The prophet Isaiah warns God's people against a foolish alliance with Egypt, urging them instead to remain true to 'the Holy One of Israel' in the face of the Assyrian threat (Is. 31:1–3).

When some denominations and church hierarchies seem to have lost their moral and spiritual centre, vulnerable to the forces of immorality, idolatry and apathy; when the Christian community is challenged by the rapid increase in alternative faiths and spiritualities; when the people of God pray and little seems to happen ... then the temptation is to lament with Jeremiah, who complained to God: 'Will you be to me like a deceptive brook, like a spring that fails?' (Jer. 15:18). Jeremiah was a prophet who struggled with opposition, unbelief, and confusion. He was a man caught in an almost unbearable tension between, on the one hand, deep anguish and despair over Israel's imminent captivity, and on the other hand, a firm conviction that God would one day restore his people. He was a tragic figure at times, subjected to misunderstanding and persecution. He was beaten, imprisoned, thrown into a cistern, and endured suffering as a true servant of God. Called to proclaim the Lord's judgment against the recognized prophets and priests of the land, Jeremiah did not shrink back. By his willingness to step out of line, to appear foolish for the Lord's sake, and to stand up to ridicule, contempt and rejection, Jeremiah is seen to be not a man of the world, but a man of God. But, vulnerable and torn, he had sunk into self-pity, even self-righteousness (see

Jer. 15:15–18) and ended up questioning God, accusing him of unfaithfulness.

The Christian community, discouraged and wearied by failure, may not speak to God as openly as Jeremiah did (perhaps honesty would be a liberating virtue!), but actions usually speak louder than words. Like Israel of old, the church has at times forsaken the Lord's ways, and relied upon the world's way of conducting its business in order to move forward, to make progress, to achieve success. Earlier on, God had spoken through his prophet, charging his people with two sins: 'They have forsaken me, the spring of living water, and have dug their own cisterns, broken cisterns that cannot hold water' (Jer. 2:13). Today, the worthless cisterns of a 'what-works' theology have been embraced too readily by a church which has been beguiled by the pragmatic 'how' rather than the prophetic 'who'.

The distinction between *relying* on what the world has to offer and *'plundering'* from the world's inventory is a crucial one. Shortly, I will be examining how the church can draw fruitfully from what the world has to offer in the conduct of its business – or, rather, God's business! – but such 'plundering' is radically different from being seduced by the promises of success offered by the prophets of pragmatism. The ultimate idolatry is the espousal of a managerial approach to pastoral ministry which supplants the call to participate in the ministry of Christ in the power of the Spirit. Jeremiah heard the word of the Lord in the midst of his despair and self-pity; tempted to turn to a stream the source of which was in the world, he was summoned to repent and stand fast as God's spokesman. Called as a prophet to proclaim only that which came from God, his task was to sift 'the valuable from the worthless, thereby removing the dross of idolatry and apostasy'.[7] I do not want to suggest that all that derives from pragmatic management methodology is worthless: as we shall see later on, sound business and administrative procedures can be of great benefit in the practice of pastoral ministry. There are some pastors, however, who succumb to the temptation to cling to what appear to be failsafe formulae for transforming church life; they need to heed the same word from the Lord as he gave to Jeremiah: 'If you repent, I will restore you that you may serve me' (Jer. 15:19).

The Old Testament prophetic literature not only warns us of the dangers of relying on the ways and words of the world, but also points us firmly in the right direction: 'Enlarge the place of your tent, stretch your tent curtains wide, do not hold back; lengthen your cords, strengthen your stakes' (Is. 54:2). Rejoicing over the future prosperity of Jerusalem, the prophet Isaiah encourages growth and expansion – 'do not hold back'. But this is accompanied by the command to 'strengthen your stakes'. The larger the tent, the deeper and stronger must be the stakes to which the cords are attached: increased size requires a firmer rootedness in the soil.

This metaphor is suggestive for all who seek church growth: our rootedness in God, in the Christ of the gospel, is essential if we are to move forward and outward into the world. Expressed in the form of a paradox, we need to be still in order to move forwards. Eager to lengthen our cords, we may fail to stake them more firmly in the ground of the gospel, in the ground of God's grace; somebody shows us a brand new technique for stretching our tent curtains more widely, and we may respond by forgetting the one whose tent it is, and focus on the mechanics of getting the tent up. When the winds of change blow, and the tent begins to flap around wildly, we may find ourselves struggling to hold on to the tent cords – in desperation, we reach out for whatever looks attractive, for whatever seems to work for others.

In the midst of these circumstances, those who are engaged in pastoral ministry need to re-focus on the one who is the source of all ministry, Christ himself. For Jeremiah, repentance led to restoration and a new reality in his calling as a prophet operating in the power of the Spirit. So it is for all in the ministry of the church. When we look within ourselves for answers, or turn to the world for solutions to church decline or ill-health, then we are in danger of losing our centre in Christ, who is the Lord of his church. As the parable of the tandem bicycle reminds us, our focus needs to be less on the race and the bike and increasingly on our 'delightful, constant companion'. Once that has been understood, the task of 'plundering the Egyptians' can be explored. It is the old, old story of Mary and Martha ... but a story that needs to be heard again and again in the midst of the clamour and clatter of the pots and pans.

The management of ministry

In his book *When the Gods are Silent* the Dutch pastor and theologian Kornelis Miskotte questions the innovative methods and techniques adopted by those who would proclaim the gospel, and chastises those who, pagans by nature, 'look for the reality of God in that which is the first and ultimate ground of experience, in the world, in the unshakable durability of things, the inexhaustible coherence of cosmic forces'.[8] So, he argues, the witness of the church must fit into 'what looks like the far narrower framework of the relationship between YHWH and his people'. Miskotte's complaint is echoed by Bill Hull, director of church ministries for the Evangelical Free Church of America, who voices the concern of many today who claim that methodology is burying the gospel message in obscurity, with the result that 'the principles of modern business are revered more than doctrine.'[9]

What Miskotte and Hull, amongst others, are concerned about is the increasing emphasis being placed upon methodologies more appropriate to the business world than to the community of faith in its privileged task of proclaiming the gospel in the world. Some have gone so far as to suggest that if the context and content of Christian ministry is Christ, then all pragmatism is necessarily excluded. In his valuable contribution to the debate, Anderson challenges the dualism implicit in such a view: 'The spiritual task of managing Christian organizations is first of all a task of managing an organization with full responsibility for its participation in the created structure of this world as God intended it.'[10] This firmly anchors Christian activity, and therefore church management, in the purpose and will of God, who ever seeks to reconcile his creation to himself in and through Christ. The church is called into being as God's chosen instrument to bring about his purpose and promise in the world. Any planning undertaken by the church must therefore be within a theological rather than a secular perspective. In Chapter One, we noted Anderson's conviction that, theologically, the future 'is both a purpose and a promise that has come to the present, rather than being extrapolated out of the present'.[11] This important distinction has a great deal to do with the present debate about the absorption of management techniques in order to accomplish the mission of the church.

Extrapolation of 'where are we now?' to 'where do we want to go?' involves much pragmatic planning: analysing past data, projecting trends based on statistical analyses and surveys, setting appropriate targets, and organizing resources in an efficient and careful way in order to meet the objective of x per cent growth in y years' time. Such is the stuff of management, and convincing and heady stuff it is at times: nor is it all wrong. Its appeal is that you can get to grips with it; it is all about efficiency and good stewardship, and it has the distinct advantage of being based on working models that offer hope. The theology of 'what works' can offer the stagnant church the possibility of digging itself out of the mud and continuing its journey along new and exciting paths. But is that what God's church is called to do? Is the Christian community summoned to grasp hold of all the good things that the world has to offer by way of management efficiency, utilizing the tools and techniques of the business world as it tries to find its feet in the twenty-first century?

Some will argue that they are seeking to be more efficient in Christian ministry. Is it not possible, however, that somewhere along the way *God*'s purposes may be bypassed in an enthusiasm to succeed and get results? In our discussion of the nature of ministry in Chapter One, we highlighted Anderson's distinction between *futurum*, which has its source in the present reality of the ministry of the church, and *adventus*, which originates in the future will and purpose of God. He illustrates the two concepts in the following diagram:[12]

PAST — PRESENT — *METHOD* → FUTURUM (future)

extrapolation

prognosis

planning/projection

PAST — PRESENT — *PREPARATION* → ADVENTUS (future)

anticipation

imagination

reflection/planning

The *futurum* framework of perceiving ministry is necessarily limited in its potential because it offers a future determined by acts in the present to bring it about. *Adventus*, however, offers a far more exciting and imaginative approach to ministry, because, by definition, it hinges upon preparation for that which derives from God's future. It focuses on an understanding of ministry which places God not so much at the centre but at the very beginning. As the diagram indicates, preparation replaces method as the context within which God's will is discerned and ultimately implemented. Anderson is rightly concerned to emphasize that planning models are not wrong or inappropriate *per se* in the practice of Christian ministry: they have their place in mobilizing the community of faith in its witness in and to the world. What concerns him most is the very real danger of losing sight of God's promise in the midst of the welter of methodology associated with the extrapolation method.

All this suggests that the minister as 'manager' needs to shift out of a linear, even bureaucratic, type of thinking in order to enter into the new things that God is always doing in the church and in the world. Some Christians disapprove of the notion of 'seeking a vision' for ministry on the grounds of its pragmatic connotations, but this is far too limited a perspective. Vision in itself is not wrong – it is only wrong if it is rooted in secular methodology isolated from the initiatives of the Spirit. Barna defines vision for ministry as 'a clear mental image of a preferable future imparted by God to His chosen servants'.[13] All that we have discussed so far is encapsulated in this definition, and the key phrase is 'imparted by God'. To have a vision for ministry is to be envisioned by God for *his ministry*. This, of course, has to do with the practice of discernment: those who are gifted by God for leadership within the church have the responsibility of seeking God's will and vision for their particular area of ministry within God's kingdom.

During my time as a lay pastor and evangelist in an Anglican church in England in the 1970s, we were privileged to participate in a liberating and transforming move of the Spirit within both the life of the faith-community and, extending outwards, within the community of the unchurched. One particular feature of this move of God was a monthly renewal meeting, which attracted Christians from many different parts of the north of England. The church building was packed, with the chancel area over-flowing, as people squeezed in to experience, for some, a fresh touch from God, and for others, gifted speakers opening up the truth of God's word. God was gracious in pouring out his Spirit in new and surprising ways amongst us, and many pastors who came to those meetings burdened and weary left with a renewed sense of calling and a new joy in their hearts.

From time to time those of us who were on the full-time staff of the church gathered to pray, seeking God's leading as we served the wider Christian community through these renewal meetings. It was evident that many people were being blessed through these meetings, and this fruit suggested to us that we were flowing in the will of God. On one occasion, however, I received a very clear 'picture' in my mind as we were together in prayer. A circle of people with their hands joined and facing inwards were standing on a large hand, opened palm up. A second hand descended over them, rather like a lid, covering the group for what seemed like a very long time. Then the second hand was lifted up, revealing the same group of people, still standing in a circle with their hands joined, but this time facing outwards. At the same time I received what seemed to be a very clear word from God that it was now time to stop holding these renewal meetings, however successful they appeared to be from a human perspective, for they were standing in the way of all that God wanted to do amongst us at that particular time. Later, we came to understand that the monthly meetings were distracting us as a church community from engaging in authentic incarnational witness within the local neighbourhood.

God graciously revealed *his* vision to us through charismatic insight, and we were guided into his purposes for us. Rather than continuing to participate in what, by all accounts, was a highly successful ministry, especially to pastors seeking refreshment and restoration, God re-directed us along a path that reflected his ministry amongst us. We discovered the joy of participating in all that he was doing amongst us, as increasingly we witnessed the remarkable workings of his Spirit in the immediate vicinity. Central to God's revelation of his will for us was our desire to acknowledge God as the holy one in our midst. We were beginning to learn the power of *adventus* over *futurum*.

In the Old Testament account of the fall of Jericho the Israelite leader Joshua faced a problem which was similar to that which confronts many in pastoral ministry today: how to penetrate the opposition and overcome! We are reminded that the mission of the church is to engage with the world, not to retreat into a ghetto-experience of 'us-and-our-God'. Prior to receiving instructions from the Lord, Joshua was apprehended by a vision from one who described himself as 'commander of the Lord's army'. Falling down to the ground in reverence, he asked him: 'What message does my Lord have for his servant?' (Josh. 5:14). The priority of 'who' and 'what' over 'how' is clear in this encounter between Joshua and God in human form. Joshua needed to learn at an early stage in his ministry the importance of responding to God's initiatives as the nation established its foothold in Canaan; central to this theophany was Joshua's acknowledgment of the holiness of the Lord.

Isaiah's commission in the eighth century BC as a prophet of the Lord is characterized by similar features. The nation of Israel had descended into an unholy mixture of idolatry, immorality, and injustice; into this furnace of apostasy God revealed himself to Isaiah through one of the most powerful visionary experiences recorded in the Bible (Is. 6). All heaven was opened up to Isaiah, as he saw the Lord in the throne-room of heaven, his own uncleanness contrasting with the utter majesty of Yahweh, surrounded in glory. Isaiah was overwhelmed by a vision of the holiness of the Lord as a prelude to his ministry as the 'evangelical prophet' to God's people.

The significance of these two Old Testament encounters between the Lord and his chosen servants should not be lost on those who are privileged to serve in pastoral ministry today. Whilst vision, at the strategic level, may be defined in terms of an understanding of God's will for a particular group of people at a particular time, it is far more important to be grasped by the holiness of God himself. It is this interpretation of vision which I want to highlight here. Authentic Christian ministry derives from an awareness of the glory of God: 'My eyes have seen the King, the Lord Almighty' (Is. 6:5). Neither Joshua nor Isaiah were permitted to move forward without a vision of the character and purpose of God, experiences which doubtless shaped the course of their respective ministries.

In contemporary church life the line between leadership and management can get blurred, and we should try to be more precise. Someone once distinguished between the two with reference to a group of people hacking their way through a jungle. Those directing operations on the ground, co-ordinating the effort to make progress and choosing how best to cut through the thick foliage, are the managers. Then someone shins up a tree, scouts around, surveying the wider scene, and suddenly cries out, 'Wrong jungle!' This person is the leader, the one who provides overall vision and purpose. So we may distinguish between visionary leader and pastoral practitioner. The specific ministry context will determine how these responsibilities are divided within the faith community. A large, thriving church may be able to sustain a leadership group which is free to distance itself from the nitty-gritty of pastoral ministry, able to concentrate on prayer and waiting upon the Lord (so the election of the seven men in Acts 6). However, in many congregational settings those in pastoral ministry may find themselves not only 'in the waiting room of heaven' but also at the sharp end of 'getting the job done'. Of necessity, they may be both leader and manager, both visionary and pastoral practitioner.

I do not want to suggest here that management is necessarily the task of a single person, and elsewhere we have acknowledged the richness of community life within the church. Schaller examines alternative approaches to management, challenging the view that people should be free to be themselves without the imposition of a system of management. He identifies three inadequate models of congregational management: doing it unilaterally, abdicating responsibility, and ignoring it and functioning as one large group – the 'happy family' model! His fourth alternative is one that he suggests is open to the pastor of nearly every congregation, which is to 'see the management of the group life of that congregation as a means to an end rather than as an end in itself, to work with the members in identifying the values and goals that congregation is seeking to promote and achieve, to facilitate setting priorities among those values and goals, and to develop a broad consensus for that system of values, goals, and priorities.'[14]

However, acceptance of the idea of management in Christian ministry begs the question: is there such a thing as a distinctly *Christian* philosophy of management? Ed Dayton, an advocate of management approaches in ministry, argues that such a concept reflects an attempt to divide the sacred from the secular: for him, they refuse to be divided. An extended quote presents his case clearly:

Now, there no doubt are men in management positions (both secular and Christian) who are operating in very unchristian ways. They are using their position to manipulate for personal gain; they are conducting their business in ways that violate accepted ethics or perhaps even the laws of the land. They may be dealing with other human beings in very unloving ways. But as I read most current management theory, it seems very Christian indeed! There is an increasing awareness that helping an individual grow as a person within the context of the organization's goal is good for the organization and

good for the individual. Like good bus driving, the *rules* of a well-
played game are reasonably obvious. The failure is not in the philosophy, or lack thereof, but in the practice. Again, we are reminded
that it is not things that are sinful, but men![15]

What is more important, then, is to adopt a Christian view of *life*
and carry that into our ministry, whatever that may be. This
argues for a Christian philosophy of management which is based
more on biblical principles of ethical behaviour and concern for
others than specific techniques or models. This observation leads
us into a further characteristic feature of a Christian approach to
church management, which has to do with caring for people.

The 'people factor' in leadership

Most management textbooks and consultants define management as an activity which seeks to 'get things done through
others'. Peter Drucker, author of arguably one of the most defini-
tive books on management, *The Practice of Management*, which
was first published in the 1950s, interprets management as 'the
organ of society specifically charged with making resources productive, that is, with the responsibility for organized economic
advance'.[16] This approach, suggests Drucker, reflects the basic
spirit of the age, an age of economic rationalism which remains
true to this day. A careful examination of his definition highlights management's role in terms of productivity rather than
people: people are essentially tools to accomplish organizational
objectives.

An alternative perspective is summed up in the statement that
management is 'meeting the needs of people as they work at
accomplishing their jobs',[17] a view which has been embraced not
only within the Christian community but also, increasingly, by
secular management theorists. Dennis Slape, a Christian leader
for whom I have great respect, once said, 'I have discovered that
if you train a man, he will become what you are; but if you serve
him, the sky is the limit as to what he will become.' In Chapter

One, we looked briefly at Paul and Barnabas, suggesting that the two present us with a contrasting study in ministry-types. Paul is the 'task-person', motivated by missionary zeal; Barnabas is revealed more as a 'people-person' whose primary concern was the welfare of others. Recognizing the inevitable tension between these two purposes within the pastoral ministry of the church, we are on reasonably safe ground in affirming that 'the glue that holds any organization together is loving communication and the communication of love.'[18]

Immediately after the death of Solomon, his son Rehoboam succeeded him as king. The Old Testament records Rehoboam's rejection of the advice of the elders who had served his father before him. Their counsel is worth noting: 'If today you will be a servant to these people and serve them and give them a favourable answer, they will always be your servants' (1 Kgs. 12:7). As a Christian leader serves others, he or she will discover that those people will remain loyal and serve in return. Our earlier discussion of servanthood as a primary characteristic of ministry is reinforced here: sadly, however, the problem with many Christian organizations is not with the principle but with the practice: 'we must take seriously our calling to be a fellowship of mutuality. Mutuality arises from the sense that we share a fundamental oneness with each other as those who are bound together by common values and a common mission.'[19]

In order to bridge the gap between principle and practice, Rush offers a number of helpful suggestions for those interested in applying a biblical philosophy of management in their own ministry situation: create a trust relationship between you and your group; give decision-making power to all individuals within the group; turn failures and mistakes into positive learning experiences for the group; constantly give proper recognition to the group and its individuals for accomplishment.[20] This reflects good management theory, and expresses the distinction between 'Theory X' and 'Theory Y' made famous by Douglas McGregor in 1960.[21] Theory X describes an approach to human motivation based on direction and control – the 'carrot-and-stick' model. Implicit in this interpretation of human behaviour is the premise that most people dislike work and will avoid it if they can; therefore, coercion and a system of reward and punishment are necessary in order to achieve organizational objectives. This approach is advocated as an appropriate strategy in the light of the perceived majority preference for security rather than personal enterprise.

However, argues McGregor, the principle of direction and control is unable to provide human beings with the deeper satisfactions which are necessary if organizations are to be maximally effective. He proposes an alternative approach, which he labels Theory Y: 'The central principle which derives from Theory Y is that of integration: the creation of conditions such that the members of the organization can achieve their own goals *best* by directing their efforts toward the success of the enterprise.'[22] The Theory Y approach to the management of human resources is based on a number of key assumptions: people do not inherently dislike work – work, in fact, is as natural as play or rest; the capacities of individual self-control, commitment and responsibility are strong motivational traits in human behaviour; and creativity and ingenuity are widely distributed among people and not confined to a select few. The symbiotic nature of Theory Y is such that both the organization and each individual member gain by working co-operatively in the pursuit of mutually beneficial objectives.

A recent example from the business world powerfully illustrates the principles of Theory Y. A Brazilian entrepreneur named Ricardo Semler joined his family's ailing engineering business, Semco, at the age of eighteen when it was on the verge of bankruptcy. He challenged the traditional corporate notion that when workers bring their bodies to the factory they leave their minds at the door. He decided that the company's major strength was its people, and his innovative management style turned the company into one of the fastest-growing organizations in the country. Semler's management philosophy is based on the principle of trust. In his book *Maverick*, which outlines his radical proposals for corporate efficiency,[23] he argues that nothing is as revolutionary as common sense! Adults should be treated as adults, not adolescents, and offered the opportunity to exercise control within their work environment.

Early on in his management career Semler noticed that workers at the company were not being consulted, and he realized that there must be a better way to motivate them. Gradually his business philosophy took shape under the guiding thesis that the goal of any organization is ultimately to do something worthwhile: profits should be regarded as a survival mechanism which serves this ultimate goal. Through a process of experimentation, key operating principles were introduced which transformed not only Semco but other companies willing to take the same radical risks. These included recycling the leadership team on a rotating basis; freeing the staff to set their own salaries and to hire and fire their own bosses; encouraging all employees to audit the company's books; developing a generous employee profit-sharing scheme; passing control back to the workforce; and promoting the concept of teamwork amongst the employees. Initially, the system was abused by a few, but the overwhelming majority respected the freedom given to them and responded by working with greater commitment and loyalty.

Semler's primary focus is on people and what is important to them: human beings are not numbers in a big corporate machine. This view also challenges the traditional emphasis on the benefits of economies of scale: small units may actually be more productive than large-scale operations because of the increase in morale and the value of people working together in smaller units. Commenting on the renowned Hawthorne experiments conducted by the industrial sociologist Elton Mayo in the 1940s, which studied the relationship between teamwork, morale, and productivity, Sayles and Strauss conclude that employees 'want more than just to have friends, they want to *belong ... [T]he shared experiences of one's immediate colleagues are among the most meaningful and potent sources of job satisfaction.*'[24]

It is an interesting exercise to translate Ricardo Semler's management philosophy into the context of the Christian faith community. At the most general level, the relational emphasis implicit in his style of management is one that has been recognized in many studies of church growth and mission effectiveness. For example, Callahan identifies twelve factors characteristic of healthy churches, concluding that the most effective churches are those that have concentrated more on his six relational factors than on the other functional or physical factors.[25] The notion of leadership rotation in pastoral ministry is intriguing, and would certainly keep the leadership on its toes; however, it is debatable whether the Spirit's anointing for leadership would necessarily correspond to a strict rotational cycle! What works within a secular context may not be appropriate for spiritual ministry. The role of church members in leadership appointment, an expression of the congregational form of church government, does at least give serious consideration to the priesthood of all believers, and apportions authority to the gathered community of faith. Care, of course, would be needed to preserve the authority of the Spirit within a community context in order to protect the congregation from any drift towards human control amongst any of its members.

Perhaps the areas which offer greatest reward for study and implementation in local church life are the principles of trust, teamwork and organizational size. Trust is an indispensable quality in people management, and is a hallmark of good leadership. We might also agree with Bonhoeffer that it is safer to speak about 'leadership' as a particular gifting than to focus on the concept of the 'leader', thus emphasizing the quality rather than the role: '... the focus of leadership is the person being led, the line of vision goes from above downwards, while the focus of the Leader is the Leader himself and the line of vision goes from below upwards.'[26] Bonhoeffer was deeply troubled by Hitler's assumption of dictatorial control, and his uneasiness is one which Christians should rightly share when faced with similar claims to authoritarian leadership within the community of faith. Fear rather than trust characterizes the group over which such control is exercised.

When Jesus began his ministry in Palestine, he developed a trust relationship with his disciples, sending them out in his name and commissioning them to go out into all the world to preach the gospel and heal the sick. He realized that they were far from perfect, and willingly risked their failure in the interests of discipling them. In our own dealings with others, we do well to remember that God is not a perfectionist ... rather, he is a perfecter, ever seeking to encourage all people into effective service within the life of the church. Similarly, wise pastoral leadership entrusts Christ's ministry to the whole people of God. Jesus was free in himself to delegate because he was secure in his own relationship with his Father: he did not need to prove himself. Some Christian leaders are unable genuinely to trust others because of their own deep insecurities, and so they become suspicious of those who seek ministry opportunities within the church. Some would prefer to remain with the *status quo*, obstructing forward movement and needed change, rather than take risks with people, even to the point of encouraging them to make mistakes! As a young Christian seeking to grow in my experience of ministry, I was richly encouraged by my pastor to spread my wings, even if it meant getting it wrong at times: I remain grateful to this day for the rich ministry learning environment he fostered within the church.

Teamwork lies at the very heart of Christian ministry. Paul's teaching about the nature of the body of Christ highlights the essential unity of the community of faith: 'The body is a unit, though it is made up of many parts; and though all its parts are many, they form one body' (1 Cor. 12:12). We should not confuse the concept of teamwork with the notion of 'every-member-ministry'. Without fail we should affirm that every Christian has something to contribute to the life and ministry of the church: teamwork, however, relates to the way in which the diverse gifts of the body are offered and received. It speaks to us of attitude rather than action. In his letter to the Philippian Christians, Paul compares relationships within the church with the Trinitarian life of God, encouraging Christians to be 'like-minded, having the same love, being one in spirit and purpose. Do nothing out of selfish ambition or vain conceit, but in humility consider others better than yourselves' (Phil. 2:2–3).

Our discussion in Chapter One of the participation of the community of the Trinity in the economy of salvation emphasized the essential interdependence of Father, Son, and Spirit in the ministry of God in the world, providing the church with a model of team ministry in the world.

The issue of size has a lot to do with the feasibility of teamwork at a practical level. The 'small is beautiful' philosophy with regard to congregational size corresponds to Semler's invitation to think small in the context of economic productivity. In Chapter Two we affirmed the value of *ecclesiolae*, or 'micro-churches', within the Christian community, and suggested that they may contribute to greater spiritual productivity in terms of more spontaneous participation and more effective social action. At times church growth literature has encouraged those in pastoral ministry to 'think big', as if size were the authentic measure of spiritual success. While we must be careful that we do not despise those who promote this interpretation of church growth, we should offer equal encouragement to those who seek to minister within the 'small is beautiful' framework. Both trust and teamwork are more easily maintained within a smaller local assembly, though sadly neither is exempt from the abuse of leadership. I have personally visited and ministered in a very wide range of small congregations and found many of them to be vital communities of faith, often making an impact in unspectacular though significant ways in the wider community.

Stephen Clark, one-time co-ordinator of the Catholic charismatic Word of God Christian Community in Ann Arbor, Michigan, argues that 'the main goal of the pastoral efforts in the Church today is to build communities that make it possible for a person to live a Christian life.'[27] Lest this be interpreted as advocacy of ghetto Christian communities, we need to recognize Clark's further concern that Christ be re-centred in the church, so building up his body in the world by means of such communities. He proposes a form of diaspora Christianity, offering an authentic Christian environment of sufficient strength to make it possible for people to live as vital Christians. Clark's emphasis is therefore on community formation rather than programmes or activities, but community *for* the world rather than just community *in* the world.

The contribution of Athens to Jerusalem

As we draw together some of the strands in our discussion so far, we are reminded of Tertullian's question, 'What has Athens to do with Jerusalem?' Specifically in our present context, what has the secular world to do with the sacred? What have management techniques and philosophies to do with the ministry of the gospel? Under what circumstances, if any, is it possible to reconcile our participation in the ministry of Christ with participation in the pragmatic approaches of secular business management? We have already acknowledged some helpful points of contact, and we need to develop these more fully later. However, the primary emphasis in this chapter has been on the two themes of vision and community. I have suggested that all who are involved in pastoral ministry should understand that they are participating in what God is doing. By faith, by revelation, they discern that which God has purposed to accomplish in Christ, and seek the wisdom of the Spirit in interpreting his future as that which comes into the present. To this we have added the dimension of building community. Throughout this book we have emphasized God's concern for people, a passion which necessarily underscores all understanding of ministry management.

But we cannot ignore the 'how' questions posed by those committed to pastoral ministry, for at the end of the day vision has to be translated into reality. Accordingly, we acknowledge that there *are* approaches and methodologies which have value within a Christian world-view: a management planning model, for example, may be a particularly useful framework for efficient utilization of available resources in order to accomplish desired church goals. Pragmatism is not to be thrown out of the window because it is capable of being corrupted: God calls his people to wise and efficient stewardship of resources. It is legitimate to 'plunder the Egyptians'. Therefore we appreciate the insights of management theorists and practitioners, but check always that they have been refined through the crucible of the cross. Critically, we also ask: do these methodologies serve the purposes of God in bringing into being the new creation he has already promised?

Immediately before writing these words I heard of the decision of a major car manufacturer to dispense with several hundred factory workers in order to satisfy shareholder demands for higher returns. The manufacturing plant is located in an area of Australia which is struggling economically. Management frequently suggests that those retrenched are free to seek employment elsewhere in the employment market, and insists that the company is bound by the dictates of its shareholder constituency. Sound arguments may be put forward that the government of the day is ultimately responsible for creating the right environment for jobs and economic growth, but the niggling question remains: is the company absolved from all blame or liability? May we not suggest that management is ultimately judged by the Christian truth of the cross? It is challenged and judged by God's ultimate purpose to build community and heal social brokenness.

Other examples may be cited. The marketing of breast-milk substitutes in contravention of a World Health Organisation international code of practice is a case in point. The reported worldwide increase in infectious diseases and malnutrition in babies has been attributed in part to the decline in breastfeeding fostered by aggressive marketing of breast-milk substitutes within the babyfood industry; the provision of free powdered baby milk in hospitals has been shown to create a dependency upon the product when mother and baby return home. Mothers are also encouraged to believe that it is the sophisticated western thing to do, and that their babies will be better served by substitute products. Companies engaging in such practices employ marketing approaches designed to maximize corporate revenue at the expense of social welfare concerns.

Environmentalists and animal-rights activists regularly protest against production and marketing practices within the 'fast food' industry. Oil spillages caused by aging pipelines have poisoned water sources in parts of Africa, and destroyed the agricultural viability of the regions affected. What is at issue here is not so much the unethical behaviour of specific companies, but the system that motivates them to value profits at the expense of wider social concerns. These and many other claims of unethical commercial behaviour give much business management a 'bad press'. However, we need to distinguish clearly between 'neutral', or value-free, paradigms which foster the efficient stewardship of resources, and the conduct of those who operate within those paradigms.

Whenever we import approaches from secular management into the community of faith, we need to ask two questions. Firstly, does the methodology serve the ultimate, eschatological, new creation purposes of God? More specifically, does it serve God's revelation of his will for us, in this place where we now live and have our being? Secondly, if so, and because the end does not justify the means, is the methodology in itself a legitimate expression of the goodness and righteousness of God? Thus we are to constantly evaluate methodology in the light of theology and God's ministry in the world. Pragmatic methodology drawn from business management is valid if, and only if, it passes through these two filters, rightly giving pre-eminence to 'who' and 'what' over questions of 'how'.

Nevertheless, the 'how' questions persist and need to be addressed. How can the minister of a local church 'plunder the Egyptians' in such a way as to benefit from all that is on offer? At one level, it is evident that administrative improvements are available through common sense application of efficient office procedures, wise introduction of computerized records, and the employment of appropriately qualified personnel. However, my concern here is with those less tangible benefits which flow from better organized personal lives (a theme which relates to personal spirituality in ministry, a topic to which we give more attention in the final chapter of this book). George Barna, one of the leading researchers in Christian ministry, discusses the importance of capturing a personal vision for one's life:

A pastor has been given a special privilege and a responsibility in leading a church. God entrusts His vision to the pastor to guide him in leading the congregation in its ministry and overall development.

In the same way, God expects each of us, whether we lead a church or not, to take command over our lives and use them to further His Kingdom ...

In much the same way that a pastor pursues the identity of God's vision for the ministry of the church, so should you, as an individual believer, seek to determine what is God's vision for your life and ministry.[28]

The biblical basis for Barna's statements is to be found in such passages as 1 Timothy 3:1–7, where Paul declares that the person who sets his heart on being an overseer/bishop/elder must be a person who manages himself and his own family well. Self-management, not only in personal conduct, but also as it relates to how we use our time, establish goals for our life, and set our priorities, is an important prerequisite for efficient church management. Linked to this idea is the concept of proactivity, a common term in current management literature. Proactivity means more than taking the initiative: it means that as human beings we are responsible for our lives. Our behaviour is actually the outcome of our *decisions*, not our *conditions*. We have the freedom to subordinate feelings to values, because God has created us with free will. Human beings are not dumb animals or puppets controlled either by circumstances or by divinely manipulated strings: freedom to choose is God's gift to humanity.

Christians need to take a leaf out of the world's book of life in this regard. It is not wrong, as some have suggested, to have a personal vision for one's life, or to set priorities. We are exhorted to seek *first* the kingdom of God (Mt. 6:33), not *only* his kingdom. We are free to play as much as we are free to pray. Paul Tournier has written a fine book called *The Adventure of Living* in which he challenges us to grasp hold of life as an adventure, to take risks.[29] In the immortal words of the English teacher Mr Keating in the film *Dead Poets' Society*, we are invited to 'seize the day!' (*'carpe diem!'*). Peter Drucker was once asked to address a major business conference in the United States and declined, though under great pressure to accept. His reason? He had set that time aside to reflect on his life's direction: at a personal level, he was going to engage in some 'corporate planning'.

The thesis of many management textbooks is that those who are most successful in managing their own lives are likely to be successful in managing at an organizational level. In fact, there are parallel processes in personal and organizational planning which are observable in the following diagram:

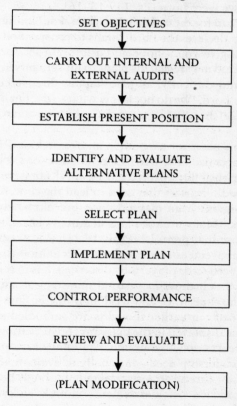

SET OBJECTIVES

CARRY OUT INTERNAL AND
EXTERNAL AUDITS

ESTABLISH PRESENT POSITION

IDENTIFY AND EVALUATE
ALTERNATIVE PLANS

SELECT PLAN

IMPLEMENT PLAN

CONTROL PERFORMANCE

REVIEW AND EVALUATE

(PLAN MODIFICATION)

In the final chapter we will consider how this planning paradigm can bring order and direction to our lives, though we will also be quick to acknowledge that adherence to a too-structured approach to organizing our time may turn our lives into businesses in the process! Models should always be used in moderation. The idea of planning is not foreign to God. God has a plan for his creation, a plan that is unfolding through history until the time comes when all things in heaven and on earth will be brought together under one head, who is Christ (Eph. 1:10). God has a purpose and plan for each of our lives; he ordained our days before we were born (Ps. 139:13–16).

He had a plan for the exiles in Babylon: 'For I know the plans I have for you,' declares the Lord, 'plans to prosper you and not to harm you, to give you a hope and a future' (Jer. 29:11). More specifically, God may reveal his plans to his servants in the face of opposition and difficulty, as Jehoshaphat discovered when he prayed to the Lord, 'We do not know what to do, but our eyes are upon you' (2 Chr. 20:12) ... and God's plan gave victory to the Israelites.

God has his plans for us, both in an overarching sense for our whole lives, and also to help us in specific situations. It is the privilege and responsibility of those in pastoral ministry to discern what is in God's heart as they seek to lead the church as his delegated 'managers'. Man may propose, but ultimately it is God who disposes: 'Many are the plans in a man's heart, but it is the Lord's purpose that prevails' (Prov. 19:21). As we noted earlier, Christian management starts with the recognition that God has plans which need to be prayerfully discerned. It is in the execution of these plans that those in pastoral ministry can most usefully draw from the experience and wisdom of the business world.

A number of our earlier thoughts are embodied in the planning sequence displayed in the diagram above. Setting objectives has a great deal to do with our understanding of *adventus*. Those in pastoral leadership need continually to evaluate their visionary manifestos, careful to resist the temptation to devise democratically produced vision statements: church leadership has to do with following the direction of the Spirit, rather than the preferences of the congregation. However, this does not mean that the Spirit bypasses the gathered community in making God's will known: 'The church requires listening leaders who will discern ... the dreams and visions on their hearts ... developing such a vision may involve dealing with difference, disagreement and conflict. Yet ... it is important for leadership to have a vision for the future which is owned and affirmed by attenders.'[30]

So God's vision needs to be communicated so that others are united in their ownership of and commitment to it. Communication, commitment and unity are three essential attributes in all forms of management organization and operation: 'The wisdom of reliable counsellors may offset your tendency to filter God's vision through your own lenses, and therefore bring you back to a more complete understanding of God's desires for you ... You and your church will be better off because you persevered and sought to clarify and expand the vision.'[31] In this way, each local faith-community will be involved in the development of its own life as an expression of God's will in that area. Vision cannot be transferred from one locality to another: it has to be discerned for each faith community.

Similarly, church growth methodologies – though they may suggest important principles which need contextualizing in specific community settings – are non-transferable precisely because God chooses to work in his way and in his time to accomplish his unique purposes in each locality. Church leaders differ in their capacity to embrace what the Spirit is doing; they vary in spirituality and competence. Furthermore, what works in one place simply may not apply to another situation. So wisdom and discernment are needed in the face of the burgeoning literature on church growth: there is no single blueprint from the Spirit offering an easy way to success and growth. Humility before the mysteries of God, a listening ear and a servant heart, and a willingness to suffer for the sake of the kingdom are more certain hallmarks of authentic pastoral ministry than a readiness to ship the leadership team to the latest church growth seminar – or the next 'feel-good' conference! We live in an age of instant results, demanding quick-fix solutions – but the Spirit of God will not bow before the demands of impatient humanity. He will direct us in helpful ways so that we may be wise and faithful stewards of the resources at our disposal, but his agenda will not normally permit him to indulge our misguided, even deliberate, efforts to short-cut his working in our lives.

Good management theory recommends the adoption of 'S-M-A-R-T' objectives – Specific, Measurable, Attainable, Realistic, and Time-related. Vaguely defined goals cannot generate clear plans: a goal to 'reach the area for Christ', commendable in itself, is hardly a 'SMART' vision! Clearly defined objectives present, for all involved in pastoral ministry, great opportunities for focused prayer, enabling a congregation to be specific in its understanding of and commitment to God's purposes. Such an approach also requires that a faith-community recognizes its own strengths and weaknesses in the light of God's vision for its future. As a result, the resources and changes needed to realize the fulfilment of that vision will be more readily discerned – this is the auditing step in the planning process.

Knowing what exactly is going on *within* the community of faith as well as *externally* within the ministry environment demands both honesty and perseverance. Business executives ruthlessly assess their internal resources of finance, human personnel and technology, and their external environment in the form of competitive threats and market opportunities. Likewise, there is value in wisely and carefully discerning congregational Strengths and Weaknesses and the Opportunities and Threats within the ministry environment, known as the 'S-W-O-T' approach.[32]

The next step in the planning process is to explore both prayerfully and pragmatically – for God is not against pragmatism, but ever seeks to protect or redeem it from ungodly influences – the various options available to fulfil God's vision in the light of the auditing process. Business executives are accustomed to distinguishing between strategy and tactics, a differentiation picked up in the church growth literature. Strategic planning is broad, whereas tactical planning addresses the details. For example, if a local congregation is convinced of a

God-given vision to engage more authentically with the elderly in the community, then it may explore a number of alternative strategies: the provision of a drop-in centre on the church premises; a visiting programme involving members of the congregation; special services geared to older folk; a special 'Alpha' initiative amongst the elderly; prayer-partnership programmes; ministry opportunities in homes for the elderly; the list is endless. These are the strategies which need to be brought before God in prayer as well as before the congregation with regard to practicality. It may appear to be entirely inappropriate to follow through some of the above options for sound, practical reasons; yet the possibility that the Spirit may lead the congregation into new strategies for ministry must never be discounted.

Once the specific strategy or strategies have been discerned, the particular details can be worked out in relation to congregational strengths and weaknesses. This is the 'nuts-and-bolts' part of planning, in which every faith-community finds itself involved at different times. Pursuing the planning sequence identified in this chapter, however, will offer opportunities for everyone to participate in God's vision for the church in its witness in and to the world. Congregational ownership of the vision, in all its myriad expressions, inevitably encourages the sort of commitment and unity which is sadly lacking in many churches today.

Perhaps enough has been presented in this chapter to indicate the feasibility of 'plundering the Egyptians' with regard to ministry management. At all times, however, we must not lose sight of the need for methodology to be subservient to the message: pragmatism must serve our theology of mission in the local community, rather than the other way round. A biblical theology of mission cannot dispense with incarnation, involvement, suffering and prayer as first-order prerequisites. John 3:16 must never be replaced as the theological foundation for mission. If the Christian community holds on to that as a priority, then pragmatism has its place. But if pragmatism is selected over theology, with the result that we lose sight of the privilege of participating in God's continuing mission in and for his world, then the faith-community is in danger of losing its distinctiveness as God's chosen instrument of witness to the kingdom of God in the world. 'You are the salt of the earth,' Jesus told his disciples. 'But if the salt loses its saltiness, how can it be made salty again? It is no longer good for anything, except to be thrown out and trampled by men' (Mt. 5:13).

Notes

1. Paul Enns, *The Moody Handbook of Theology* (Chicago: Moody Press, 1989), p. 334.
2. Kruger, *Home*, p. 26.
3. Calvin, *Institutes of the Christian Religion*, 2.2.16, pp. 236–7.
4. See, for example, Donald A. McGavran, *Understanding Church Growth*, rev. edn. (Grand Rapids: Eerdmans, 1980); C. Peter Wagner, *Your Church Can be Healthy* (Nashville: Abingdon, 1979).
5. Sakari Pinola, *Church Growth: Principles and Praxis of Donald A. McGavran's Missiology* (Abo: Abo Akademi University Press, 1995), p. 261.
6. From an unknown author, revised by Theron Messer.
7. R. K. Harrison, *Jeremiah and Lamentations: An Introduction and Commentary* (Leicester: IVP, 1973), p. 104.
8. Quoted in Anderson (ed.), *Theological Foundations for Ministry*, p. 649.
9. Bill Hull, 'Is the Church Growth Movement Really Working?' in Horton (ed.), *Power Religion*, p. 142.
10. Anderson, *Minding God's Business*, p. 23.
11. ibid, p. 48.
12. ibid, p. 50.
13. George Barna, *The Power of Vision* (Ventura: Regal Books, 1992), p. 28.
14 Lyle E. Schaller, *Effective Church Planning* (Nashville: Abingdon, 1979), p. 52.
15 Ted W. Engstrom and Edward R. Dayton, *The Art of Management for Christian Leaders* (Waco: Word, 1976), pp. 38–9.

16. Peter F. Drucker, *The Practice of Management* (London: Mercury Books, 1961).

17. Myron Rush, *Management: A Biblical Approach* (Wheaton: Victor Books, 1983), p. 13.

18. Dennis Slape, *As Eagles Rise: A Strategy for People Ministry* (Unley Park SA: The House of Tabor, 1984), p. 104.

19. Stanley J. Grenz, *Created for Community: Connecting Christian Belief with Christian Living* (Grand Rapids: Baker Books, 1998), p. 222.

20. Rush, *Management: A Biblical Approach*, pp. 32–47.

21. See Douglas McGregor, *The Human Side of Enterprise* (New York: McGraw-Hill Book Company, 1960).

22. ibid., p. 49.

23. Ricardo Semler, *Maverick* (Random House Australia: Melbourne, 1993).

24. Leonard R. Sayles and George Strauss, *Human Behaviour in Organizations* (Englewood Cliffs NJ: Prentice-Hall, 1960), p. 84.

25. See Kennon L. Callahan, *Twelve Keys to an Effective Church* (San Francisco: Harper & Row, 1983).

26. Quoted in Anderson, *Minding God's Business*, p. 64.

27. Stephen B. Clark, *Building Christian Communities* (Notre Dame: Ave Maria Press, 1972).

28. Barna, *The Power of Vision*, p. 152.

29. Paul Tournier, *The Adventure of Living* (London: SCM Press, 1960).

30. Peter Kaldor *et al*, *Winds of Change: The Experience of Church in a Changing Australia* (Homebush West NSW: Lancer, 1994), p. 41.

31. George Barna, *A Step-by-Step Guide to Church Marketing: Breaking Ground for the Harvest* (Ventura: Regal Books, 1992), p. 131.

32. For an application of 'SWOT' in church management, see David S. Luecke, *New Designs in Church Leadership* (St Louis: Concordia Publishing House, 1990), pp. 134–42.

Chapter Eight

Participating in the Dance of God in the World

... let us run with perseverance the race
marked out for us.
Hebrews 12:1

Augustine's phrase, *'noverim te, noverim me'* – 'may I know you, may I know myself' – sums up the essence of true spirituality. The crux of this insight is that spirituality is measured in terms of relationship rather than activity. This is not to embrace passivity, however, for the spiritual person is someone whose heart is caught up in God and therefore in his compassionate love for the world. Those in full-time Christian ministry are not usually torn between activity and passivity; more often, their difficulties arise from trying to cope with the many demands placed by others on their time. The truth is that many in pastoral ministry are called to counsel and help people who are driven to exhaustion, whilst they themselves are suffering from the same disease! The cry, 'Physician, heal yourself!' is rather too close for comfort, and cannot be shrugged off: one pastor's wife wept openly in front of a large gathering of Christians, complaining that she felt as if she had been 'raped by the church'. Pressure on her husband, violation of their privacy, and emotional exhaustion had taken their toll.

In this final chapter we address the vital issue of how to engage in incarnational ministry without being swallowed up in the process. The theme of this book is that participation in the ministry of Christ is a liberating privilege, releasing us from the pressures and burdens of 'doing things for God' in our own strength. The reality, however, is that the actual is often very far from the ideal in the ministry experience of many pastors. The word 'burnout' has been used over and over again to describe the condition in which many Christians find themselves as they seek to serve the Lord. So the question may be phrased as follows: how is it possible to burn brightly without burning out? During my student days at theological college an Anglican bishop informed us of a series of meetings he was leading in a few days time in a university city in the north of England. His topic had to do with the quality of the Christian life. 'But there's only one thing I have to say at the moment,' he observed wryly, 'I'm shattered!' So it is with many pastors; called to proclaim the richness and joy of life in Christ, they frequently discover a vast gap between the words they speak and the lives they are living. A quiet desperation begins to take over as they struggle to fulfil their vocation as ministers of the gospel. In vain they call on all their coping mechanisms, fervently praying for greater trust in the Christ who promises to give rest to all who are wearied and burdened (Mt. 11:28). In vain they remind God that 'those who hope in the Lord will renew their strength. They will soar on wings like eagles; they will run and not grow weary, they will walk and not be faint' (Is. 40:31).

Sadly some are overwhelmed to the point of throwing in the towel and seeking employment elsewhere. The 'call to ministry' has turned into a bitter pill in their mouths. Is there nothing to say to those who feel betrayed by those whom they sought to serve, betrayed even by God himself? I would like to offer a number of suggestions which, taken together, offer those in ministry not only the possibility of survival in ministry but the prospect of *revival*. The title of this chapter reflects this more positive hope: to be revived is to be given fresh life, and that is precisely what many are longing for. The areas we examine have to do with appreciating our essential humanness, which also involves connecting with others in community; welcoming the gift of spirituality; exercising self-management in life; and embracing the journey of life as a dance. As we look at each of these in turn we shall note areas of overlap between each one, and the twin themes of honesty and the need for self-examination will become apparent.

Hope in our humanness

Our humanity is a gift from God. In the early days of the Christian church, Gnostic influences led to a sharp distinction being made in some quarters between spirit and matter, with the result that the material creation, including human flesh, was regarded as evil, to be subordinated to the 'spirit' realm. Whilst some interpreted this teaching as a licence to indulge the flesh, most adherents pursued an ascetic line. Gnosticism's dualistic understanding of human life has unfortunately penetrated Christian thought to greater or lesser degrees throughout the history of the church. In the context of contemporary Christian ministry, it finds expression in the frenetic race to accomplish what we believe to be God's will, to the exclusion of all else, including our own health and well-being. So we 'hammer ourselves as we rush away from our basic humanness, as we try to evade genuine intimacy and tenderness, as we deny our finitude and mortality'.[1]

In Chapter Three, I quoted de Chardin's famous dictum that 'we are not human beings having a spiritual experience; we are spiritual beings having a human experience.' This must not be interpreted in such a way as to truncate our humanity in favour of the spiritual dimension: we must affirm that we are undoubtedly created *human*, formed from the dust of the ground as creaturely beings. To fail to look after ourselves as the summit of God's good creation results in a diminishment of our lives and, ultimately, in the denial of our potential as human beings. When we truly discover our humanity, when we realize afresh that God has made us with infinite tenderness and love and invites us into a journey of discovery with him – a discovery of our true selves as those who have been created in his image – we will rejoice once again in our humanity and seek to glorify our Creator *in our very humanness*.

Our true calling as Christians cannot be measured by displaying to others – let alone to God – how spiritual we are. Of all people, Christians are privileged to enjoy life as a gift: we are free to embrace every opportunity to experience the fullness of our humanity. Hans Küng was once asked why we should embrace Christianity. His reply was: 'So that we can be fully human.' He understood clearly that participation in the life of God offered people the opportunity to realize their potential humanness in all its richness and God-given glory. Peterson's insight into the twin blessings of play and prayer is particularly helpful to those who are caught up in what I described in Chapter One as 'the bondage of oughtage and mustery'! 'Prayerfulness and playfulness … are life-enhancing not life-diminishing. They infuse vitalities, counteracting fatigue. Playing and praying counter boredom, reduce anxieties, push, pull, direct, prod us into the fullness of our humanity by getting body and spirit in touch and friendly with each other.'[2] The snare of super-spirituality, in which we exalt prayer over play, has dogged the church for centuries. There is an amusing anecdote about a bishop who made a visit to a church known for its ultra-pietism. Sitting cross-legged on a table, he casually addressed the children: 'Tell me,' he asked them, leaning forward, 'what is grey, has a bushy tail, and eats nuts?' There was an uncomfortable silence, until one little boy put up his hand, and answered uncertainly: 'Please, sir, I know the answer should be Jesus, but it sounds like a squirrel to me!'

SQUIRREL or JESUS

The holistic conjunction of play and prayer leads us away from legalism and into liberty – indeed, the more we discover play as gift from God, the richer will be our praying. Christians in ministry suffer more than others from the pressure to perform, to 'get it right'. This is not a bad thing in itself: excellence in any calling is surely something to which all should aspire. However, when the mad chase becomes a way of life, so that we find ourselves living to work rather than working to live, then something has gone very seriously wrong with our lives. The sad truth is that many are blind to the disease that afflicts them. The Spirit of God comes to us in gentleness and urgency to open our eyes, not only to the truth about God and the world in which we live, but also to the truth about *ourselves*.

Too often those involved in Christian ministry endure lives that are characterized by a quiet desperation, a resigned commitment to snatch a few moments of enjoyment in their stressful, frustrated lives. If I may take exegetical licence with Paul's letter to the Romans: 'What a wretched man [or woman] I am! Who will rescue me from this body of death?' And the response must surely be Paul's: 'Thanks be to God – through Jesus Christ our Lord!' (Rom. 7:24–25). Only in Christ do we discover the difference between running the race that *he* has marked out for us, and running someone else's race (see Heb. 12:1). Just as the task – and privilege – of the community of faith is to discern that which is on God's heart for their ministry, so each of us is responsible individually for discerning and doing that which God has called us to do, no more and no less, so that our participation in ministry is grounded in God's revelation of his good and perfect will for our lives. Dancing to the tune of other Christians – or even to the tune we impose on ourselves! – is less exhilarating than dancing in the arena of God's grace: 'I hear the Spirit saying: let the party begin, let the banquet be set, let us enter into the play of new creation! The Spirit choreographs the dance of God and also directs the steps of creatures entering God's dance.'[3]

As we invite the Spirit to lead us into a new awareness of ourselves, we may find ourselves recoiling from being truly open to his searching gaze. Some may fear losing control, a common encumbrance to effective Christian ministry; others may struggle with the prospect of entering unknown territory as the Spirit brings to the surface that which has been hidden for many years. My former colleague John Court contrasts two models of ministry:

> ... the first is impelled forward by love, the second is pressed forward by fear. Fear of what would happen if ... Fear of what will people say ... Fear of stopping lest the lurking dangers should catch up. That kind of activity is like running away from a hungry tiger – the faster you run the harder it is to keep going, and ultimately you are devoured. The first kind of running is more like that of the athlete

who is not concerned about what lies behind but sees the finishing line ahead and is inspired to keep on going until the task is accomplished. The second kind gets no satisfaction in stopping because the fear catches up and leaves a hollow anxiety and guilt.[4]

Too many in pastoral ministry have bowed to the pressure of what has been demanded of them, incapable of facing the truth that deep down there may be an emptiness in their soul, a bankruptcy masked by busyness and activism. Gradually – and painfully at times – confronting and resisting these fears in my own life, I have discovered the true significance of what it means to be made in the image of God, to understand not only *who* I am, but *whose* I am (a theme which we explored in Chapter Two in our discussion of community life). The realization that I have been created for relationship with God has released me into a life which is the greatest joy and the greatest happiness – even though I face troubles and sorrows along the way.

When busyness and pressure threaten to overwhelm us, we need to take time out to reflect on our identity as those who have been created in the image of God. The biblical affirmation is that we are 'fearfully and wonderfully made' (Ps. 139:14), and the physical complexity of our bodies is testimony to that truth. I recall holding my first-born child in my arms shortly after his birth and, though not a Christian believer at the time, I breathed a silent thanksgiving to the God I did not yet know for this miracle of perfect life. Beyond our physical design, however, are the intangible realities of our meaning and value: 'Our lives are intelligible precisely because we can have faith that our existence is the result of the actions of an all-knowing, intelligent God. Our lives have meaning because God meant or intended us to be.'[5] Our value lies in the fact that God created us – we are his handiwork. God does not love us because we are valuable: rather, we are valuable because God loves us. There are people who collect paintings or antiques because of their value, perhaps as a status symbol or an investment; and they may quite legitimately enjoy the pleasure that such ownership affords. The danger lies in the temptation to love possessions because of their value, rather than to value them because we love and enjoy them.

But that is not God's way with us: his is the '*agapē* love that does not look for value in what it loves ... but ... creates value there'.[6] Pitt-Watson relates a personal story which illustrates this truth, describing how his exhausted and tearful three-year-old daughter, Rosemary, was handed a rag doll on the family's arrival in Melbourne after the long flight from London. Through the years Rosemary clung to that doll, and it became the most precious thing she possessed: 'In time the rag doll became more rag than doll and began to get a bit dirty. The sensible thing to do was to face the fact that the rag doll had never been worth much and was now no more than a bundle of dirty rags that ought to be trashed. But that was unthinkable for anyone who loved my child. If you loved Rosemary you had to love the rag doll. That was part of the package.'[7] Rosemary's love for her rag doll was not contingent upon any intrinsic value that it had. For the world-weary pastor caught on the treadmill of activism in order to please God, the story reminds us that we do not have to drive ourselves in order to satisfy God or be loved by him. We are loved because the God who is love chooses to love us. Our value does not depend upon what we achieve – a liberating truth for all in pastoral ministry.

But the relational dimension in *imago Dei* goes beyond the vertical, and propels us into vulnerable 'horizontal' community life. In Chapter Four, I recounted the incident of the visit of a missionary to the church in which I was involved at the time, who had come to speak to us one evening. Before he had the opportunity to do so, the Lord graciously ministered to him through the gathered, worshipping community. Here was a man who had come amongst us to serve us; he was lonely, exhausted and almost at breaking point. In a miraculous and gentle way, the Lord restored him through those to whom he had come to minister. He was blessed amongst us, and out of that blessing he blessed us. This sort of experience is a healthy reminder to us that our true humanity is found only in community. When we put a protective bubble around ourselves, cutting ourselves off from

[margin annotations: RAG DOLL; GOD'S LOVE EXEMPLIFIED]

others, our humanity is diminished. We can do this for many reasons: for example, past hurts and pains often lead to an unwillingness to expose ourselves to others in case we get hurt again; that is understandable, but it is not what God wants for our lives. He longs to heal us so that we are free to enter into rich relationships with each other. When we persevere with what I call the 'John Wayne' syndrome – 'I don't need anyone; I can stand on my own two feet!' – we are denying ourselves the very help we need to live a fulfilled human life. To try to 'go it alone' is to be less than human.

The pressure to perform, coupled with the demands and expectations of those around them, lead many in Christian pastoral ministry to experience the stress of loneliness and isolation. This can be avoided if all involved – pastor and congregation together – think of themselves as community before they think of themselves as individuals. In fact, if you amputate all the connections in life in order to try and discover your 'pure self', you might be horrified to find nothing left! At the human level, I can only know who I am in community – as I wrote in Chapter Two, I am a father, a husband, a neighbour, a work colleague, a brother in Christ: I am who I am in a web of intricate relationships. To be made in the image of God implies a willingness to live vulnerably, opening ourselves to one another, learning from each other, giving and receiving in a way that demonstrates that life in God's family is healing, refreshing, and wonderfully liberating.

The motif of adventure was introduced in Chapter Two, and we return to it here as a further expression of *imago Dei*. A few years ago I was challenged by a sign at a roadside church that declared: 'Some people never sing; they die with all their music still inside them.' To be made in God's image is to be enthused by the same spirit of adventure that animates him. God's music is the music of life, the music of adventure, the music of going on a journey full of anticipation and a sense of discovery. To be willing to take risks, to step out into the adventure of living, which is God's gift to us all, is to see life through new eyes. It is to put on 'the spectacles of the Spirit' and to discover that there is a whole new way of life available to us in God which has to do with enjoying our humanity and God's good gifts to us in his creation.

Ted Engstrom relates the following homily composed by an old monk called Brother Jeremiah, who, reflecting on his many years, concluded that he had taken life too seriously. This is what he wrote:

> If I had my life to live over again, I'd try to make more mistakes next time. I would relax. I would limber up. I would be sillier than I have been this trip. I know of very few things I would take seriously. I would take more trips. I would climb more mountains, swim more rivers, and watch more sunsets. I would do more walking and looking. I would eat more ice cream and less beans. I would have more actual troubles and less imaginary ones.
>
> You see, I am one of those people who live prophylactically and sensibly and sanely, hour after hour, day after day. Oh, I've had my moments, and if I had it to do over again, I'd have more of them. In fact, I'd try to have nothing else. Just moments, one after another, instead of living so many years ahead each day. I have been one of those people who never go anywhere without a thermometer, a hot water bottle, a gargle, a raincoat, aspirin, and a parachute. I would go places, do things, and travel lighter than I have.
>
> If I had my life to live over, I would start barefooted earlier in the spring and stay that way later in the fall. I would play more. I would ride on more merry-go-rounds. I'd pick more daisies.[8]

To be truly human is to take life less seriously than we often do. It is to sing the song that God has put into our lives, and not to drown it in the clamour of activities that will inevitably surround those who seek to serve others. The English mystic, Evelyn Underhill, writing at the beginning of the twentieth century, described many Christians as 'deaf people at a concert': 'they study the programme carefully, believe every statement in it, speak respectfully of the music, but really only hear a phrase now and again. So they have no notion at all of the mighty symphony which fills the universe, to which our lives are destined to make their tiny contribution, and which is the self-expression of the Eternal God.'[9]

Only the Spirit can make the music of God come alive in all its richness and splendour. As the Spirit draws us into the life of the Trinity, we enter into new possibilities for our lives. We discover that to be fully human is to rejoice in relational love; it is to be free to make more mistakes and take more risks in life! This understanding of life as participation in the community life of the Trinity liberates us from any approach to ministry that would set us apart from the natural order of things. We rejoice in our God-given humanity, acknowledging that God accepts us in the midst of our human struggling and failure.

Pauline theology declares that God's power is perfected in human weakness, and throughout the Bible we note examples of this principle in action. In the Old Testament, ordinary human beings like Moses, Jeremiah and Gideon are summoned by God despite their self-confessed inadequacies – perhaps because of them! Welker explores the biblical truth that God uses frail, inadequate human beings to accomplish his purposes. Drawing from Ezekiel 36:26–28, he asks why the gift of the Spirit is accompanied by a heart of *flesh*: 'Why is the gift of the Spirit not sufficient *by itself*? If not a heart of stone, why does not God nevertheless grant some sort of *firm* heart? Why does God not simply come out and grant the firm, *pure* heart for which Psalm 51 asks …?'[10] His response is that fleshliness, which he defines in terms of sensitivity, vulnerability, frailty, and perishability, characterizes creaturely life: 'A life that kept itself *untouched*, *untouchable*, and invulnerable, that remained insensitive to complex external influences – such a thing neither can nor should exist … Fleshly life is placed *in the service* of the action of the Spirit.'[11]

This is a profound insight, and has all sorts of pastoral as well as personal implications. We are weak, vulnerable, imperfect creatures, yet God delights to work through us precisely because of our weakness and frailty. God is not a perfectionist, demanding that we reach a certain standard of purity, of strength, of human sufficiency, of spiritual accomplishment. His strength is made perfect in our weakness. Illuminated by this truth, we are freed from the 'messiah complex' that afflicts so many pastors and Christian leaders: *his* strength in *our* weakness; *his* deity in *our* humanity. Peterson argues that our pastoral ancestors had their source in a 'grace-filled relationship with God'. Aware of their mortality, they gained true wisdom: 'how to live as a *human*, not as a *god*; how to live into and up to human limits but not beyond them'.[12] Today we seek to live as gods, rather than as human beings dependent on God.

In his book, *Opening Blind Eyes*, John Claypool describes his desperate striving for self-worth through workaholism: he sought significance, even fame, through his own zealous efforts. Eventually he joined a small group of people and there discovered the grace of God at a deeply personal level; he experienced a transition from what he describes as a spirit of acquisition to a spirit of awareness. The turning point came when an Episcopalian priest declared: 'what we need is to hear the gospel down in our guts. Jesus said, "You are the light of the world." He did not say that you have to earn light or become number one in order to get light. He simply said, "You are light."'[13]

The spirituality of absence

Spirituality involves both absence and presence, withdrawal and engagement. The title of this book alludes to this reality. All who are involved in Christian ministry are privileged to dance in the light of God in the darkness of the world. There are times when the Spirit's spotlight will focus on our need to draw aside from active participation in the confusion, sorrow and pain of the world: in deliberate non-involvement, we embrace the disciplines of solitude and silence in order to rediscover the joy of participating in the rapturous dance of the Trinity: 'This is why we humans love to play in the midst of the seriousness of ordinary life – play bespeaks eternity. Play is a gesture of hope. It takes us momentarily out of the realm of suffering and lets us glimpse deathless joy. It is a gesture of hope in the midst of ugliness and destruction.'[14]

At times our withdrawal may be akin to what St John of the Cross has called 'the dark night of the soul', a process in which the soul is held by grace throughout a period of dryness and distaste in order to achieve the sweetness of divine union with God. The Spirit may lead some through this refining process whereby the soul is denied its customary gratification, not as an end in itself but as a means by which the all-sufficiency of God's grace may be truly apprehended. The darkness of which we speak here has nothing to do with the darkness of the sinful world in which we live; rather, it refers to a wilderness experience in which the individual consents to the purifying ministry of the Spirit. St John of the Cross describes this 'contemplative purgation' as follows:

> Poor, abandoned, and unsupported by any of the apprehensions of my soul (in the darkness of my intellect, the distress of my will, and the affliction and anguish of my memory), left to darkness in pure faith, which is a dark night for these faculties, and with my will touched only by sorrows, afflictions, and longings of love for God, I went out from myself … This was great happiness and a sheer grace for me, because through the annihilation and calming of my faculties, passions, appetites, and affections, by which my experience and satisfaction in God were base, I went out from my human operation and way of acting to God's operation and way of acting …
>
> This dark night is an inflow of God into the soul, which purges it of its habitual ignorances and imperfections, natural and spiritual … Through this contemplation, God teaches the soul secretly and instructs it in the perfection of love without its doing anything or understanding how this happens.[15]

The experience of 'the dark night of the soul' is not so much to be sought as to be embraced when it comes: mystics teach us that it is to be received as gift. We must not reproach ourselves if we distance ourselves from the afflictions implicit in the 'dark night' experience: St John of the Cross may be 'leading us into deeper waters than we care to go. Certainly he is talking about a realm that most of us see only "through a glass darkly" ... but perhaps he has stirred within us a drawing toward higher, deeper experiences, no matter how slight the tug. It is like opening the door of our lives to this realm ever so slightly. That is all God asks, and all He needs.'[16] Whether the Spirit leads us into joyful dance or dark night, the purpose is the same: that we might realize afresh our dependence upon God as the source of all life, and if of all life, then also the source of all ministry in and for the world.

We need to embrace a 'theology of absence' so that others can find the peace of God in our presence. Henri Nouwen argues that this type of meditative concentration is the necessary precondition for true hospitality: 'When our souls are restless, when we are driven by thousands of different and often conflicting stimuli, when we are always "over there" between people, ideas and the worries of this world, how can we possibly create the room and space when someone else can enter freely without feeling himself an unlawful intruder?'[17] Hospitality requires first of all 'that the host feels at home in his own house'.[18] The poet T. S. Eliot once declared that 'At the still point of the turning world ... there the dance is ... Except for the point, the still point, there would be no dance, and there is only the dance.'[19] Withdrawal, an absence from ministry activity, is necessary if we are to get in touch with that still point, so that we have something genuine and profound to offer both friend and stranger in our midst.

In 1999 an Alaskan adventurer named Robert Bogucki was found wandering in the Great Sandy Desert in Western Australia. He had started out on his journey without any clear understanding of what he was looking for: he simply wanted to spend some time on his own with nobody else around, and perhaps 'make peace with God'. Bogucki's desires echo the longings of many people today. All of us need to get to that still centre (Eliot's 'still point'), wherever and however that may be found, in order to make sense of life and give us some sort of hope that the future will hold out purpose and meaning for us. Increasingly, people are turning to some form of spirituality in order to 'find themselves': the failure of materialism, consumerism and secular humanism to fill the void in the human soul has propelled many into the wilderness – in some cases, literally, as for Bogucki – in search of inner satisfaction.

Throughout this book I have argued that the Christian church urgently needs to rediscover a spirituality which resonates with the culture of the day. Many people today are turning to mystical experiences because of the emptiness and bankruptcy of their soul. In their search for meaning and truth, they are exploring many different expressions of spirituality. The diverse offerings under the umbrella of the New Age Movement, psychic phenomena, medieval mysticism, Orthodox spirituality, other faiths and religions besides Christianity, even the occult are all drawing their adherents from far and wide. Throughout the twentieth century psychologists have been deeply suspicious of religious phenomena and claims, but in recent years there has been a growing awareness amongst some within the discipline that the religious dimension in human beings cannot be dismissed so readily: 'Spiritual longings occur within the very heart of personality; they are not the stirrings of some part of persons independent of the rest of personality.'[20]

One significant development within the Christian scene is the re-emergence of Celtic spirituality. The phenomenal success of the Irish dance ensemble *Riverdance* has been the catalyst for a mushrooming interest and involvement is all things Celtic throughout the world. The appeal of Celtic spirituality outside Christian circles is augmented by the popularity of singers and music bands, and whilst their success has undoubtedly given great pleasure to many people, others have been encouraged to explore their spiritual longings through the medium of Celtic paganism rather than Christianity. Celtic spirituality speaks powerfully to third-millennium humanity in its search for a transcendent reality which is at the same time down-to-earth and more authentic than that which is conveyed in many contemporary Christian churches.

The renewed interest in Trinitarian theology in the church is significant in our understanding of the burgeoning fascination with Celtic spirituality: 'the distinctive tenor of Celtic Christianity is one of a life-affirming integration which finds its theological centre in the vision of God as divine creativity and community, which is the Christian doctrine of the Trinity.'[21] The creative dimension in Celtic spirituality finds expression not only in music, but in poetry and art. The concept of 'soul friend' is central to personal spiritual growth within the Celtic tradition; it corresponds to the notion of 'spiritual direction', and enhances the importance of community inherent in Celtic spirituality – the Irish *anamchara* means 'soul friend', and there is a Celtic proverb which asserts that 'a person without an *anamchara* is like a body without a head'.

But there is more to Celtic Christianity than creativity and community. Other significant emphases are a holistic approach to life, in which body, soul and spirit are viewed as interrelated aspects of humanity; an openness to the direction of the Holy Spirit in all of life, in which a listening silence is central; a simplicity of lifestyle based upon the gifts of God's good creation; the importance of symbols, ritual and liturgy in worship; a deep respect for human life and the dignity of the individual; an understanding that all of life is sacramental, including the natural world; an awareness of life as a pilgrimage, expressed both spiritually and literally – retreats and pilgrimages to special sites, such as Iona and Lindisfarne, are encouraged; the centrality of prayer and the disciplined life within a natural rhythm of work and rest; and a missionary zeal, embracing a concern not only for the soul but for the whole person.

Many of these themes have been addressed throughout this book, and they help us to understand why Celtic Christianity has grown in popularity in recent years. Whilst wisdom is needed to ensure that our adoption of the Celtic stream into mainstream Christianity does not also introduce pagan elements into the life and worship of the church, it is evident that it offers genuine opportunities for personal and corporate spiritual growth. The symbol of the knot reflects the passionate Celtic belief in the

Trinitarian God, whose communal life is the basis for all human life: only in community with God and with each other can human beings discover their true identity and purpose. This was the message which the Celtic preachers took into the villages and towns, sharing their faith wherever opportunity presented itself. Celtic spiritual discipline was never regarded as an end in itself but as a means of enabling effective witness to Christ in the pagan world.

The spirituality of presence

Spirituality is therefore more than contemplation: ultimately its goal is compassion. The American priest and theologian Matthew Fox rejects all interpretations of spirituality which isolate the contemplative dimension from engagement in and with the world. He contrasts two types of spirituality, which he labels 'climbing Jacob's ladder' and 'dancing Sarah's circle'.[22] The ladder theme, claims Fox, has dominated the history of spirituality, with its (misinterpreted) implication of ascent to God and of various stages, or steps, which the Christian pilgrim must go through in order to reach God 'up there'. Fox suggests that Greek ideas, especially the Platonic notion of an upward progression from the concrete to the abstract, lie behind this narrow and unbiblical understanding of true spirituality. He contrasts this paradigm with the more authentic proposition that 'God is not spatially up but in one's midst ... The question is not so much *where* God is as *when* will the people allow God to be among them?'[23]

The earthiness and sheer celebration which is characteristic of Jewish spirituality is made explicit in Fox's allusion to God's promise of a child to Sarah, though she was past the age of child-bearing (Gen. 18:11–15): when that promise is fulfilled there is joy and laughter, for God has *come to* her in crazy, glorious, and imaginative possibility. Fox quotes the feminist thinker Adrienne Rich, who challenges the purist aims of the spirituality of ascent; in one of her poems she invites us to embrace a spirituality which is more sensual, down-to-earth and imperfect:

Let us return to imperfection's school.
No longer wandering after Plato's ghost.[24]

One particular way in which Fox develops the contrast between a 'ladder-spirituality' and a 'dance-spirituality' is by insisting that the 'proper dynamic of our spiritual lives is in/out and not up/down.'[25] In the up/down schema there is the suggestion of individual escapism, whereas dancing with others is all about involvement and shared experiences. Ladder-climbing conveys the idea of strenuous effort and the fear that one might never reach the top; dancing invites us into an enterprise that stimulates and refreshes. The in/out paradigm is described by Fox in terms of mysticism and prophecy. Through mysticism we enter into the transcendent joys of life and living, encountering God, one another, and all of creation in the innermost depths of our being: we are then equipped and motivated to re-enter the world in all its confusion and pain, speaking truth and life out of that which we have received. Dancing Sarah's circle requires us to look around, so that we might express the energy of the divine life *amongst others* and so draw them into the dance.

This incarnational dimension in spirituality moves all those who are involved in pastoral ministry away from solitude for its own sake and towards servanthood as they immerse themselves in the realities of everyday life. This is one of the distinctive features of the Holy Spirit's work in the life of the Messiah, who came amongst men and women to serve them and give his life for them. So it is meant to be in the lives of those who seek to follow in his footsteps. The prophet Isaiah draws out the essential link between servanthood and the Spirit in Isaiah 11, 42 and 61, texts in which justice and mercy are prominent. Only the Spirit can grant to his people the strength and wisdom needed to engage compassionately with the world.

The Spirit's ministry in the pastoral activity of the church has both a paschal and a Pentecostal dimension. He calls us to suffering involvement in the world, and equips us with Pentecostal power to sustain us in that mission. But he is also the same Spirit who refreshes us in joyful Trinitarian dance. We cannot put a wedge between the Spirit who draws us into intimate communion with God and the Spirit who leads us out into compassionate involvement with the world. To focus on one whilst ignoring the other is to misunderstand not only God but also ourselves. For all ministry is *God*'s ministry, who alone has the power and grace to confront the misery and mystery of life and bring order out of chaos, and life out of death. In ourselves we cannot help the world: perhaps we need to learn absence so that God's presence may be mediated rather than simply our own. Henri Nouwen suggests that 'We have to learn to leave so that the Spirit can come.'[26]

The Spirit who comes, however, is not always obvious by his presence. He works in hidden and at times obscure ways to accomplish God's purposes in the world. Our theology of the Holy Spirit may need to be stretched a little here, for we are accustomed to certain paradigms which define his actions, paradigms which are dictated by our theological or ecclesiastical persuasions. My thesis in this chapter is that the Spirit is at work in human life not only to enhance our spiritual faculties but also to free us to be more fully human. If we are honest with ourselves we will admit that our energy levels are at times insufficient for the occasion, and sometimes we struggle when faced with the simplest of tasks. As human beings we may need to learn how to negotiate with others so that we are not overwhelmed by their demands. As an Anglican minister in England, I was encouraged when my churchwardens approached me at an early stage in my incumbency and inquired searchingly if I was taking sufficient time off to enrich my own personal life: I was thankful that I did not have to plead with them for recreation time!

If, however, we allow ourselves to be sucked into a ministry practice that denies us the opportunity to manage our own lives effectively, then we may find ourselves denying those whom we serve the freedom to discover and nurture their own humanness. To serve others is to encourage them into wholeness, into an awareness and experience of what it means to be made *imago Dei*. But the culture of western society, with its emphasis on success, achievement, competition, and technological advance,

militates against this *shalom* life of God. Sadly, the Christian
faith community has too easily capitulated to secular values:
Eugene Peterson blazes in indignation against the pastors of
America who have 'metamorphosed into a company of shopkeepers': 'And there must be any number of shopkeepers who by
now are finding the pottage that they acquired in exchange for
their ordination birthright pretty tasteless stuff and are growing
wistful for a restoration of their calling.'[27]

The Spirit of God challenges us in two profound ways as we
embrace our calling to ministry: firstly, do we recognize him in
the ordinary affairs of life as he seeks to bring the culture of the
kingdom of God into the commonplace? Secondly, lest we are
tempted to diminish his supernatural grace at work in
manifestations of charismatic power, do we acknowledge his
desire to transform our own lives, and respond openly and
expectantly to his *chrisma*, his anointing – what some refer to as
'unction' – upon us for ministry? Both dimensions of the Spirit's
enabling are necessary.

The first speaks to us of the hidden service of the faithful, no
less powerful for its hiddenness. Foster calls this the 'discipline
of service', and lists a number of ways in which this may be
expressed 'in the marketplace of our daily lives': the service of
small things, the service of guarding the reputation of others,
the service of being served, the service of common courtesy, the
service of hospitality, the service of listening, the service of
bearing the burdens of each other and the service of sharing the
word of Life with each other.[28] In these and other unspectacular
ways the Spirit is at work in human life. An authentic 'spirituality of presence' acknowledges the gentle breeze of the Spirit no
less than the wind and fire of Pentecost: in the routine tasks of
ministry the Spirit is just as present and active as in the dramatic
and evidently supernatural manifestations of divine power, in
which unpredictability and surprise may be characteristic elements. In fact, Christian ministry in the power of the Spirit has
more to do with the ordinary than the extraordinary.

A pastor once dreamt that he was in a fairground, enjoying
the many different rides on offer; he was especially captivated by

the thrills of the huge roller-coaster and was making his way towards it when he found himself being re-directed to the merry-go-round. The dream persisted, and he woke up with the scenario fresh and alive in his mind. The pastor was considering his future, and was keen to explore exciting new vistas in ministry; through this dream the Lord called him to rededicate his life afresh to the ongoing task of ministry in the local community (the merry-go-round). Like many in ministry, the attractions of running towards the big thrills of 'roller-coaster ministry' are tempting, especially if the merry-go-round becomes predictable and boring. But it is in the very routine of everyday life that we are called to make a difference, and that is where the Spirit of God is pleased to minister his grace and hope.

In the French film *Ça Commence Aujourd'hui* ('It All Starts Today'), the film director Bertrand Tavernier pays tribute to the many people in society who are seeking to make a real difference to those who are caught in the endless cycle of despair and poverty. Set in a depressing industrial town in northern France, the hero is a schoolteacher, Daniel Lefebvre, who engages compassionately with families and children as they try to cope with crippling unemployment, an under-funded welfare system, and the resulting family dislocation and poverty. No spectacular solutions are offered; Lefebvre is determined not to be overwhelmed by the social deprivation around him. His life is portrayed as a daily struggle to bring life and joy into people's lives: Tavernier's passionate cry for justice actually contributed to needed changes in the French welfare system.

The film ends with an imaginative and creative transformation of the school yard and buildings into a colourful celebration of life, communicating hope in the midst of the squalid conditions in which many of the town's inhabitants live. Though fictional, the film was based on the real-life experiences of one of the screenplay writers, and throughout I was struck by the compassion and gentle strength of Lefebvre, and asked myself: is this not the context within which the Spirit of God works to reveal God's grace and love? The film is not explicitly religious or Christian, but it communicated the truth that God may be at work by his Spirit amongst suffering humanity in more ways than we care to think. And if we are inclined to be dismissive about the claim that the Spirit may be at work through the lives of those who do not overtly confess Christ, we 'may easily miss him if [we] have any preconceived ideas, for he may be working at a carpenter's bench'.[29]

Christian ministry requires us to notice what God is *already doing* in the situations and lives around us, and to participate in his acts of love and kindness. At times we may receive gracious gifts from God to enable us to fulfil that which he requires of us: a word of wisdom, special strength and courage, faith to believe in God's power to heal, supernatural insight, perhaps the gentle prompting to reach out with a touch or a smile. Such gifts may be granted to us without our awareness, or we may be acutely aware of their presence in our lives. In our weakness and dryness, as we cry out to God for greater power and authority, the Spirit may respond with a fresh anointing for ministry. It is precisely because the task of ministry takes place on the merry-go-round of daily life that we need the Spirit's energy, power, and encouragement in our lives. A spirituality of presence is earthed in the predictability of the merry-go-round, not the thrills of the roller-coaster.

The discipline of self-management

In today's frantic world, the call to manage our personal lives in order to experience the *shalom* of God is as urgent as ever. In Chapter Seven a planning paradigm was presented for effective ministry in a local church setting. I suggested that such a paradigm may also be applied to bring order and direction to our personal lives; indeed, efficient self-management is desirable in those who are called to manage others. Adlai Stevenson shrewdly observed that it is not the days in our life that count but the life in our days!

Tom Sine is only one among many Christian writers who have addressed the issue of reordering our lives so that we are free both to enjoy life and to serve others.[30] Sine recounts a life-changing experience during work on a project in rural Haiti: the people amongst whom he laboured had a 'Gospel-rhythm' to their lives, always having time to stop and talk with passers-by: 'On many warm Haitian evenings during my sojourn we would visit the homes of friends. They would open their homes to us and serve us food and drinks. We would spend a whole evening telling stories, laughing, singing, and playing with the children to the flicker of kerosene lamps ... I thank my Haitian friends for helping me discover a more biblical approach to my time.'[31]

The concept of time management, so familiar in business circles, is regarded with hesitation, even suspicion, by some Christians. After all, have we not been 'bought at a price' (1 Cor. 6:20)? Does not our time now belong to God? This interpretation, besides failing to exegete the biblical text accurately (it has to do with the sexual misuse of our bodies), suffers because it falls short of a true understanding of our essential humanness. I have already suggested that the more fully we acknowledge our humanity as gift of God the more likely will we be to give expression to that gift in response to God and his call to serve others. The management consultant Stephen Covey identifies four dimensions of human life – physical, mental, social/emotional, and spiritual – and comments that wise, regular, and consistent exercise of all four dimensions 'is the single most powerful investment we can ever make in life – investment in ourselves, in the only instrument we have with which to deal with life and to contribute.'[32]

Covey argues that all four areas need to be 'sharpened' regularly because they are interrelated: improvement in one area has a positive effect in other areas. Therefore we do our intrinsic humanity a disservice by neglecting, for example, the social dimension of our lives and concentrating on the other three. In the context of Christian ministry, our holistic nature demands that we do not sacrifice growth in other areas of our lives in our single-minded pursuit of spiritual excellence. We do well to remember that Jesus 'grew in wisdom and stature, and in favour with God and men' (Lk. 2:52): in Covey's parlance, his life was in balance, or 'optimally synergetic', as he matured in each of the four dimensions of his humanity.

David Cormack, who once worked at Shell International as Head of Training and Organization Development, has put forward a helpful course on the effective use of time, in which he outlines nine basic skill areas in personal time management: establish a vision for your life; translate this into clear targets; identify priorities for action; prepare and follow appropriate plans; organize yourself; manage demands on your time; develop the energy required; act according to the steps outlined; and, finally, learn through reviewing.[33] Although caution needs to be exercised to ensure that life does not become over-organized to the point where it ceases to reflect the 'Gospel-rhythm' about which Sine rightly enthuses, the principles which Cormack, and other time management gurus, expound need to be examined more thoroughly than Christian ministers are wont to do. I have worked with many groups of Christians, leading them through the skill areas outlined above, and have discovered that the majority are woefully inadequate in one or two areas. The most common weaknesses are usually in the areas of vision building, identifying priorities, and taking action.

Here we look briefly at the first three of Cormack's checklist steps: establishing vision, translating vision into targets, and identifying priorities. They will point us in the direction of taking greater responsibility for our lives. In Chapter Seven I suggested that Christians need to be more proactive in establishing a vision for their lives. We often do this at a 'macro' level in our lives – for example, all of us have a vision for a better world in which to bring up our children, to see poverty reduced and justice extended throughout the nations – but relatively few people articulate a personal 'micro-vision' for their lives: Cormack encourages us to be specific about what we would like to accomplish in our lives.

Larry Crabb suggests that all of us have been created by God with two fundamental needs, or legitimate thirsts: relationship and impact. He defines the thirst for impact as 'a desire to be adequate for a meaningful task, a desire to know that we are capable of taking hold of our world and doing something valuable and well'.[34] Distinguishing between casual, critical, and crucial longings, Crabb suggests that whilst all human beings have a crucial need for Christ at the core of their being, legitimate desires for ourselves, our families, and the needs of the world around us must not be neglected: these may be labelled 'critical longings'. Casual longings have to do with personal preference and convenience.

As we examine ourselves and reflect upon what is important to us, we begin to articulate a vision for our lives, which may have a number of components, such as our time with God, family life, our social relationships, Christian ministry and leisure time. The next step is to translate this into achievable targets. For example, if I decide that I need to give more of my time to improving my relationships with others outside my immediate family ('sharpening my social saw'), I may decide to meet someone new each month for the next six months, and spend at least one evening with them to get to know them better. Notice that this is a 'S-M-A-R-T' target, according to the language of time management (see Chapter Seven)! Many people are reluctant to quantify their goals in life in this way, but there are significant benefits to be gained, so long as the process remains our servant rather than our master. I know of one woman in England who deliberately decided to try one new experience each month in order to widen her appreciation of life as God's gift to her. One month she climbed a mountain (small, but still a mountain!); another month she visited an art gallery she had never been to before. Each month opened up to her a larger vista of God's good creation and her life has been enriched immeasurably by her conscious choice to establish attainable targets for her life.

The area of identifying priorities is where many people fall flat on their faces. If we reconsider the story of Mary and Martha in this context (Lk. 10:38–42) a number of key time management principles are discernible. Martha learns from Jesus not to confuse the urgent with the important: 'Mary has chosen what is better' – Martha perceived an immediate need and chose to react to the urgent; Mary invested her time in the important. Secondly, we notice that Jesus wanted both sisters to sit at his feet: Martha lost sight of this goal by focusing on the preparations for the meal, with the result that the activity became her goal. Thirdly, our activism can trap us into criticism of others: Mary was rebuked for not pulling her weight. Finally, Martha was clearly not at peace within herself, for she had become worried and upset: inner anxieties are often the result of a sense of over-responsibility, and this may lead to dysfunctional stress. These four consequences of mistaken priorities are common in the lives of many in Christian ministry: misplaced urgency, activity-centredness, proneness to criticism and dysfunctional stress.

Because we are relationally dependent, wrong priorities can be damaging not only for us but also in the lives of others. Conversely, right priorities are wonderfully liberating. Keith Miller writes of his attempts to become a better father and husband: at the beginning of each year he notes in his calendar such events as his wedding anniversary and family birthdays, and inserts 'commitment to family' against that day.

> I remember the first time an invitation to participate in a big meeting came on one of the children's birthdays. I was very interested in the meeting but said 'no'. The man, who was a friend, must have sensed my hesitation, because he asked, 'Why can't you come? This is an important convention and your witness might reach a lot of people.'
>
> I was a little embarrassed to say that it was 'my little girl's birthday', but I went on to tell him, 'You can get half a dozen speakers in an hour, but I am the only daddy she's got.'
>
> He was quiet on the other end of the line for a few seconds, and I thought he had rejected me as a fool. Then he said quietly, 'I wish I could do that.'[35]

The truth is that we are freer than we think we are to make the right decisions in life. We are free to say 'no' if the quality of our life in God is likely to be significantly diminished by undertaking a specific course of action. The principles of time management encourage us to evaluate the whole of our lives within the holistic paradigm suggested earlier. Those who are involved in full-time Christian ministry do not have to succumb to the pressure to conform to certain expectations placed upon them by others. Faced with the demand not to teach again in Jesus' name, Peter and the other apostles replied, 'We must obey God rather than men!' (Acts 5:29). Today, faced with the demand to 'do this', 'do that', that same response is apposite: 'No! I have a life to live, and God is calling me to life in him! I choose not to bow down to your demands.'

Of course, saying 'no' may become a convenient habit in order to avoid responsibility and ease the burden of ministry, but the opposite extreme – that of saying 'yes' in all circumstances – is more usual in Christian ministry. By acknowledging that we are not indispensable and by exercising the discipline implicit in the personal time management process, the rewards of living life to the full become more accessible. Jesus' call to discipleship was never intended to be an arduous journey, in which we grit our teeth as we climb the steep and narrow path of faith: certainly we will experience difficulties and pain, but his call is essentially one of joyful union with him and with others, a community life in which ministry is an integral part of the passionate dance of life. At times we need the courage to say 'no' in order to hear God's welcome and resounding 'yes' to the choices we make in life.

Dancing the journey

In several places throughout this book we have explored the ontology of human existence. As an antidote to activism, the notion of 'being' has been recommended above that of 'doing'. As creatures who have been made in the image of God, who does what he does because he is who he is, human beings do well to take stock of their own lives, and to ask, with Eliot, 'Where is the Life we have lost in living?'[36] Immediately preceding this searching question, Eliot remonstrates against the incessant, and ultimately fruitless, pursuit of idea and action which drives us further from God, rather than towards him:

The endless cycle of idea and action,
Endless invention, endless experiment,
Brings knowledge of motion, but not of stillness;
Knowledge of speech, but not of silence;
Knowledge of words, and ignorance of the Word.
All our knowledge brings us nearer to our ignorance,
All our ignorance brings us nearer to death,
But nearness to death no nearer to God.[37]

As they examine their busy lives, many in Christian ministry may discover with regret that these words have a hollow echo: the abundant life that Jesus promised in John 10:10 has given way to a frantic pursuit of knowledge, experiment and action. Instead of life, they have, for the most part, experienced only existence, a cheerless and depressing struggle to survive from day to day.

Two motifs which offer hope for the struggling pastor – indeed for all Christians – and which I have highlighted in this book are *community* and *journey*, both of which come alive in the context of life as a 'dance'. Community reminds us that we are not alone in this world: we are, to use Douglas John Hall's language, 'being-with' creatures. Only as we willingly and vulnerably connect with others will we begin to experience fully God's life within us: 'The life of Christ is coming out of me only when I am gladly ruled by a passion to know you, to bless you, and to be known by you so that together we can enjoy fellowship with Christ and with each other.'[38] Honest self-examination – perhaps through some of the suggestions proposed in this chapter – will reveal to us how truly open we are to live in vulnerable relationship with one another.

However, the way into this community life begins with the realization that God's call to life in the world has its genesis in his gracious invitation to dance with him! Lovingly, gently, and with infinite patience God teaches us the steps of the divine dance: when we stumble, he does not leave us helpless on the floor, nor does he point a disapproving finger at us. The Spirit who dwells within us, smiles over us as he reaches out a hand to pick us up and lead us on in the dance: 'The face of God, shining for joy, is the luminous source of the Holy Spirit. The light floods over us, and our faces become mirrors which reflect that light and diffuse it.'[39] When we *know* that God is smiling at us with joy we are encouraged to learn the steps of his dance, and then creatively to choreograph new steps, new sequences, which flow out of his life within us. They are still his steps, but we are the ones who are bringing them into being!

In the film *Strictly Ballroom* a professional dancer is castigated for his persistent desire to introduce new steps into his routine in the competitive world of ballroom dancing; he is 'spoiling the show' and his supposed arrogance in inventing a new way of dancing is met with hostility and anger. Eventually, his originality and creativity win the day. The film ends in joyful celebration as competitors and spectators alike crowd onto the floor and rejoice in the freedom of dance: all the people are caught up in the carnival. That is how it should be with God and his creatures: 'let the people of Zion be glad in their King. Let them praise his name with dancing and make music to him with tambourine and harp. For the Lord takes delight in his people ...' (Ps. 149:2–4). The community of the faithful dance with joy in the presence of their God. Of course, now we experience only the firstfruits of such joy, but that knowledge should make us all the more eager to appropriate everything that God has for us.

To know God in this lively way is to start tapping our feet to the rhythm of life – deep calls to deep as the Spirit draws us into the Trinitarian dance. This is a dance which is irresistible to those whose eyes have been opened. Caught up into the life of the triune God, we experience his grace in the steps of the dance – here there is neither striving nor weariness, for the dance is God's dance, not ours! We have observed that those in pastoral ministry are tempted to side-step the gift of the Spirit and to rely upon human effort to achieve 'success' in ministry. This is not God's way for us! As Pinnock prays, may our theology make explicit what the heart has always known: 'Let God not be defined so much by holiness and sovereignty in which loving relatedness is incidental, but by the dance of trinitarian life.'[40]

As we gain confidence in dancing, we discover that the experience of 'being-with' is accompanied by an awareness that gradually we are being transformed within. It is not just the steps that are changing as we are encouraged to experiment and innovate: we ourselves 'are being transformed into his likeness with ever-increasing glory, which comes from the Lord, who is the Spirit' (2 Cor. 3:18). We begin to enjoy the dance and long for others to enjoy it with us, those who are on the outside looking in, even those who scowl because they do not know what fun they are missing. The life of God, who is full of compassion and steadfast love for all people, invades our hearts so that we begin to love as he does. We discover that we are beginning to dance new theological steps, and though some may frown, others are drawn into the dance!

So we begin to dance the journey. It is a journey which is less linear, more circular and satisfying. As the music plays, we expend our energies in the shared dance of life. Commenting on his distinction between 'climbing Jacob's ladder' and 'dancing Sarah's circle', Fox notes the transformations that have taken place in the egos and spirits of those who have made the transition from climbing to dancing: 'Joining hands and weaving about a chapel, church or room as a curved line in motion, as a spiral or a circle, is truly a spiritual conversion for many who have never been invited to put their bodies back into worship.'[41] This sort of dancing embraces people of all kinds, young and old, rich and poor, experts and learners, black and white. The essence of mission is learning to take this dance out of the church building and into the streets and open spaces of our neighbourhoods. This is the privilege of Christian ministry: caught up in the dance of the Trinity, we discover that our dancing, energized and orchestrated by the Spirit within us, brings light into the darkness around us. Here there is no drudgery in ministry, nor talk of mere survival: dancing in the dark may be the harbinger of revival not only in the soul of all who minister in Christ's name, but in the soul of a bruised and hurting world.

Notes

1. Francis McNab, *Getting There: Coping with Frustration, Stagnation, Burnout* (Melbourne: Spectrum Publications, 1982), p. 38.
2. Peterson, *Working the Angles*, pp. 54–5.
3. Pinnock, *Flame of Love*, p. 37.
4. John H. Court, 'Drawn or Driven', *Australian Ministry Digest*, 6:4 (Oct.–Dec. 1999), 8–9.
5. Stanton L. Jones and Richard E. Butman, *Modern Psychotherapies: A Comprehensive Christian Appraisal* (Downers Grove: IVP, 1991), p. 42.
6. Ian Pitt-Watson, *A Primer for Preachers* (Grand Rapids: Baker, 1986), p. 48.
7. ibid., p. 48.
8. Quoted in Ted Engstrom, *The Pursuit of Excellence* (Grand Rapids: Zondervan, 1982), p. 90.
9. Source unknown.
10. Michael Welker, *God the Spirit* (Minneapolis: Fortress Press, 1994), p. 165.
11. ibid., pp. 166, 168.
12. Peterson, *Working the Angles*, p. 31.
13. John R. Claypool, *Opening Blind Eyes* (Nashville: Abingdon Press, 1983), p. 57.
14. Pinnock: *Flame of Love*, pp. 43–4.
15. St John of the Cross, *The Collected Works of St John of the Cross*, tr. Kieran Kavanaugh and Otilio Rodriguez (Washington DC: ICS Publications, 1991), pp. 400–1.
16. Foster, *Celebration of Discipline*, p. 92.
17. Henri Nouwen, *The Wounded Healer* (New York: Doubleday, 1972), p. 90.
18. ibid., p. 89.
19. T. S. Eliot, 'Burnt Norton' – I (Four Quartets) in *Collected Poems* (London: Faber & Faber, 1963), p. 191.
20. Benner, *Care of Souls*, p. 86.
21. Oliver Davies and Fiona Bowie, *Celtic Christian Spirituality* (London: SPCK, 1995), p. 21.
22. See Matthew Fox, *A Spirituality Named Compassion* (San Francisco: Harper, 1979), pp. 36–67.
23. ibid., p. 41.

24. Adrienne Rich, 'Stepping Backward' in *Poems: Selected and New* (New York: Norton, 1975), p. 9.
25. Fox, *A Spirituality Named Compassion*, p. 46.
26. Henri Nouwen, *A Living Reminder* (Minneapolis: Seabury Press, 1977), p. 45.
27. Peterson, *Working the Angles*, p. 3.
28. See Foster, *Celebration of Discipline*, pp. 117–22.
29. Taylor, *The Go-Between God*, p. 40.
30. See also Robert Banks, *The Tyranny of Time* (Homebush West NSW: Lancer, 1983); Gordon MacDonald, *Ordering Your Private World* (Crowborough: Highland Books, 1984).
31. Tom Sine, *Wild Hope* (Tunbridge Wells: Monarch, 1991), p. 271.
32. Stephen R. Covey, *The Seven Habits of Highly Effective People* (Melbourne: The Business Library, 1990), p. 289.
33. David Cormack, *Seconds Away!: Fifteen Rounds in the Fight for Effective Use of Time* (Eastbourne: MARC Monarch Publications, 1986).
34. Larry Crabb, *Understanding People: Deep Longings for Relationship* (Grand Rapids: Zondervan, 1987), p. 114.
35. Keith Miller, *Habitation of Dragons* (Waco: Word Books, 1970), p. 141.
36. T. S. Eliot, 'Choruses from "The Rock" ' (Chorus I) in *Selected Poems* (London: Faber and Faber, 1961), p. 107.
37. ibid., p. 107.
38. Crabb, *Connecting*, p. 54.
39. Jürgen Moltmann, *The Source of Life: The Holy Spirit and the Theology of Life* (London: SCM, 1997), p. 14.
40. Pinnock, *Flame of Love*, p. 47.
41. Fox, *A Spirituality Named Compassion*, p. 53.

Subject Index